# COUNSELING TODAY'S SECONDARY STUDENTS

## Practical Strategies, Techniques & Materials for the School Counselor

### KENNETH HITCHNER • ANNE TIFFT-HITCHNER

JOSSEY-BASS
A Wiley Imprint
www.josseybass.com

Published by Jossey-Bass
A Wiley Imprint
989 Market Street, San Francisco, CA 94103-1741   www.josseybass.com

Jossey-Bass books and products are available through most bookstores. To contact Jossey-Bass directly
call our Customer Care Department within the U.S. at 800-956-7739, outside the U.S. at 317-572-3986
or fax 317-572-4002.

Jossey-Bass also publishes its books in a variety of electronic formats. Some content that appears in
print may not be available in electronic books.

**Library of Congress Cataloging-in-Publication Data**
Hitchner, Kenneth W.
     Counseling today's secondary students : practical strategies, techniques, and materials
    for the school counselor / Kenneth W. Hitchner, Anne Tifft Hitchner.
      p.    cm.
     ISBN 0-7879-6698-3
     1. Counseling in secondary education—United States.  2. Student counselors—United
States.  I. Tifft-Hitchner, Anne.  II. Title.
    LB1620.5.pH545  1996                          96-15628
    373.14—dc20                               CIP

FIRST EDITION
*HB Printing* 10 9 8 7 6 5 4 3

# ABOUT THE AUTHORS

**Kenneth W. Hitchner** is the author of several books on school counseling, including a *Survival Guide for the Secondary School Counselor* and the *School Counselor's Letter Book* (The Center for Applied Research in Education, 1987, 1991). He received his B.A. degree in English and social studies from Dickinson College, Carlisle, PA. After doing graduate work in school counseling at Bucknell University, he went on to earn Ed.M. and Ed.S. degrees in school administration from Rutgers University. Mr. Hitchner has thirty years of school counseling experience, working in three different New Jersey school districts prior to his arrival at East Brunswick High School. He is a past vice-president of the New Jersey School Counselor Association, has given numerous presentations at state and national conferences, and has been published in the *Journal of College Admissions*, the College Board's *College Prep*, and the *New Jersey Reporter*.

**Anne Tifft-Hitchner** is the co-author of *Making A Difference In College Admission* and the *School Counselor's Letter Book*. She is the recipient of a B.A. degree in chemistry from Georgian Court College, Lakewood, NJ, and an M.A. degree in philosophy of science from St. John's University, New York, NY. She has taught students in middle school through junior college, doing most of her teaching at East Brunswick High School in the content areas of chemistry and physics. The author has also taught English at The Peddie School in Hightstown, NJ. Ms. Tifft-Hitchner has served extensively as a student advisor, both at the high school and college levels. She presently chairs the Hightstown-East Windsor chapter of the Mercer County, New Jersey Human Relations Commission.

# ABOUT THIS BOOK

Much has happened in the public and private school arena since the publication of our book, *A Survival Guide for the Secondary School Counselor*, in 1987. Now a "notebook" is really a lap-top computer; and lap-top computers have replaced yellow legal pads. Personal Typing is now called Keyboarding and is taught on a computer terminal instead of on a typewriter. Fax machines prevail. Don't mail it. Fax it! Of course that carbonized wonder, the drop-add slip, is still with us as we continue to complete them by the thousands.

We are a world of rapid change. "Rapid change"—a phrase that aptly describes the world situation in the twenty-first century. Political, economic, social, and technological evolution is transpiring at a faster pace than ever before. Impermanence has become the norm.

On the educational front, schools are engaged in a serious examination of current practices, as they look to address the preparation of their students for the new century.

One important happening in school counseling is the shift in the counselor's role from that of sole *deliverer* of guidance and counseling services to *orchestrator* of said services, working in collaboration with teachers, administrators, parents, and community members. Professional counselors are fast becoming practitioners *and* educational leaders: counselors are making their roles more central to the actual instruction and consequent learning that takes place. It's in the *consulting* aspect of the counselor's role where the most movement is visible.

Across the nation, the major stumbling block to all of this continues to be excessive counselor caseloads. Where heavy caseloads are a factor, the very students who need counseling the most—especially educational counseling —are often the very ones excluded from such services. But, as Bob Dylan wrote some time ago, "The times they are a-changin'." Counselor/student ratios are coming down, albeit slowly, as administrators and boards of education come to grips with the fact that guidance and counseling must be central to a school's mission. National organizations such as the American School Counselor Association, The College Board, and the National Association for College Admission Counseling are at the forefront, pressing to make ratio reduction a reality.

As we look to the twenty-first century, two major educational issues continue to have a negative impact on the well-being of our nation: (1) the low retention of students at the secondary level, especially within the inner-city and (2) the low retention of students at the collegiate level.

On the positive side, we see a very real and purposeful thrust for education to align itself more with business and industry. It's a marriage of convenience. Educators are paying more attention to addressing the needs of business and industry at the secondary and collegiate levels, while business and industry are giving more heed to the preparation of today's students for tomorrow's world. American students will have to compete in an international market as the country moves with great rapidity toward a global economy. That's why such terms as problem solving, cooperative learning, human relations, communications, and multicultural education are far more than buzz words. Higher education, business, and industry are not nearly so concerned about whether students have a 4.0 or a 3.75 grade point average as they are about whether those same students can express themselves well orally and in written form, and can relate properly to both peers and adults.

Nowhere has role assessment become more vital than in school counseling, as the profession moves from traditional reactive services to planned, sequential, and developmental programs—programs supported by a sequence of connected *activities* that can utilize counselor strengths in the most effective manner.

*Counseling Today's Secondary Students* addresses these considerations. This book can be a valuable practical tool—an encouraging force for any counseling department that seeks to enhance its existing programs or create new ones. It might be especially helpful in the dozen or so states that have developmental school counseling models in place.

The book has been divided into four sections that mirror four major adolescent growth areas: (1) middle/secondary school educational development; (2) personal and social development; (3) post-secondary educational development; and (4) career development. The activities listed in each section are meant to directly *and* indirectly enhance your personal skills, as well as the personal skills of your counselees. The book does more than just describe an activity: it sets forth the rationale for implementation, and outlines the methods for putting the activity into place.

Furthermore, the book is designed to help a counseling department become less reactive and more proactive at its philosophical base. Once counselors know where they stand as to role and function, they are much more amenable to shifting from a reactive to a proactive posture. An increasing number of departments are discovering the numerous benefits of proactive counseling, but the adoption of the process demands a strong sequence of comprehensive and developmental activities. A counseling department can also use this book to develop a plan of goals, objectives, and priorities that incorporate the appropriate activities.

Knowledge is not useful until it translates into action. It's one thing to have a creative thought, quite another to move on such thinking. An activity becomes truly successful when *everyone* in the department and the school at large gets behind it. In football, the quarterback is not the only player; so, too, with counseling programs and activities. Each play is the shared responsibility of the entire school staff.

Collegial utilization of *Counseling Today's Secondary Students*, then, can go a long way toward promoting the growth of a school counseling program.

Kenneth W. Hitchner
Anne Tifft-Hitchner

# ACKNOWLEDGMENTS

We are grateful to the following people for their special assistance in the preparation of this book: Curtis Lippincott, Robert Sullivan, Charlotte Grodzki, Barbara Leifer-Sarullo, John Cosse, Dorothy Chard, Arthur Thomas, Martin Barlow, and Nora Kashinsky.

Our appreciation to the many school counselors and college admission officials, too numerous to mention, who provided valuable input and support for the writing of the text.

Special thanks to Connie Kallback, our editor at Simon & Schuster, for her fine counsel and continuous encouragement.

# CONTENTS

# SECTION III
# POST-SECONDARY
# EDUCATIONAL DEVELOPMENT—161

# SECTION IV
# CAREER DEVELOPMENT
# FOR THE SECONDARY STUDENT—277

# SECTION I

# EDUCATIONAL DEVELOPMENT OF THE SECONDARY STUDENT

◆ ◆ ◆ ◆

Educational development is the essence of the school counselor's mission. You can see it in your work with the gifted and talented, the underachiever, the college bound, the special education student, and the families of your counselees. It is at least implicit in your dealings with disaffected students, administrators, supervisors, and other staff personnel.

But what is educational development? It is the attempt of a school system to assist in the *maturation* of young people by developing their desire to know, and their capability of accessing information and then processing it. At its root is the conviction that young people must use their minds to become whole, valuable human persons.

What might be the counselor's role in this educational development? To help. To advise. To encourage. For in this age of specialization, who else *is* there to look after the whole child? The throat doctor doesn't talk about toes. The soccer coach doesn't advise on figure skating. It's rare to find a chemistry teacher comfortable in advising a student on his or her linguistic studies. So who does it? The counselor does it. *You* do. You help, advise, encourage—and you often do all three simultaneously.

With the exponential growth of information available in today's society, the prime directive of educational development should be to *teach* students *how* to learn. Far too many secondary school students have not mastered the elements of time management nor developed appropriate study skills. Many remain in the dark as to the academic courses they should be

1

pursuing to broaden their knowledge base as well as to properly prepare themselves for future endeavors. Students must enroll in the "right" courses as early as grade six, commensurate with their future educational and career plans. If you are a middle or junior high school counselor, you play a vital role in affording your counselees the appropriate head start.

A significant portion of any school counselor's advisement time should be spent on educational planning, i.e., course selection and the design of a program of studies for *subsequent* academic years. We must counsel for the future. Placing students in appropriate courses according to abilities, interests, values, and career aspirations continues to be one of the most serious and vital responsibilities of the school counselor.

Another critical issue: scholastic achievement. Counselors recognize that a student's difficulty in not turning in homework assignments can be one facet of a much larger problem, that is, across-the-board underachievement. There can be both superficial and/or deep-seated reasons for lack of academic success. Your challenge, then, is to help the student improve his or her position. And what a challenge it is!

*All* students need help and encouragement with scholastic matters, but it's especially critical for those from low-income and/or under-represented groups, where the difficulties can be more pronounced. We need to know what the youngster was coming from *and* what he or she is going toward.

School counselors are directly involved in the adolescent maturation process. A critical factor is time! Counselors need enough *time per student* to develop probable plans early on, and to see these plans through to completion.

# CHAPTER 1

# FOSTERING A LOVE OF LEARNING

Has the joy gone out of the journey? Some would say that it has, but let's really think through the question: Are today's young people caught up with joyless concentration on the goal rather than on the enjoyment of the trip—the trip of learning? Are we making nervous wrecks out of our young people, especially the academically talented? Whatever happened to the concept of learning for learning's sake? Was it left back in kindergarten? Or did it ever take hold, considering that parents fret over which kindergarten experience will get their child into an Ivy League school.

A recent study indicates that American teenagers are more "strung out" than their Asian counterparts. According to an international survey conducted in 1994 by Harold W. Stevenson, professor of psychology at the University of Michigan, U.S. teenagers may be more likely than their Asian peers to be under school-related stress. The report was based on tests and questionnaires administered to over eight thousand eleventh graders in Minneapolis, Minnesota; Fairfax County, Virginia; Alberta, Canada; Sendai, Japan; Taipei, Taiwan; and Beijing, China. The findings indicate that Asian teenagers are pressured to be *academically* successful, while American students—and their parents—want it all: the youngster must get good grades in school *and* be popular, *and* be good at athletics, *and* hold down a part-time job.

And of course nobody knows better about the stress-filled years of secondary schooling than the students themselves. Some have been intensely self-directed since birth and are their own greatest propellants, while others willingly point a finger at society with its continuing love affair with "success"—and at the schools in particular that historically have done little or nothing to tame the sea. But how could the schools have done any taming? They've been too busy piling on the pressure to even consider the impact that all of this has been having on our youth.

### WHAT THE STUDENTS ARE SAYING

- "Heavy competition can have positive effects. MHS is extremely competitive, but then this is good because it motivates me to try harder."

- "The outside world is very competitive, and the competition here prepares students well."

- "There is healthy competition and unhealthy competition. Often, students forget the reason they're in school—to learn. They create unnecessary pressures. Fun, enjoyment, and understanding are often missing elements because students become totally absorbed in getting good grades."

- "Unhealthy competition is rampant at EW. How many of us have come in contact with students who seem to know everyone's GPA, class rank, SAT scores, and to which colleges they have applied, been accepted, or rejected?"

- "How about the students who are forever quibbling over points and persuade their teachers to raise their grade."

- "I'm totally amazed at the kids who try to figure out who's smart and who isn't. They even pick their friends by that."

- "Students seem to be more concerned about grades than actual learning. We have been taught to try to do better than everyone else; at times this competitive spirit can take us over the edge."

- "Education should be a cooperative effort, and students at TR seem unwilling to share their knowledge for fear that they'll be giving another student an edge."

- "Let's have competition for achievement, rather than for grades."

- "Some kids in this school don't have a competitive spirit; this super competitive environment doesn't favor them."

- "The overemphasis on class rank and GPA creates unnecessary additional pressures."

### BODIES OF STONE

At the opposite end of the spectrum are the disaffected students, many of whom sit impassively facing the teacher as if chiseled in stone (except when it comes time to shrug shoulders). For them the joy has turned to indifference. On the one hand, the classroom is a useless place to be; on the other, the school building is a warm, fuzzy place—one big social hall in which to "hang out." Disaffected students will often do just enough to pass.

There are multiple causes for disaffection, and though it might be productive for you to be familiar with some of the causes (child abuse/neglect, separation/divorce, poverty, substance abuse, lower ability level than peers), the bottom line is that the student has quit and no longer cares. This type of student seldom reacts to encouragement or positive feedback of any kind. These youngsters are down so far that they can't get themselves back up.

Stanford Education Professor John Krumboltz, a notable contributor to the school counseling movement, in a keynote address in 1993 at the H.B. McDaniel Conference, stated, "Today's schools may be unwittingly teaching students to hate learning." School counselors, he asserted, can help counteract the problem. Krumboltz believes that counselors must expand their role into the realm of academic achievement if they are to engender a love of learning in students. That's good news for those critics who think school counselors have forgotten the basic mission of schools, education; and that they're spending too little time on academic matters and too much time on youngsters' social and emotional problems. Krumboltz himself is one of those critics. "Too often, counselors are given jurisdiction over only emotional problems or career guidance which places them on the fringe of the educational endeavor. Students don't learn to love learning because no one has made love of learning a big enough goal."

Another respected critic, Ernest Boyer, in his 1983 work, *High School: A Report on Secondary Education in America*, suggests that counselors should have a caseload of no more than 100 students each. Much like Krumboltz, Boyer believes that counselors should be functioning in an educative, rather than a therapeutic or crisis-intervention role.

## CONSULTATION AND LEARNING

Consultation is the process by which a first party (consultant) helps a second party (consultee) solve a problem that concerns a third party (client). School counselors can be consultants to an individual, group, or an entire organization. In the school setting, counselors act as consultants in providing an *indirect* service to students by working *directly* with staff personnel and parents.

The concept of the school counselor as consultant has been articulated rather recently, yet counselors have been acting in this capacity for years without realizing it. Consultation is a collaborative effort between you and the consultee, that might include your "teaching" staff and parents certain problem-solving techniques. Most of the skills that you would be teaching are already in your repertoire by virtue of formal training and practical experience. But remember that consultees usually know what is best in their own situations. Don't impose solutions! The key word is "collaborative"—involved parties need to be working as a team toward solutions. And so helping one staff member, be it professional or support, can literally mean helping hundreds of students.

Some educators see consultation as an efficient use of counselor services—so much so that a few of them even go so far as to suggest that because of budgetary restrictions, this should be the counselor's main function. Hardly! You can't consult about a student unless you are working on *your* part of the student's progress.

While individual counseling is—and should be—your primary role, you will find that consultancy broadens your range and gives your efforts greater support. You can utilize your knowledge of human development to do more for youngsters, all the while fostering a love of learning.

YOU MIGHT BE CONSULTING WHEN . . .

- as a high school counselor, you communicate with a middle school counselor.

- as a specialist, you communicate with a generalist, or vice versa.

- you sit with a group of parents and discuss the issue of study skills.

- you meet with a teacher to explore certain behavioral principles he or she might employ with a problem student.

The where, when, how, and why of consultation is an excellent discussion topic for an informal weekly department meeting or a more formal workshop.

### NERVOUS ADMINISTRATORS

The consultancy concept also embraces the idea that school counselors can work within the system to influence meaningful organizational change, including making an impact on the curriculum. Because of your unique position as a receiver of feedback from students, graduates, teachers, parents, community members, and college officials, you are in a position to suggest certain soft and hard modifications, e.g., a particular subject area needs more emphasis; a major curricular area could stand some upgrading; an alternative program is warranted for a special group of students. Of course, any suggesting is done with the idea of improving the learning environment, thereby making life more pleasant and productive for your affected students.

As you increase your effort in the consultancy area, your principal might get a bit nervous. (There are still principals who are.) He or she may not cotton to seeing you as an agent for change, despite the fact that you have been acting in this capacity for some time. You'll want to move slowly and tactfully as you explain your aims and credentials. Remind him or her that counselors as student advocates are interested in the *whole* school.

### FINAL WORDS

Effective consultation can also be a real image-builder. Try adding a 10 percent consultancy component to your direct servicing efforts. A good way to keep your feet wet in this matter is to make a conscious commitment at the beginning of any academic year to get more involved in this aspect of counseling. This might mean communicating more with teachers, or parents, or the community at large. Your initial target population should be those individuals whom you perceive to be receptive to your service.

Tracking your efforts can be interesting and productive: maintain a log for a year on those occasions when you *think* you are consulting. At the end of the year, the results might surprise you.

# FIVE INITIATIVES FOR FOSTERING A LOVE OF LEARNING

Counselors can be a positive influence in the student's choice of courses—the student's choice of learning. Krumboltz believes that such influence is the key to fostering a *love* of learning among students. In his address, he suggested five initiatives for working toward that goal; note the amount of consultancy involved:

1. Help parents help their own children by consulting with parents, running group counseling sessions for them, and referring parents to other agencies and specialists who conduct parent education classes. "Most parents have good intentions but miss the connection between their actions and their intentions."

2. Consult with administrators on policies affecting students. Counselors should examine school policies to see that all students are having positive learning experiences.

3. Help teachers adapt to individual differences. "Counselors can help teachers realize that some students may be bored in class because they are not sufficiently challenged, while others in the same class are fearful, worried, and anxious because the same activities are proving to be overwhelmingly difficult. Counselors are often in the position to lend support and encouragement."

4. Develop counseling programs for students. "Counselors need to be sensitive to complex issues that underlie low academic achievement. Counselors who can see beyond the facades generated by fear and who gently confront self-defeating thinking are in a powerful position to help youngsters reshape their lives."

5. Publicize goals, activities, and shared successes. "How easy it is for administrators to ax the counseling budget because no one has heard of any counselor achievements."

# CHAPTER 2

# EDUCATIONAL ACHIEVEMENT EXPLORED

## SELF-ESTEEM: TOO EASY AN ANSWER?

If we look to our students for evidence of improved scholarship, then praise them exuberantly for even the smallest advancement, we might be falling into the trap of praising prematurely—or, more precisely, praising for nothing. Some people believe that educators, eager to stroke underachieving students, have promulgated a dangerous myth: merely improving the youngsters' self-esteem is a sure-fire way of improving their scholastic performance and solving many of society's social ills.

Many have hopped onto the self-esteem train, including Jack Canfield, who has authored a series of books on the topic. Canfield argues that the schools should be doing more to enhance self-esteem. The issue has become so pronounced that it has spawned an entire movement overseen by the National Council of Self-esteem. The extremists within the movement believe that one should give positive feedback regardless of quality of performance—trophies for everyone, even for those on a team who didn't win a single game. Does it really enhance self-esteem when everyone is awarded a trophy? What effect would this have on the following year's effort when an in-the-cellar record culminates in apparent approval and satisfaction?

In the 1940s and 1950s, B. F. Skinner and Norman Vincent Peale thought there'd be an assurance of a happier life if only we would accentuate the positive and eliminate the negative. The 1960s and 1970s brought psychologists Abraham Maslow and Carl Rogers, both of whom have had a profound influence on educational achievement in terms of children feeling good about themselves.

But have we gone too far afield with "feeling good"? More than a few educators, including school counselors, believe we have. Ability grouping is a case in point: society continually seesaws back and forth between heterogeneity and homogeneity—heterogeneity is now in, homogeneity is out—that is, except for honors and advanced placement programs. Teachers are being asked to modify their instruction to please everyone, and include more individualization where necessary—a feat difficult to achieve with a class size of 30 and a greater-than-ever ability spread. (For example, all but honor students are placed in one English level; the rationale is that the more capable can stroke and mentor the less capable.)

Meanwhile, critics argue that too many are bored. The more capable are not being challenged enough; the less able are not being remediated enough. Many school counselors, privy as they are to annual lists of non-graduates, are noting that the list correlates strongly with those who failed Senior English. *Should* all students, college prep or not, take the same course?

As a school counselor you are very much an advocate of self-esteem. You know that students who have a strong sense of their own worth are in a better position to make positive life-enhancing decisions. But you should also know that this aspect of the counseling movement is under attack. Across the nation, self-esteem materials and programs are being closely scrutinized, if not outright challenged, by communities that believe them to be instruments that undermine parental authority, interfere with student focus on the academics, and even promote sinning.

The media has contributed to the problem. They've helped oversell self-esteem as a national quick-fix that can explain away various addictions, dependencies, and irrational and self-defeating behaviors. In the February 17, 1992 edition of *Newsweek* magazine, reporter C. Sarler writes that the United States has received international criticism for our preoccupation with self-esteem as a national reluctance to grow up.

### Self-esteem Defined

Everyone seems to have a different definition of the term. One's self-esteem refers quite literally to the extent to which one admires and values the self. We can think of it as the product of three "selfs": self-respect, self-confidence, and self-competence. A person's valuing of self stems largely from mastery or accomplishment. Unfortunately, mastery and accomplishment have gotten lost in the quest for self-aggrandizement or "feeling good." This "loss" is the precise point where self-esteem has gotten a bad rap with the public.

What is self-esteem, then? It is the idea that one's actions, thoughts, feelings, and beliefs count for something; that one has or will accomplish something—for oneself and for society. Self-esteem is learned and in constant flux. It is not merely a K–6 nurturing process. It is pliant, and must be continuously shaped; it is very much affected by life's big and little successes and failures. The person with a high level of self-esteem eventually takes ownership of his or her learning, choices, and ultimately the end results. (See Chapter 12.)

### *What You Can Do to Get the Self-esteem Train Back on Track*

- Understand how the media and public are misconstruing and misrepresenting the issue. Knowledge is power. Such knowledge should enable you to appropriately and fully respond to community challenges of counseling programs.

- Remember that your mission is to help youngsters enhance their personal competence in the educational, personal, and social realms; develop greater responsibility; and improve their confidence. When a student is able to master today what the student was unable to master yesterday, he or she develops an "I can do it!" attitude. And getting there becomes a bit like *The Little Engine That Could*: "I think I can, I think I can."

- Introduce interventions intended to modify in-school behaviors. Empathy and talk are cheap. Engage your counselees in real problem-solving. Whether it be on an individual or group basis, students *can* be *taught* everything from how to cope with being cut from an athletic team, to how to approach a teacher for assistance, to how to be a peacemaker rather than a fighter.

- Get involved with accountability activities; self-esteem levels are measurable to some extent. For example, you can communicate with teachers through periodic performance reports; make phone calls to parents for their perspective and support; phone and/or send notes to attendance officials and assistant principals. All of these communicative devices are intended to see whether or not your interventions are having an effect.

- Multicultural counseling strategies can come into play here. Don't lose sight of the fact that *your* beliefs about adolescent self-responsibility that involve the capability of making wise decisions might differ markedly from those of your concerned parents, especially the parents of certain minority youth and/or religious persuasions.

- Listen! You have to listen carefully to parental concerns in your district. Never become defensive! Good listening builds trust. It's also the first component of good communication.

- You should remain informed about challenges to counseling philosophy and programs on the state and national levels. Programs can be strengthened by *properly representing* self-esteem, and by involving parents in program development. The establishment of a local Guidance Advisory Committee can go a long way toward broadening ownership of counseling and guidance activities, and similarly keeping these same activities "necessary" in the eyes of the community. An advisory committee, composed of parents, teachers, business leaders, and counselors, can conduct bi-monthly evening meetings.

- Employ such terms as mastery, competence, responsibility, and accomplishment regularly. Again, mastery leads to more mastery. Even in the college admission process, you influence levels of self-esteem as you walk your counselees through the admission process, showing them that what they want *is* important, and at the same time reminding them that they must adhere to regulations, procedures, deadlines, and ethical considerations to attain it.

*Other Unexpected Advice*

- Although we mentioned previously about the importance of praising for any little advancements, *do* expect much from your counselees. For the most part, they will live up to your expectations; naturally, you need to be realistic about the standards you set. Many youngsters underestimate their capabilities as can be seen in the college admission process, where they have trouble uncovering "reach" schools.

- As you take delight in the efforts of your counselees, try to be *specific* with your laudatory comments: "Congratulations on your research paper; your English teacher told me you did a great job." Or "I like the way you've 'moved out' and have begun visiting college campuses."

- Continually examine yourself for tone of voice and body language. Most of what we communicate is through tone of voice, facial expressions, and the rest of our demeanor.

- What words are you using? Your counselees can forget what you said to them, but they never forget how you made them *feel.* A negative comment might seem insignificant to you, but it can touch a raw nerve in certain youngsters; the simplest positive comment can cause a youngster to swell with pride.

- Talk *with*, not *at*, your counselees. Professionally trained counselors usually have no trouble with this one, but parents often are unaware of the implications. It's like the song from *Midnight Cowboy*: "Everybody's talkin' at me; I don't hear a word they're sayin'." You are important to your counselees, and your words are taken to heart.

- Smile a lot! A smile says, "I like you; I care about you."

- Let students do a little homework. Listen to their ideas, then suggest that they transform the ideas into action. When youngsters take on a responsibility and then achieve a goal, it can increase their feelings of self-worth.

- Laugh a lot! It's contagious—and a great stress reducer. Laughter can even boost self-confidence.

- Reach out to parents. "I'm as close as a telephone" should be a phrase you use often. Sound communication with parents can make life easier for everyone, especially the developing adolescent.

# LEARNING STYLES

*Single-Sex Education: The Good and the Bad of It*

*Too many girls speak quietly, do not contradict boys, seldom argue, and listen carefully. Too many girls write everything down and simply repeat it. Boys talk loudly, contradict and interrupt girls, prove contentious, and talk before they listen. Boys propose theories, explain things. . . . I am too impatient to accept the intellectual timidity of the obviously brilliant woman, too cynical to accept the assertive ignorance of the stupid man. I make equal demands on my students, men, and women both, and set goals for them just beyond where they are. . . . What this means in practical terms in the classroom is easy to say. Women have to talk up, speaking in voices that can be heard. They have to develop capacities for assertiveness in vigorous discourse and in their writing. . . . Intellectually in the classroom there should be no difference between men and women.*

—*Jacob Neusner*
*How to Grade Your Professors and Other Unexpected Advice, 1984*

That was 1984. The situation has improved somewhat in the classroom since that time, but unfortunately there are only pockets of enlightenment—much remains to be accomplished regarding equal educational opportunity for women and for people of color.

No problem for women in law and medicine. About 50 percent of law and medical school entrants are now women. But we are still experiencing real problems in engineering (computers included), mathematics, and science. Physics is a disaster. The under-enrollment of women in these occupational areas continues to be a source of consternation to educators and others.

Society looks to school counselors to help rectify any shortages, but to be optimally effective, counselors need to: (1) sensitize themselves to the many factors that prevent young women from considering certain nontraditional careers; and (2) familiarize themselves with intervention techniques that might be potentially useful in helping female counselees surmount any established barriers.

School counselors are by no means the only educators on whom society is leaning. *Exercised* administrative leadership is a crucial factor. And classroom teachers can be positive models, as well as positive promoters.

Let's examine how Anacapa Middle School in Ventura, California is working with the problem. In the February 1995 issue of *NEA Today*, middle school teacher Pam Belitski is quoted as saying, "Creating all-girl math classes in middle schools to boost girls' achievement and create equal opportunity may seem extreme, but research and my own experience shows that it works."

At Anacapa, optional single-sex mathematics classes for girls were established in 1994. A year later, enrollment had risen from 30 to 90 girls. The creators argue that the learning style of girls is different from that of boys, and that such classes offer an opportunity for girls to enhance their problem-solving skills, become divergent thinkers, heighten their self-esteem as to mathematical aptitude, and become aware of gender and stereotyping issues without the distraction of having boys present. To accommodate the way girls think through math problems, Belitski's teaching is more concept-oriented than number-oriented. She finds the classroom atmosphere a lot less competitive and a lot more cooperative.

School counselors recognize that middle school years are ones when students make important decisions about their futures—decisions that can have some bearing on students' success or failure in mathematics and science classes. Middle school counselors and teachers can help build positive attitudes regarding mathematics: *strengthened attitudes can stem from strengthened skills.*

Of course, the flip side of the argument is that none of this is necessary—that single-sex classes are actually disadvantageous to girls. The argument is that higher performing mathematics students are often boys, so in all-girl math classes, there is an absence of positive role models. Lack of role models is the reason often cited for eliminating homogeneously grouped classes; segregation by sex is a form of homogeneous grouping. Furthermore, critics of single-sex classes argue that the school should be a setting where young people prepare for life: it should be a microcosm of the real world.

Another negative vote for single-sex classes comes from the young women themselves: many of them resent the implication that girls are "not as good as" boys. This is especially true of high-achieving girls who *want* the opportunity to compete against the best, even if they happen to be boys. A valedictorian from Presque Isle, Maine felt that her sex had been insulted; to take care of the low-achievers, she claimed, there should be an "All-Timid" Math.

People talk about single-sex classes for girls, but what about boys? To allow for equality of opportunity, one school instituted an all-boys math class to balance an all-girls class. The results after one year of the experiment showed the following: in seventh grade, the CTBS math scores of the boys were 3 to 10 percentiles higher than the girls; after ninth grade, during which time the students were in single-sex math classes, the boys' scores were 14 to 22 percentiles higher than the girls'. A one-year experiment proves nothing; additional classes will have to be studied, but some interesting questions have been raised:

1. Does the disparity of scores in the seventh grade indicate that *earlier* single-sex education would make a difference?
2. Are the boys more intimidated by the girls than vice-versa?
3. Should serious and controlled research be undertaken on the single sex issue, despite Title 9?

Many of the same pros and cons have been advanced about women's colleges. But they've been around for generations and are doing a rather good job of preparing young women for life in the real world.

## *Advanced Placement: A New Look at an Old Program*

For nearly a half century, the College Board's Advanced Placement program has been serving the needs of many of our most capable students by way of teaching college courses in a high school setting—everything from Calculus and Pascal to Art and Latin.

But as the number of AP courses—as well as students pursuing them—has proliferated, an increasing number of colleges and universities are restricting the number of credits they will award to incoming freshmen. Some institutions refuse to accept *any* credits in lieu of college work, arguing that as they've redesigned curriculums, AP course content and accompanying tests have not kept pace with the changes. No problem for Amherst College—they've never accepted credits. Its faculty has consistently voted to require freshmen to take the college's full load. Then again, it should come as no surprise that some colleges feel "more comfortable" awarding credit only for work pursued under their auspices. (Some high schools also do not include coursework taken elsewhere in computing their students' rank and grade point averages.)

The Advanced Placement program now covers 16 subjects and 29 separate tests. Statistics and environmental science will become part of the portfolio in the 1996-97 school year. A record number of 425,000 students in the nation are currently enrolled in one or more AP courses. The shifting attitudes of various colleges and universities is impacting on how school counselors are advising their students toward this particular College Board program. As policy variance becomes more pronounced, the tracking of relative information has become more complex.

CONSIDERATIONS IN ADVISING YOUR STUDENTS

- Take the time to explore why a particular counselee wants to pursue an AP course. It might not be in his or her best interest to do so. Here are reasons to ponder—from the more acceptable and erudite to the less acceptable and down-home practical: (1) to intellectually challenge the student, (2) to greatly enhance the student's knowledge in a given subject area, (3) to reduce family tuition costs, (4) to make the transcript look good, (5) to give mom and dad something to brag about, (6) all of the above.

- Remind your students that there has been some belt tightening. Some collegiate institutions are now requiring a minimum score of 4 (5 being the highest) rather than 3. A score of 3 is considered a middle ground in which college faculty believe student ability varies greatly. The 5's are spectacular, the 4's solid, the 3's can be elusive.

- Know that informal studies indicate that students who scored a 3, and are now in college, seem to experience more trouble with advanced course work than their higher scoring counterparts. Colleges and universities that accept 3's might not be doing their students any favors. Unduly sweating it out as a freshman can wreck havoc on one's self-confidence.

- Be aware that decisions on whether to increase minimum acceptable test scores, or even whether to accept AP credit at all, continue to largely reside with individual academic departments within a college or university. This can make your advisement all the more complicated. Only a handful of institutions like Clemson University and Amherst College have institution-wide policies.

- Work at getting your students to become less concerned about the awarding of credit and more concerned about the development of their intellect—just as we need to continually remind our students that the primary reason for taking a foreign language is to become bilingual, not to get into college. Higher Education continues to look favorably on the pursuit of advanced placement work in large part because of the critical thinking skills built into the instruction. AP work *is* great preparation for college.

# CO-CURRICULUM AND THE EDUCATIONAL EXPERIENCE

As you know, students who participate in co-curricular activities have a "leg up" on acceptance to college, especially to the 150 or so that emphasize such participation in their search for a diversified student body.

Along with other educators, we prefer the term "co-curricular" which implies a broad definition of the word "curriculum," and suggests that co-curricular participation is an integral part of the educative process.

Whether it be sports, honor societies, student government, or hobby clubs, co-curricular activities provide students with real-life opportunities outside the classroom to acquire new skills, and to accept and then handle said responsibility, an undeniable advantage when enrolling in a college or university.

A report released in June 1995 by the National Center for Education Statistics, *Educational Policy Issues: Statistical Perspectives*, highlights the correlation between co-curricular activities and student success, along with the availability of these activities to all students. The results are based on data obtained by NCES from the 1992 National Education Longitudinal Study.

While almost every school that participated in the study offered some sort of co-curricular program, the size and affluence of the school, whether public or private, dictated how many activities were offered. As you examine Table 1, note that student participation was drastically different. Although four out of five seniors said they participated in an activity during the fall of 1992, those students from less affluent schools were less likely to participate.

Here socioeconomic status (SES) became an important variable in participation. According to the study, almost 75 percent of low SES students engaged in at least one activity, compared with 87 percent of high SES students. Also, the students from low SES were more likely to be involved in vocational or professionally-oriented activities, e.g., Future Teachers of America, 4H, and Audio/Video Clubs.

Since co-curricular participation can be an integral part of the educative process, we believe that such participation can positively impact on a student's educational achievement.

## *Promotional Points to Consider*

Along with administrators and faculty, counselors should be most concerned about the breadth and quality of a school building or district's co-curricular program. Because of their interest in the whole child, counselors are in a favorable position to effect change. The expansion of any co-curricular program can rest with a school district's philosophical statement and goals and objectives. The tie needs to be there; the statement and goals and objectives need to be examined. All too often people are incapable of properly defending the existence of a co-curricular program. Just as students should be taking a foreign language for reasons other than college admission, so too should they be engaged in co-curricular activities for reasons other than making their transcripts look good.

- In some secondary schools, counselors voluntarily serve as club advisors. Here they can have an extra stake in the program.

- All co-curricular activities, including sports activities, should be listed in an annually updated student/parent handbook. The piece doesn't have to be the ultra-attractive but rather expensive spiral bound that can be personally produced by Premier School Agendas, Bellingham, Washington; rather, it can be something your administration produces internally by means of desktop publishing. The issue isn't so much what route you select, including black & white or color scenery along the way, as it is that you select a route. Functional handbooks that include study hints and weekly calendars are a virtual must for today's students.

- A school district's economic condition can sometimes determine the breadth and depth of any co-curricular program. You might have to double your efforts to help make certain activities "necessary" in the eyes of the powers that be.

TABLE 1

**Percentage of public school seniors participating in selected extracurricular activities by SES of student and influence of school, 1992**

| Selected Activity | All Students* | Low SES Students | | High SES Students | |
|---|---|---|---|---|---|
| | | Less Affluent Schools | More Affluent Schools | Less Affluent Schools | More Affluent Schools |
| Any extracurricular activity | 79.9 | 74.7 | 73.0 | 86.8 | 87.6 |
| Sports (individual and team) | 42.4 | 34.3 | 33.2 | 48.6 | 53.1 |
| Performing Arts | 27.5 | 25.0 | 20.7 | 32.0 | 29.2 |
| Academic Clubs | 26.2 | 20.2 | 20.5 | 36.2 | 32.3 |
| Vocational/ Professional Clubs | 20.8 | 29.2 | 25.6 | 16.0 | 11.8 |
| Honor Societies | 18.1 | 10.3 | 10.0 | 30.8 | 29.9 |
| Publications | 17.0 | 17.6 | 9.5 | 22.4 | 20.0 |
| Student Governments | 15.5 | 12.6 | 9.9 | 17.5 | 20.9 |
| Service Clubs | 15.2 | 10.0 | 9.4 | 25.0 | 21.1 |
| Hobby Clubs | 8.5 | 8.2 | 6.9 | 9.4 | 9.6 |

*Includes students in middle two quartiles.

Source: *Educational Policy Issues: Statistical Perspectives, June 1995; Extracurricular Activities and Student Engagement*

# SUGGESTED READINGS/CONTACTS

American Association of University Women (1995), *Growing Smart: What's Working for Girls in School*, 1111 16th St., N.W., Washington, DC 20036 (a report that details a variety of programs and strategies that can be easily employed by educators, parents, and community members).

American Association of University Women (1992), *How Schools Shortchange Girls*, 1111 16th St., N.W., Washington DC 20036.

Glasser, William (1990), *The Quality School*, HarperCollins, New York, NY 10022.

Premier School Agendas, Inc., 2000 Kentucky Street, Bellingham, Washington 98226; or 593 Skippack Pike, Bluebell, Pennsylvania 19422.

Sadker, David and Myra (1994), *Failing at Fairness: How America's Schools Cheat Girls*, Charles Scribner's Sons, New York, NY 10022.

# CHAPTER 3

# ACADEMIC LONG-RANGE PLANNING: FOUR- AND SIX-YEAR PROGRAMS OF STUDY

Clearly, we must promote the actions of families in the long-range planning of the education of their children, with special emphasis on grades 6 through 12. The term "promote" is significant because it denotes the development and fostering of this particular activity. Of course, such proactive planning should be tentative in nature due to the numerous variables that can affect planning, including the need for continual curriculum review and enhancement, and the changes that occur in the intellectual, social, and emotional growth of a given student. No matter what, long-range educational planning has far more positives than negatives. Finding the time to meet with parents, whether on a group or individual basis, is certainly a step in the right direction. If a financial planner can do it, so can you.

It serves no purpose to argue that parents should totally assume the educational planning role. Educational demands have changed; many of today's parents are either not sufficiently knowledgeable about the process, or are incapable and/or unwilling to help. This then becomes another arena in which a school counseling department must take the lead in bridging the gap. And "lead" can mean calling parents into the school to "show them the way," so to speak. To empower them.

In many high schools, student programs of study are constructed a year at a time with little or no thought to post-secondary educational plans or career objectives. But placing students in appropriate courses according to abilities, interests, values, and career aspirations is one of the most serious and vital responsibilities of the school counselor. Just think of the "down the line" importance such responsibility has when you and the family ultimately do a little post-secondary educational planning.

A study conducted in 1990 by the California State Department of Education indicated that many youngsters who claimed they planned to attend college were not even enrolled in college preparatory courses at the ninth- and tenth-grade levels, especially in the areas of mathematics and science. Families should be made aware of *all* options available to their offspring and the courses that lead to each option.

An educational plan (see Figure 3-1) that keeps track of credits or units earned, specific coursework required for graduation, as well as course recommendations for post-secondary education, can be a valuable blueprint to help ensure that *all* students reach their maximum potential.

Note that in the four-year plan, graduation requirements can be preprinted.

Five-year plans whereby students take Algebra I and the first level of a foreign language in grade eight are quite common today. A surprising number of schools, however, still do not offer such acceleration. Accelerated students are usually the academically talented, yet there are a handful of secondary schools where eighth-grade Algebra I is available to *all* college-bound students.

Honors Biology should be offered at the ninth-grade level for the academically talented. High schools that do not have this kind of science acceleration (ninth-grade Honors Biology) are usually those that wonder why their Advanced Placement science programs are so under enrolled in grades eleven and twelve. If your community wants a strong AP science program, then you've got to get your talented students moving "up front."

A six-year plan is especially appropriate where the first year of college preparatory mathematics and foreign language are offered at the seventh-grade level. In a few schools, such as Abington Senior High School in Abington, Pennsylvania, and East Brunswick High School in New Jersey, a six-year sequence of college preparatory mathematics, with the first year of study commencing in grade seven, is in evidence. The program *can* conform to that recommended by the Commission on Mathematics of the College Entrance Examination Board and/or the National Science Board Commission on Pre-College Education in Mathematics. The sequence mathematics might be as follows:

| | | | |
|---|---|---|---|
| Grade 7 | Algebra I Honors | Grade 10 | Pre-calculus Honors |
| Grade 8 | Algebra II Honors | Grade 11 | Discrete Math Honors or Intro to Calculus |
| Grade 9 | Geometry Honors | Grade 12 | AP Calculus AB or BC |

Note that Honors Geometry is held until grade 9, in part to get as close to PSAT/SAT testing as possible. This type of super-accelerated student usually has little or no problem pulling it all together at a later date by way of self-study or through sheer mathematical inclination. Remember, research indicates that the more years of mathematics study, the higher the college admission test score.

Increasingly, we are seeing the first level of foreign language study beginning in grade 6 or 7. When a youngster is in grade 6, grade 12 can seem a long way off, but languages are more readily learned at an earlier age — yet another reason for doing some long-range planning.

FIGURE 3-1

FOUR-YEAR EDUCATIONAL PLAN

Student Name _____ Initiation Date _____

| GRADE | 9 | 10 | 11 | 12 |
|---|---|---|---|---|
| **SUBJECT AREA** | | | | |
| English:<br>(4 yrs.) | English I | English II | English III | English IV |
| Social Studies:<br>(3 yrs.) | Global Studies | _____ | US History I | US History II |
| Mathematics:<br>(3 yrs.) | _____ | _____ | _____ | _____ |
| Science:<br>(2 yrs.) | _____ | _____ | _____ | _____ |
| Fine/Practical Arts:<br>(1 yr.) | _____ | _____ | _____ | _____ |
| Foreign Language: | _____ | _____ | _____ | _____ |
| Physical Education/<br>Health:<br>(4 yrs.) | _____ | _____ | _____ | _____ |
| Elective: | _____ | _____ | _____ | _____ |
| Elective: | _____ | _____ | _____ | _____ |

What about youngsters who drastically change their goals during their secondary school experience? First, we should encourage the pursuit of coursework that brings out the best of everything in a youngster — sometimes the more inclusive the approach, the better. (A few high schools now *require* all students to take Algebra I.) Second, once a four- or six-year educational plan has been developed, there should be enough flexibility built into the plan to accommodate change! Although there is much to be said for long-range planning, there's much to be said for day-at-a-time planning as well. Day-at-a-time counselors are often "options open." They can be creative and energetic types who are not afraid to make a few waves for their clients where necessary. Helping young people realign their paths can be a crusade with some of these professionals, even if it means expending an inordinate amount of time to do so.

Change is an okay thing with your counselees. Indeed, as we move toward the year 2000, students will have to be optimally flexible. The twenty-first century promises to be a century of even more rapid change. As your counselees proceed from semester to semester, grade to grade, you need to be continually on the lookout for those promising "diamonds in the rough." If there must be a race, then young people should have the opportunity of *entering it at any given point on the course!*

# COUNSELOR LIAISON TO SUBJECT AREA DEPARTMENT

Of course, to construct an educational plan and effectively counsel a family, you should know what you are talking about; and the most evident source of that information is that group most involved with the welfare of students: the teachers. One reason for developing sound communication with any teaching faculty is that they can be fonts of expertise. Take any instructional department: the combined experiential knowledge of all the teachers is impressive. You and your counselees can tap into this rich supplemental source for guidance in selecting the proper courses to take; teachers can tell you the respective levels of difficulty, as well as offer a more *detailed analysis of specific courses*. As counselors, we probably "lean on" teachers most heavily in the subject matter area, but teachers can also be excellent resource people when it comes to college majors and certain occupational fields.

Whether or not teachers are willing to communicate with counselors can depend on the amount of rapport established between counselor and teacher. Counselors often reach out to various teachers, but are teachers comfortable in going to counselors to help solve student problems?

One solution: The Counselor Liaison Program, an innovative rapport-building concept. It can *indirectly* enhance the personal skills of your counselees in that it can improve communications between a counseling department and various subject area departments. The jist of the program is that one counselor is assigned as a liaison to each subject area department, or if the counseling department is small, one counselor could service two departments. The counselor representative presents two short presentations, fall and spring, to subject area teachers. An added bonus is that at these meetings teachers have the chance to voice any concerns that might affect both departments. The counselor rep then takes all information back to his or her department meeting for a full staff presentation.

One department eased into the picture with a brief questionnaire to the faculty. (See Figures 3-2 and 3-3.) A rather loose program had previously existed, but the intent was to expand the concept.

FIGURE 3-2

---

Date: _____

Dear _____ :

For the past several years the Counseling Department has had a communications program in place whereby designated counselors have acted as liaisons to various subject area departments.

Plans are to improve and expand this program for the coming academic year. For example, we are considering defining the role of the liaison more precisely to ensure a greater similarity of purpose and involvement.

You are one of twenty-seven teachers whom we are asking to complete the enclosed questionnaire. We value your thoughts and opinions!

Would you kindly return the completed questionnaire to us by Monday, September 16.

Sincerely,

Robert Altman
Counseling Department Chair

---

FIGURE 3-3

LIAISON QUESTIONNAIRE

Teacher: _____

1. The idea of having a counselor/liaison to the various subject area departments is (*circle one*)

   an excellent idea     a good idea     a mediocre idea     a poor idea

2. If you believe the concept to be worthwhile, how do you personally view this particular role? For example, what specific tasks do you see the counselor/liaison performing?

3. In what general or specific ways can counselors be more helpful to you in your role as a classroom teacher?

4. How can the counselors better assist you and/or your department at the time students are programmed for their next year's courses?

5. What role do you see the counselor playing in the teacher/counselor relationship? What services would you find most helpful?

6. How often do you enter the counseling office to avail yourself of counseling and guidance services? (*circle one*)

   never     seldom     occasionally     often

7. If you circled "never" or "seldom," is there something the Counseling Department could do to cause you to become a more frequent visitor?

8. Are there questions you have about guidance and counseling procedures that could be more fully explained? If so, what procedures would you like to know more about?

You should share at least some of the findings with the participants, so do so through a thank you letter:

FIGURE 3-4

---

TO: _____

FROM:   Robert Altman

RE:       Liaison Questionnaire Participation

On behalf of the Counseling Department, I would like to thank you for your efforts as to the liaison study conducted during September. We appreciated receiving your well-placed and insightful comments concerning the proposed role and function of the department liaison, as well as those that pertain to counselor/teacher relationships.

Twenty-five of the twenty-seven teachers surveyed responded to the questionnaire. The results of question #1, "The idea of having a counselor/liaison to the various subject area departments," are as follows: excellent—13, good—9, mediocre—2, poor—1.

A number of commonly mentioned issues became apparent, such as class size, counselor visitation of classes, counselor accessibility, and the placement of students in certain subject areas.

All of this information will become food for thought, and we intend to carefully examine the data over the next several weeks.

Thanks again for your involvement!

---

Now a "sharing" memo (see Figure 3-5) is sent from the chairperson to his or her staff.

FIGURE 3-5

---

Dear Colleague,

Enclosed please find participating teacher comments in regard to the inter-departmental liaison study. We will discuss the findings and the entire liaison topic at a future department meeting.

I have included most of the rendered comments in the attached seven pages. But I took the liberty of eliminating repetitive answers where appropriate. It is interesting to see commonly mentioned issues such as class size, counselors getting out and visiting classes, etc.

Please study the findings, and perhaps make some random notes as to your perception of the role and function of the liaison.

Robert Altman

---

Figure 3-6 shows an announcement to all subject area chairs stating that the counseling department wants to move forward with the newly improved program. This is followed by the "Tractenberg" memo shown in Figure 3-7.

## FIGURE 3-6

TO:        Ms. Kathryn Hall, English Chair

FROM:   Dr. Kenneth Molsen, Counseling Chair

RE:        Subject Area/Counselor Liaison Program

DATE:    September 12, 199X

In an effort to improve communication between the Counseling Department and your department, we will be expanding the counselor liaison program this year. As you are aware, for the past several years a counselor has been assigned to your subject area department to act as a liaison between our two departments. This academic year the counselors would like to present two twenty-minute presentations, one in the fall and one in the spring to discuss issues of common interest. Throughout the year the designated counselor will be available to meet with you or any member of your staff on any concerns or issues that involve both our departments.

Donald Tractenberg will be your liaison for this school year and he will be contacting you to arrange a date and time for his presentations.

Thank you for your consideration.

## FIGURE 3-7

TO: Kathryn Hall, English Chair

FROM: Donald Tractenberg

DATE: September 20, 199X

As the Counseling Department's liaison to the English Department, I would appreciate the opportunity to address your department sometime in the near future for purposes of exploring common concerns and issues.

As we near the time for the programming of students for the next academic year, it might be appropriate to speak to your department sometime in November or early December.

I would need only twenty minutes for the presentation.

Anything you might do would be most appreciated.

c.c. Dr. Kenneth Molsen

It should be apparent that with a rather sophisticated Counselor Liaison program in place, the school counselor would be in a more favorable position to advise families on important educational matters, including that of long-range planning. Communication with faculty members needs to be especially close just prior to the programming of students for the following academic year.

# CHAPTER 4

# HOMEWORK AND STUDY ISSUES

The assignment of homework is a major issue among educators: some are for it, some against. Some school systems have well-delineated policies on the subject, others have none; even teachers within the same building have varying opinions as to the type and quantity of work that should be assigned.

While a component of the school reform movement of the 1990s reflects an emphasis on increased amounts of homework, research on the subject reveals a mixed bag. Sometimes homework is associated with higher levels of achievement, sometimes not. Many parents favor "burning the midnight oil" when necessary, while others complain that family life is interrupted by the inordinate amount of time required to complete assignments. Teachers are griping as well; often it is the case of students not completing assignments or ignoring them altogether. Some educators have simply abandoned ship and assign no homework at all.

On the whole, though, it is thought that if a youngster continues to ignore a half-dozen or so English assignments, several chemistry lab reports, and a few foreign language vocabulary drills, he does serious damage to his sense of self-worth, to say nothing of what he does to his course grades. Such blatant disregard for the norm is perplexing to parents, but not to school counselors. They've seen it all before. Counselors recognize that a student's refusal to turn in assignments is simply another aspect of underachievement, an irresponsi-

29

ble lack of action. It's no mean task for a counselor to get his or her counselee to see the problem for what it is, and then act on it. What *can* be most helpful is a meeting of the minds: parents, students, teachers, and counselors coming together and laying their cards on the table, so to speak. This can be accomplished through an open and honest discussion of the issue either in private conference or via small- or large-group presentations conducted during the school day or in the evening.

Here are some ideas and materials you can utilize in developing a presentation for teachers, parents, and students.

# RATIONALE FOR ASSIGNING HOMEWORK

The rationale for assigning homework incorporates at least four perspectives: (1) Today's society expects more than in the past; the future might well be worse. There's just too much to learn, and the mountain of information needed to be learned continues to rise rapidly. As a result, teachers are unable to cover sufficient amounts of content material during the school day. (2) Homework needs to be viewed as a means of *supplementing* classroom instruction. Nothing more, nothing less. (3) The research on memory loss and retention high-lights the importance of distributed practice and review. Students need to practice what they learn, including those foreign language vocabulary words. (4) The purposeful assignment of homework can promote independent learning. Students who grow in self-direction and who develop sound time-management skills will learn much more on their own than those who do not develop such skills. Enhancement of these skills can pay big dividends at the collegiate level.

Homework comes in all sizes and shapes. The following suggestions should be implemented *where appropriate*.

# ACTION PLAN: EIGHT SUGGESTIONS

1. What is sorely needed in our schools is a solid agreement on the part of students, parents, and teachers as to the role homework should play in a building or district; it should be followed by a careful explanation to all involved parties of the reason that homework is assigned. First, district policy, if any, needs to be examined. If no such policy exists, then perhaps one per building is in order. The rendering of an explanation is no guarantee that all students will understand or comply; on the other hand, failure to highlight the value of homework can mean that some students will regard the process as a meaningless exercise, meaningless busy work. Any message of explanation must be reinforced periodically.

2. Homework needs to be relevant. Relevancy has always been a critical piston that drives motivation and meaning; today's young people seek it as never before. Rather than reading about a war, a student might interview a veteran. Or rather than studying an entire list of spelling words, a student can study a separate and personal list of misspelled words.

3. So often we forget that students learn through their mistakes—as often as the students themselves do. The four "re's" are applicable here: *re*write, *re*view, *re*think, and *re*work. The process entails learning from one's mistakes by correcting them; much growth and development takes place from surmounting errors. When a student misses three out of ten mathematics problems, he or she should be expected to rework them. Students don't improve their positions by making mistakes and then moving on. This is not an acceptable practice on the athletic field, and it should not be an acceptable practice in the classroom.

4. Requesting students to do anything is of little or no value unless they know how to do it. For example, requiring students to turn in a five-paragraph essay on *Macbeth* is fruitless unless students are familiar with the logistics of writing a five-paragraph essay. Teachers should not assume that a topic has been taught to *all* students by a previous instructor. Sometimes students submit poor reports because they lack the appropriate skill in the components needed to bring the task to a successful conclusion.

5. Long homework assignments can be divided into shorter segments. This is both a practical and psychological maneuver. By assigning one-half of the week's vocabulary words to be learned for Wednesday, you assure that students will begin studying by Tuesday rather than waiting until Thursday. Asking students to submit at least *one* college application by early October has both psychological and practical benefits. It gets students moving and thwarts procrastination; it also shifts the counseling department into high gear from a processing standpoint. An English teacher asking for a certain number of note cards each day can get students started on a term paper project.

6. There is nothing wrong with occasionally asking parents to review and sign-off on homework. This is a good way for parents to see the type and quality of work their youngster is doing at school. Furthermore, it's a tactic that can solidify parent/school communications.

7. Teachers should not assume that *all* students have access to the materials needed to complete assignments. We should examine whether or not students have access to particular reference sources, transportation to the local library or beyond, and even to the newest of computer technologies. Similarly, it might be profitable to recap what has been assigned at the very end of a class period to ensure that the *proper* school books and materials go home for that evening.

8. Homework needs to be checked! Students learn early on not to put in time and effort on work that is not checked. If homework is truly important, then it should be monitored in some manner by student, peer, or teacher. Research reveals that a teacher placing comments on a student's work can pay big dividends in terms of intellectual growth.

And as for intellectual growth, all roads to good grades seem to lead to *time on task*—the amount of time students expend on homework and study. Numerous research projects, including a large-sample path analysis conducted by Timothy Keith of Duke University in 1982, indicate that after controlling for other variables, earned course grades are generally commensurate with the number of minutes a student devotes to homework and study. In short, the more time on task, the higher the grade.

# HOMEWORK AND STUDY: NOT SYNONYMOUS TERMS

In private conferences or evening presentations we often hear parents lament the fact that their youngsters never bring any work home. It's certainly an issue worth exploring, especially if some sort of pattern seems to be emerging with an individual teacher or subject area department.

A more significant issue, however, is the misunderstanding that students have about what constitutes homework and what constitutes study. They love to lump the two together: when homework is done, so is study. But the two terms are *not* synonymous. When are young people going to learn that homework might translate into doing mathematics problems on pages 36 through 38, while studying might mean outlining a World History chapter, or rewriting the day's Lab Biology notes? Some counseling departments do little or no advising about *study* habits; others are "into it" in a big way. Parents and teachers need to be on base, too.

You can do much to attack this area by making it an agenda item for a group orientation program or a study skills seminar; it can be a great middle school topic. One middle school ensures that all of its counselors are doling out the same advice: "*All* students should be spending a *minimum* of twenty minutes of homework/study time each day (five days per week) per major subject." If Jennifer carried five majors, she would put in 100 minutes of preparation time daily. Of course, when you first inform the Jennifers of the world about this suggestion, they either look at you in utter disbelief, or fall off their chairs laughing. However, it only takes a few years of persistent suggesting for most students to get the message—much like the time it takes to hold the line on schedule changes.

Since many students have no concept as to what actually constitutes study, and similarly are unable to properly differentiate between that and homework, here are a few examples.

## *Study Examines Effort Versus Ability*

Harold Stevenson and James Stigler compared American and Asian beliefs about school success. Asian students stated to the authors that "studying hard" was more likely to lead to success in school, whereas American students said that one's ability was a greater factor than effort.

The study relates quite well to the time-on-task findings of the aforementioned Duke University study. Stevenson and Stigler comment that American students' belief in ability is mistaken, in that it hurts youngsters: students with high ability can "find little reason to work hard;" youngsters who think they have lower ability doubt they can master their lessons through continuous and persistent effort—and so they have little reason to work hard.

Asian students are *confident* that the *time* they invest will lead to mastery. When these same students receive a low grade, they don't see themselves as slow; rather, they take the posture that they'll just have to double their efforts to reach their goal.

School counselors and teachers can help young people develop an "I can do it" attitude by instilling in them the idea that a tough subject *can* be learned if one keeps at it—and the earlier the instillation the better! Of course, this is where the influential home comes into play. And for every non-caring parent in America, there appears to be at least one caring one.

FIGURE 4-1

## HINTS TO HELP YOU STUDY BETTER

Dear Student:

We often hear students exclaim that they have no homework. You must remember that even though no specific assignment has been made, there is still homework: it's called "study." We strongly recommend that you spend a *minimum* of twenty minutes of homework/study time (five days a week) on *each* of your major subjects. If you have no studying to do whatsoever, you should still complete the 100-minute minimum: pick up a good book and *read*! Remember that extensive readers tend to score higher on standardized tests, including those for college admission.

*Note:* The four re's are where it's at! Study, in contrast to specified homework, includes but is not limited to:

1. The *rewriting* of lecture notes and lab reports.

2. The *reviewing* of lecture notes while they are still fresh in one's mind. In terms of understanding material, one hour spent as soon after a lecture as possible is worth several hours several days later.

3. The *rethinking* of theorems in geometry so that one knows them verbatim and can apply them to problems not previously assigned.

4. The *reworking* of foreign language vocabulary words by making up English sentences and transcribing them into the foreign language.

5. The outlining of a history chapter for purposes of review for a chapter or section test. The rewriting of any material has been shown to be a most beneficial technique in improving recall or comprehension.

6. Get a good night's sleep before a test—no cramming! Research indicates that sleep helps to "seal in" information.

7. If you have no studying to do—**Read!**

Psychologist, Nicholas Zill, co-authored a study sponsored by Child Trends, Inc., a non-profit, non-partisan research organization in Washington, D.C. Zill slices it down the middle. He believes that there are plenty of hard-working families that want to do well by their children; on the other hand, Zill and co-author Christine Nord were surprised to discover that nearly half of all U.S. high school students have parents who don't attend back-to-school nights, class plays, athletic events, etc. "The social environment in many of our schools tends to run counter to the messages children get at home—namely to study hard and behave in class." The authors found that only 38 percent of U.S. students in grades 6-12 said their friends thought it very important to put in the effort needed to achieve high marks.

Bob Herbert in a *New York Times* article of March 1, 1995, thinks we are fast becoming a nation of nitwits. "In an era in which the ability to acquire and properly process information has become profoundly important, America insists on being, to a large extent, a nation of nitwits. . . Some African-American students unable to extricate themselves from the quicksand of self-defeat, have adopted the incredibly stupid tactic of harassing fellow blacks who have the temerity to take their studies seriously. According to the poisoning logic of the harassers, any attempt at acquiring knowledge is a form of 'acting white,' and that, of course, is to be shunned at all costs."

As a school counselor, you know that such harassment is cross-cultural. It's not "cool" to be smart—whether you're black, white, female, or whatever.

## Scholastic Achievement and Self-Concept

Some of those "doubting" lower ability students were studied as early as 1945. Prescott Lecky, in his fascinating work, *Self-Consistency: A Theory of Personality*, suggested that students' level of achievement might be related to the perceptions they had of themselves as learners. He noticed that some children made the same number of spelling errors per page, no matter how difficult or easy the material: an observation that caused him to wonder whether the children might be responding more in terms of how they *thought* they could spell as opposed to their actual spelling abilities. To test this hypothesis, a number of the children worked with a counselor who helped them explore their feelings regarding their spelling capabilities. As a result of this communication, and without the children engaging in any additional drill, there was a noticeable improvement in their spelling. It seemed that as their self-perceptions changed, so did their performance.

Lecky's unsophisticated pioneering research opened the door to the unbelievable possibility that how students feel about their abilities may, for better or worse, consciously or unconsciously, affect their academic performance. The seed was thus planted that suggested that scholastic achievement might not be just an expression of students' abilities, but of students' perceptions of their abilities—which when positive can help them to feel confident and capable—but when negative, can cause them to feel hesitant and uncertain.

Numerous studies over the past quarter century, including that of Donald Hamachek (1992), have concluded that there *is* a moderately strong concurrent relationship between students' scholastic achievement and their concept of their own ability. Furthermore, a growing body of research indicates that not only is scholastic self-concept clearly differentiable from general self-concept, but that scholastic self-concept is even more highly correlated with scholastic achievement than is general self-concept.

Although it has been argued that students first have to do well in school to have a positive self-image regarding their scholastic abilities, the position has also been taken that a positive self-image is a prerequisite for doing well in school. If nothing else, all of this suggests that self-concept and achievement are dynamically interactive and reciprocal. Several studies conducted in the 1980s and targeted at high school students have uncovered the fact that self-esteem rises significantly and commensurately with improved scholastic achievement. Therefore, there is evidence to demonstrate that following an improvement in achievement, students with previously low self-concepts tend to have improved self-perceptions.

The debate as to which comes first, a positive self-concept or scholastic achievement, is undoubtedly more academic than practical. The important thing is that you appreciate their interactive and reciprocal dynamics, and understand that each is mutually reinforcing. The relationship between the two becomes more apparent at the middle school level when students are better able to interpret and internalize feedback from their scholastic performance. As middle school students acquire a clearer understanding of relationships between ability and scholastic achievement, they become more sensitive to performance feedback, which in turn makes their self-perceptions of ability more accurate.

High self-concept students seem to approach school-related tasks with confidence, and success with those tasks reinforces this confidence. Conversely, the opposite pattern is likely to occur for students with low scholastic self-concepts.

## SUGGESTED READINGS

Hamachek, Donald (1992), *Encounters With The Self,* (4th ed.), Harcourt, Brace, Jovanich, Fort Worth, Texas.

Keith, Timothy (1982), *Time Spent on Homework and High School Grades: A Large-Sample Path Analysis,* Journal of Educational Psychology, Vol. 74, No. 2.

Lecky, P. (1945), *Self-Consistency: A Theory of Personality,* Island Press, New York, NY.

Stevenson, Harold and Stigler, James (1992), *The Learning Gap: Why Our Schools Are Failing and What We Can Learn From Japanese and Chinese Education,* Summit Books, 1230 Avenue of the Americas, New York, NY 10020.

Zill, Nicholas and Nord, Christine W. (1994), *Running in Place: How American Families Are Faring in a Changing Economy and Individualistic Society,* Child Trends, Inc., Washington, DC.

# CHAPTER 5

# BRINGING THE SERIOUS UNDERACHIEVER AROUND

Bringing a serious, passive, scholastic underachiever around is one of the most difficult of counseling tasks. Everyone underachieves to some extent, of course, so how do we identify a youngster who could use some help? Perhaps the key words here are "serious," in that an otherwise capable student has a grim-looking academic record; and "passive," in that the student is for the most part unresponsive to proffered instruction. Aside from those characteristics, underachievers come in all shapes and sizes.

## PROFILE OF THE UNDERACHIEVER

### Characteristics of the Underachiever

1. Most are boys.
2. Standardized testing usually reflects average to superior achievement.
3. Many underachievers have well-educated parents who place a high premium on education.
4. Many are articulate, well mannered, and personable.

5. Many have low self-esteem.

6. Personal attitudes toward in-class assignments and homework are frequently negative.

7. Problems tend to exacerbate during the middle-school years as additional independent effort is expected.

8. Underachievers tend to "sponge off" their harder working peers when it comes to the completion of assignments.

## Reasons for Underachievement

The reasons for serious underachievement fall into three broad categories:

1. Difficulty with interpersonal relationships.

2. Overriding emotional problems.

3. Curricular/instructional issues, including teaching methodology.

### INTERPERSONAL RELATIONSHIPS

A youngster's difficulty with interpersonal relationships can stem from (1) continual criticism by an adult (usually a parent) that eventually erodes personal confidence; (2) a rebellious attitude toward a family member, i.e., an overly strict parent, a highly successful older or younger sibling, or a laissez-faire parent who supplies little or no support; and (3) a sheltering parent who interferes with a youngster's normal growth in self-direction.

### EMOTIONAL PROBLEMS

Overriding emotional problems can include a fear of succeeding: it is much easier to say, "I'm not going to try" than "I tried and failed." Putting oneself on the line can be a most difficult task for certain young people.

### CURRICULAR ISSUES

Sometimes boredom can set in with one or more subject areas. Also, instructional techniques might be a mismatch with the individual student's learning style. (See Chapter 2 on educational achievement.)

As we do our best to light fires under our more serious underachievers, especially seniors, we are more and more mindful of the impact individual learning style can have on: scholastic achievement, the role relevancy plays in the educative process, and the disillusionment and discouragement that can be felt by thousands of youngsters who discover themselves hopelessly out of step with the traditional high school. (One million students dropping out of high school each year *is* an appalling statistic.)

## *Solutions to Underachievement*

Once a serious underachiever has been identified, you will want to develop a plan of attack. Here are some points to consider:

1. Employ the assistance of parents when necessary. At the very least, keep parents apprised of what's happening.
2. Be prepared to shift gears and modify any mutually developed plan.
3. Academically talented students are generally motivated by projects that allow for creativity and application.
4. Serious underachievers can display considerable enthusiasm in particular subject areas. You might want to identify the areas and then capitalize on such enthusiasm, remembering that positive attitudes in one or more areas can have a beneficial affect on others.
5. Summer enrichment programs within the school district or on a college campus can be the avenue to pursue in certain cases.

## *A Team Approach*

Here is an example of how a counselor, several teachers, and an administrator implemented item number 4 and capitalized on an underachiever's love of music in order to promote some forward movement.

There are school districts that have established grade-point-average minimums for participation in co-curricular activities, e.g., an earned marking period GPA of at least 2.0. Exceptions to any written policy is usually made by the local board of education. In "Eric's" case, it is the principal who is asking the counselor to construct the letter, recognizing to some extent the influence of the counselor. Counselors will often take the initiative themselves and approach the administration. Note the use of the word "professional" in Figure 5-1—a term all too infrequently employed by school counselors. The principal then follows through with a letter to the superintendent of schools. (See Figure 5-2.)

### Postscript

A formal contract was drawn up by the administration. The board of education did approve the waiver. At the mid-point of the first marking period, and after the family had signed the contract, Eric had earned a 3.40 grade point average. Again, the above case represents a team approach to solution number 4. It also reflects the power and influence of the school counselor within the advocacy role.

FIGURE 5-1

TO:         Andrew Vodola, Principal

FROM:    Betsy Falkner, Counselor

RE:         Eric Williams

DATE:     July 15, 199X

This memorandum is in response to your suggestion that I place in writing my thoughts and concerns regarding sophomore Eric Williams, and his possible participation in our Marching Band program for the coming school year.

In my professional opinion, Eric exhibits many of the symptoms of a youngster with Attention Deficit Hyperactivity Disorder (ADHD). I have arrived at this conclusion through my counseling of Eric, teacher reports, and psychiatrist Dr. Lawrence Smilo's letter of April 7. (See enclosure.)

In spite of the fact that we still did not have solid medical documentation as to the existence of ADHD necessary for the development of a formal written 504 Plan, we nonetheless moved forward this past academic year on an informal basis, and modified Eric's schedule (dropped the fourth level of German and added a marking period of Composition to support the English program). The established interventions were of some help. Eric did fail American Literature and World History; however, he is currently enrolled in summer school for both subjects and doing well.

At this point I believe it is in Eric's best interest to engage in Marching Band for the school year 199X-9X on a probationary basis. (Musical activities are extremely important to this youngster.) Furthermore, I would recommend that he be allowed to do so for the first half of the first marking period. A check of Eric's academic progress would be made at that time.

FIGURE **5-2**

| TO: | Dr. Arthur Whelan |
|---|---|
| FROM: | Andrew Vodola, Principal |
| DATE: | July 20, 199X |
| RE: | Eligibility Appeal—Eric Williams |

In a letter dated July 6, 199X from Karen Dufty, private advocate for Eric Williams who will be a sophomore, she requested a waiver of the 2.0 GPA requirement in order that Eric might be able to participate in Marching Band. Upon receipt of the letter, Eric's status was discussed with Ms. Falkner, Eric's guidance counselor, who then submitted a memorandum dated July 15 (copy attached).

In her response, Ms. Falkner supports granting a waiver for the first half of the first marking period. During this "extended probation" period Eric's academic progress would be closely monitored and teacher grades obtained at the mid-point of the first quarter (October 11). If his progress warrants, namely the equivalent of a 2.0 GPA, Eric would be allowed to continue as a member of the Marching Band until the end of the first quarter (November 16). At the conclusion of the first quarter, his academic progress would again be reviewed to ensure adherence to Board Policy regarding GPA and credits. If he did not meet the requirements, he would be removed from the Marching Band.

After reviewing all of the documentation—report card grades one through nine, transcript, sophomore course requests, attendance data, discipline reports, referral reports, teacher comments, and standardized test scores, it is apparent that Eric has above average intelligence and is capable of obtaining a 2.0 grade point average. He also has sufficient credits to comply with the policy.

In the final analysis I support and recommend Ms. Falkner's approach of allowing Eric to participate in the Marching Band until October 11. On that date, his teachers will be requested to submit a letter grade reflective of his progress to date. If at or above a 2.0 GPA, he will be permitted to continue until the end of the first marking period (November 16); at which time the normal review will occur for GPA and credit compliance with the Board Policy.

## Further Words

- The establishment of rapport between you and your counselee is crucial to the eventual success of any interventions you might decide to implement. So, too, is the uncovering of how previous counselors have tried to work with the underachievement problem; for that matter, the gathering of such information from multiple sources such as family and current and past teachers can be most helpful. We must do all of this because repetition of unsuccessful attempts can become part of the problem.

- Your counselee needs to be completely aware of your nonjudgmental attitude and the open "anything goes in this office" atmosphere that you support and to which you adhere.

- Term usage is most important. The student's past performance may leave much to be desired, but you will want to refrain from using such terms as poor, failing, lousy, etc. Let your counselee pick up on it and employ his or her own terms.

- In your initial session, it can be helpful to keep threatening materials, such as progress reports, report cards, and testing information, out of sight. The timing of the employment of these documents is important.

- Work toward a mutual acceptance of where your counselee stands as to achievement versus aptitude. Many students, even as late as middle school, do not understand the difference between these two terms.

- Now move toward having your counselee express, in his or her own words, the fact that he or she has indeed been underachieving these past several years. Such expression can be very therapeutic for the student. Keeping the mood light and offhanded can produce the needed results.

- The sharing of standardized test results can be part of bringing the underachiever around. The tactic can also backfire if not handled smoothly and judiciously. It is surprising as to the number of students who have never seen their actual scores and/or had them simply but explicitly interpreted for them. Oh, yes, we mail the scores home with explanations, but some parents don't take the time to study the explanations, let alone sit down and explore the findings with their offspring.

- In your interpretation of scores, consider placing greater emphasis on national percentiles in contrast to local ones. It can be argued that since many students sit for college admission testing on a national basis, and then go on to rub shoulders with students from around the country, it's beneficial for students' total developmental growth to emphasize national standing. That is not to say that local percentiles or stanines should be ignored, but national results can certainly be a more positive thrust.

- Establish reasonable expectations. "Too easy" can translate into boredom. "Too difficult" can make success unlikely.

- Specificity is the key! Initial goals should be specific *and* short-term.

- Teach study skills that include organizational tips.

- Causes of inappropriate behavior can be *subconsciously* affecting your counselee.

- Some underachievers experience a rebirth when they see their future laid before them. Post-secondary educational planning and/or career planning can trigger such a response.

- Judge any new growth not by what your counselee says (he or she may tell you what he or she thinks you want to hear), but by tangible evidence, e.g., positive teacher reports and/or improved marking period grades. Any new-found success needs to be documented!

- If it looks as if the student is indeed beginning to shift into second gear, praise him or her sparingly. Remember that when students begin to come alive, they're often embarrassed by adult praise. Also remember that not doing well for heavy underachievers can be a badge of honor. As you know, peer pressure to not do well can be relentless and most persuasive.

- Any success needs to be passed back to the student, for it's the student who has been advancing, and he or she needs to internalize the fact that he or she has been doing the bulk of the work.

- Know when to refer!

# LIMITED COUNSELING

"Limited counseling" is an alternative counseling methodology for those students experiencing developmental problems that center on such issues as scholastic underachievement and peer relationships. The aim of the methodology is to attack the problem in one or two sessions—a limited period of time. Counselor caseloads in some schools virtually dictate this approach because it permits school counselors to use their time more efficiently within the individual counseling process. The limited-time model is but one more tool in a counselor's repertoire of techniques. The approach is popular with students who are looking for both limited contact with their counselors and for practical interventions. At times, even a single session can be sufficient for certain youngsters, while it might only be the beginning point for others.

## *Assumptions That Underlie the Technique*

1. Students can effect meaningful change within a short period of time.

2. The problem that the student presents to the counselor *is* the problem. The counselor will not take time to search for any serious underlying problems. That is not to say that the student does not have other concerns and that they are of equal or greater importance; but the counselor will focus on the topic about which the student really wants to talk. Other topics can be dealt with later.

3. The student possesses the necessary resources to solve the problem, even though the student may not realize that he or she has said resources. Where appropriate, the counselor will guide the student toward greater recognition and implementation of any internal and external resources.

4. A relatively small change is all that's required to break a particular established pattern of thoughts and behaviors.

### Developing Short-Term Manageable Goals

Effecting minimal change with your counselee often entails the implementation of short-term manageable goals. It's a little like concentrating on the "here and now." Discussion of the problem is generally kept to the minimum in favor of time spent on goal development.

An instrument that addresses and is dedicated to obtaining short-term gains in scholastic achievement is the well-focused Student Performance Report (see Figure 5-3). Note the absence of extraneous material on the form. Report coverage can be as brief as ten days or as long as a marking period segment. You're really earning your stripes when you can get your counselee to adopt a self-directed posture and agree to be the requestee. In essence, the student begins to assume ownership for the problem. Even when the parent is the requestee, your counselee should be the first to see any teacher-supplied information. (Note the printed warning to teachers on the form.)

The "Assignments" area is a critical one, yet often problematic with the underachiever. When check marks begin to appear in the Up to Date column, progress in the elevation of course grades should become apparent.

Some of the principles of Reality Therapy (Chapter 13) could be applicable with Limited Counseling in that you and your counselee would be dealing with immediate and concrete issues within a solution-oriented framework.

There are certain disadvantages to the employment of limited counseling in the school setting. One is remembering that you might be focusing on a problem to the exclusion of other more serious ones. Therefore, you will want to move with care around the problem presented initially. Once the initial problem has been solved to your counselee's liking, you might want to explore for any other associated or underlying ones.

## FINAL WORDS

The waste of a human mind is indeed a tragedy. If you're a real supporter of individuality, and you believe your counselee to be one-of-a-kind, then you will always analyze the situation carefully and *separately*, and tailor any solutions to that one-of-a kind person. Good luck!

FIGURE 5-3

## STUDENT PERFORMANCE REPORT

Counselor: _____      Request Date: _____
(Due)

Date: _____

Requested by:    Parent    Counselor    Student
(*circle one*)

Student: _____      Teacher: _____      Course: _____

Desired Report Coverage: (*check one*) Past Ten Days Only __ Current Marking Period ___

Assignments: Up to date?    Yes    No    If not, number missing _____

Test grades? _____    Quiz grades? _____    Lab grades? _____

(*Circle one*)

**Class Participation**

1. Enthusiastic
2. Dominant
3. Adequate involvement
4. Passive

**Attention Span**

1. Long
2. Average
3. Short

**Classroom Behavior**

1. Good
2. Normal give and take
3. Immature

**Response to Constructive Criticism**

1. Accepts
2. Rejects

**Independence**

1. Works well independently
2. Relies on others
3. Never seeks help

**How Peers React to Student**

1. Good
2. Accept
3. Tolerate
4. Reject

Note: The information provided below may be shared with the student/parent.

General Comments:

# CHAPTER 6

# WORKING WITH THE GIFTED AND TALENTED

The term "gifted and talented" conjures up a picture of a person with well-above-average capabilities, yet a substantive definition continues to be elusive. The federal government has defined giftedness by way of five identifying characteristics: (1) intellectual capability, (2) creative capability, (3) visual and performing arts skills, (4) leadership skills, and (5) psychomotor skills. (Leadership and general creativity propose problems in the use of standard measurement.) Additional data is still needed to define the title more precisely.

In her book *Smart Kids with School Problems*, Priscilla Vail claims that "Gifted people frequently have clusters of the following ten traits: rapid grasp of concepts, awareness of patterns, energy, curiosity, concentration, exceptional memory, empathy, vulnerability, heightened perceptions, and divergent thinking."

Much has transpired in the past decade as to identification of the gifted and talented, but classification remains complicated in that students are gifted in many different ways. Unfortunately, the ultimate decision-maker is the school budget: separate classes and/or individual instruction do cost money.

Although purists insist that there is such a category as "gifted and talented" and that inclusion in the category is readily measurable, they seem to restrict giftedness to academics. This category is most obvious in a school setting, and it is most often attended to. Some people prefer to employ other terms such as "academically talented," "honors," or "exceptional." If "gifted" is limited to academics, then these terms would be acceptable.

It wasn't that long ago that educators and other professionals began to realize that "academically talented" students needed a different educational program from that of mainstream students. In the beginning, the testing instrument used for identification was solely the intelligence quotient (IQ) test. As we became more sensitive and knowledgeable about the gifted, e.g., the other traits exhibited and the limiting factors of the IQ test itself, it became readily apparent that the picture could be framed more appropriately, and that testing alone was not a good indicator for providing that frame. (An ongoing problem with IQ tests is the difficulty in determining exactly what they measure, and the fact that the instrument measures only convergent thinking.)

A distinction has been made in the *type* of academic talent young people possess: some are called "intellectually-minded" and others, "creatively-minded." Each behaves differently from the other: for the intellectually gifted, the left brain is more dominant in its functioning. The creatively gifted are considered right-brained, or the right hemisphere of the brain is more dominant in its functioning. Instruments continue to be developed to better measure both left- and right-hemisphere brain function.

Left-brained people are great at learning mathematics, math-related sciences, and foreign languages. They might have prodigious vocabularies, but might not be that proficient in creative writing. As convergent thinkers, they tend to be careful in analysis and conservative in nature, and quite self-directed. They soak up knowledge like a sponge.

Conversely, right-brained people are often visually minded and exhibit good kinesthetic control. Furthermore, they are intuitive thinkers, possess colorful vocabularies, and vivid imaginations. This kind of person often excels in the visual and performing arts, athletics, mechanical operations, and social relationships. In school, they're thought of as bright, but not necessarily strong in certain academic areas. These divergent thinkers often have a zest for living, are adventurous in nature, and liberal in their outlook. The creatively gifted seem to be falling through the cracks in our schools, though; a good number of them are not being sufficiently challenged.

While we have discussed two categories of gifted and talented youth, such slotting in no way implies that all gifted and talented youth fit neatly into one of these two categories. Not by a long shot!

## STUDENT COURSE SELECTION

The ramifications of incorrect course placement of the gifted and talented student are much the same as for any other student:

1. failure
2. extreme frustration
3. depression
4. adverse effects on career and college planning
5. loss of self-esteem (the loss can come from two directions: if the course is too difficult, the student feels inadequate; if it is too easy, he or she feels undervalued)

In working with all of your counselees, you will have to carefully evaluate each student's abilities and interests, and then compare them to course content and the real demands of a given course.

Most courses do not present placement problems. Tenth-grade health follows ninth-grade health; U.S. History II follows U.S. History I; the college-bound student (or possibly all students) must begin with Algebra I. The difficulties ensue with questions like *which* English course to take, or *when* to start a high school science or mathematics sequence.

When you place a student in an honors or an accelerated program (the two terms mean totally different things), you must consider not only the course in question, but also the student's ability to handle subsequent courses in subsequent years. For example, some school systems continue to exercise a considerable amount of control over eighth-grade Algebra I placement. Given the requisite ability needed, it is likely that the student who does well in that course will also do well with Geometry in grade nine, Algebra II in grade ten, and so forth.

Real problems can emerge with ninth-grade Biology, however. The student may well have the inquiry and largely verbal skills needed for Honors Biology, but will he or she have the mathematical and conceptual skills necessary for Honors Chemistry by grade ten? What to do? You will need to check his or her mathematical placement to certify that subsequent courses will correspond.

Because of the press for students to have some sort of Calculus experience by the end of grade twelve, some of the larger schools in the nation now offer sections of *both* honors Algebra I and regular academic Algebra I in the eighth grade. Even rarer are those schools that offer a six-year sequence in college preparatory mathematics by introducing Algebra I in seventh grade. (See Chapter 3.) In that situation and at some point in time, the sequence usually includes an honors course in Probability and Statistics or Discrete Mathematics. Also, Algebra II will then directly follow Algebra I; Geometry will then be studied in grade nine.

Appropriately placing the gifted and not-so-gifted can be a real hassle at times. As a counselor, for example, would you or would you not encourage marginal Fred to attempt an honors course? If you would, you should feel obligated to Fred to help him monitor his progress carefully, lauding and encouraging him if he succeeds, or helping him to "bail out" if the boat starts to sink.

In many middle and junior high schools there can be considerable amount of course and/or level "tryout" on the part of students. That's as it should be. Counselors can keep a sharp eye on the progress of their young, impressionable counselees. Fortunately, middle and junior high school counselors have more time for personal and academic counseling than do their high school counterparts.

A certain amount of *sensible* experimentation with honors work is healthy. What isn't healthy is when parents want their kids in honors courses so that they can brag about it at the neighborhood cocktail party.

# GIFTED AND TALENTED WOMEN

Many boys wear their talent as a badge of honor; they dream of becoming President of the United States, or the CEO of a billion-dollar company, or a pro football player, or the Bill Gates of a new industry. Girls are much less likely to do so. Why?

Betty Walker and Marilyn Mehr think they have found the key. In their book *The Courage to Achieve*, they describe the study of academically gifted women: they interviewed graduates of Hunter College High School, a New York City public school whose female students had been recognized as the brightest in the nation (IQs over 130), from 1910 through the 1980s. They found that while 92% went to college, very few had earned graduate degrees. And from women in their the early twenties through 92 years of age, they received a similar response: being exceptionally bright was not an asset.

"Even though Hunter women did not suffer from any noticeable lack of self-esteem, only a few were able to admit that they knew they were bright and were proud of it. . . . Excellence requires that people recognize and 'own' their specialness; that they view intelligence as a clearly positive trait. . . . If smart women do not acknowledge their abilities, they will never set high goals. . . . [W]omen seldom see themselves as "heroes" in adventures of their own making. If they cannot envision themselves as leading players, they will be satisfied with supporting roles."

A common complaint voiced by the women surveyed was that they had very little counseling on the high school level. They felt that such counseling could have helped in two areas: counselors could have addressed personal and emotional problems, and counselors could have provided a bridge to the outside world by helping the young women set goals that would develop their special talents.

We are still contending with a society that has different values for different sexes. What, if anything, should be done about it? Walker and Mehr claim that to overcome negative conditioning, girls need help in learning how to pursue the nontraditional and make their own choices independently.

"The influence of counselors is critical at this age because adolescence requires girls to separate from their parents and establish their own identities. . . . Young women need teachers and counselors working along with parents who encourage them to explore and experiment, to develop visions and dreams about futures that are foreign to their culture and times. . . . [T]hey need to hear the voices of teachers, counselors, role models, and friends cheering them on, a chorus of encouragement to their achievements."

## COMMON PROBLEMS WORTH EXPLORING

It's important to understand that early maturing children are not always gifted. Gifted children are not always early maturing. Many a middle-schooler is intellectually ready for senior high school, but is far too young emotionally and/or physically. Great care must be taken in placing students in extraordinary circumstances.

Smart kids do have school problems. Vail calls them "conundrum kids": some are obviously learning disabled with high though hidden intellectual potential; some are gifted with subtle learning disabilities; and many are "average," where giftedness and disability mask each other; they comprise about 20–30% of any school population. The gifted and talented do have their own unique problems. They can suffer from an impaired self-image, caused in part by years of extreme anxiety and unrelenting pressure to excel academically.

And they need a counselor as much as the next guy—maybe even more—and so do their parents. Once identified, the gifted student will display symptoms that warrant counselor intervention. (Gifted students are more reluctant to seek counseling than their non-gifted counterparts.) Symptoms can become evident within five broad areas: (1) perfectionism, (2) frustration, (3) insecurity, (4) depression, and (5) college and career planning.

The gifted and talented often think like adults. Their thinking process exhibits much of the same confidence that adults project in their thinking, yet these youngsters are quick to reject parental advice. For many of them, the greatest of life's pressures—and the consequent anxiety—occur within the school setting. It would be great if you could ease some of that anxiety through humor. Unfortunately, some gifted and talented are humorless.

Other problems that these youngsters and their parents experience, and ones that you can explore together, might include:

- a loss in enthusiasm for learning

- doing poorly—or even failing—maybe for the first time in one's life

- being shunned by family and friends for not going to a "good" college

- being kidded as a freshman about size as he/she sits with juniors in an honors mathematics class

- being too focused on the academics, and not enough on the non-academics

- reaching out and leveling with parents who may have unrealistic expectations; not only can a youngster be misplaced in a particular course, he or she can be misplaced in a particular school

- helping a student sort through his or her priorities to keep things in perspective

- helping a student who is not gifted in some areas work effectively with his or her weaknesses; some do not do well in classes that require the employment of certain physical skills, i.e., Home Economics, Physical Education, Industrial Arts & Technology

- counseling a high achiever who looks upon cheating as a practical, not an ethical issue

- helping a counselee deal with the frustration of getting into a "hot" college, which he or she views as a ticket to a "hot" career

- helping students wend their way through the bureaucracy as they search to satisfy special objectives

- counseling a youngster who feels he or she has dishonored the family name and is contemplating suicide

## A WORD OF WARNING

If a child is "different," he or she is a target for loneliness and misunderstanding. The gifted and talented are often observant enough to recognize that they don't fit in. This will more than likely cause pain. Sometimes it causes suicide. One of our great tragedies is that there are few adults who have the insight and then take the time to reassure those youngsters that somewhere, sometime, there is a place for them. As a school counselor, please give them enough support so that they can achieve their ultimate and celebrate their specialness.

Vail offers us this poem:

**The Wall**

They laughed at me.
They laughed at me and called me names,
They wouldn't let me join their games.
I couldn't understand.
I spent most playtimes on my own,
Everywhere I was alone,
I couldn't understand.

Teachers told me I was rude,
Bumptious, overbearing, shrewd,
Some of the things they said were crude.
I couldn't understand.
And so I built myself a wall.
Strong and solid, ten feet tall,
With bricks you couldn't see at all,
So I could understand.

And then came Sir,
A jovial, beaming, kindly man,
Saw through my wall and took my hand,
And the wall came tumbling down,
For he could understand.

And now I laugh with them,
Not in any unkind way,
For they have yet to face their day
And the lessons I have learned.
For eagles soar above all birds,
And scavengers need to hunt in herds,
But the lion walks alone,
And now I understand.

—By an anonymous eleven-year-old boy, in tribute to Henry Collins,
Director of The Association for Gifted Children, London

# SUGGESTED READINGS

Ingram, C.F. and Todd, S.M. (1983), *You and the Gifted Child*. Springfield: Charles C. Thomas.

Vail, Priscilla L. (1987), *Smart Kids with School Problems: Things to Know and Ways to Help*. New York: E. P. Dutton.

Walker, Betty A. Ph.D. and Mehr, Marilyn Ph.D. *The Courage to Achieve: Why America's Brightest Women Struggle to Fulfill Their Promise*. New York: Simon & Schuster.

# CHAPTER 7

# WORKING WITH THE LEARNING DISABLED

The hidden handicap that we now designate as "learning disability" (LD) has been around ever since people have tried to process information. The issue has taken on increased significance through the years as societies have continued to place more and more emphasis on learning and education.

Learning disabilities take many forms: visual, auditory, motor control, communication, logic, etc. Emotional disturbances and behavioral difficulties are often secondary results. As the child grows into adolescence, however, secondary results can become primary concerns. Optimal attention to any disability requires a total approach to the educational, psychological, physiological, and medical needs of the individual youngster.

The federal government defined learning disabilities in the 1975 Public Law 94-142: The Education of All Handicapped Children Act. It is vital for families to know that there *are* federal and state laws that protect the civil rights and assure educational opportunities for all handicapped students. The laws require that a free and appropriate public education be provided to any handicapped student in the social and educational setting that best meets his or her needs. The law also provides a structure for handling and resolving complaints that pertain to identification, program, and placement. When families fully understand the regulations that govern the delivery of special education services within the school setting, they can participate more confidently with Child Study Team members who serve the LD student. For example, the law is quite clear as to:

- Who is responsible for evaluating the handicapping condition
- Which youngsters are eligible for services
- Which services must be offered
- How the Individual Education Plan (IEP) is developed
- Parents' rights, responsibilities, and involvement in the process

P.L. 94-142 also legislates financial assistance to the states so that they in turn can provide special education for all of their handicapped students. Furthermore, the federal statute stipulates certain minimum standards of service required to qualify for federal monies. All states except New Mexico prepare an annual plan that explains how P.L. 94-142 regulations will be implemented within the state education system.

Labeling youngsters as "uneducable," "behavior problems," "underachievers," etc, continues to plague the development of those youngsters. Authorities agree that a number of youngsters are doomed to failure in school—and in life in general—unless their disabilities are discovered early, appropriately diagnosed, and then afforded remediation by way of educational, psychological, physiological, social, and medical services.

## SYMPTOMS OF LEARNING DISABILITY

An LD student is normally considered to possess near-average or above-average intelligence, but, for apparent or not-so-apparent reasons, there is a gap between potential and achievement. Just as each of your nondisabled counselees is unique, so too is each of your disabled: each displays a different combination and severity of problems. A learning disabled youngster is one who has one or more significant deficits in the essential learning processes.

The symptoms of learning disabilities are a diverse set of characteristics that affect a student's growth and development. One or more of these symptoms can be located in *all* youngsters at some time or other during their development, but an LD youngster usually has a cluster of symptoms that do not disappear with advancement in age. The most frequently displayed symptoms include:

- short attention span
- poor memory
- difficulty in following directions
- inadequate ability to discriminate between and among letters, numerals, or sounds
- low reading skills
- weak eye-hand coordination
- difficulties with sequencing

Other symptoms might be:

- erratic daily performance
- stating one thing, but meaning another
- responding poorly to discipline
- difficulty adjusting to change
- immature speech
- inability to follow multiple directions
- forgetting easily
- difficulty in sounding out words
- impulsive behavior
- late gross or fine motor development
- reversal of letters or placing them in incorrect sentences
- limited physical coordination

Again, it's important to understand that a youngster is not necessarily learning disabled if he or she exhibits a few of the aforementioned symptoms, since many individuals display some of them at one time or another. On the other hand, if a person has a cluster of these problems, he or she should be examined for the possible existence of a disability.

## INCLUSION OF LD STUDENTS IN REGULAR CLASSROOMS

The big move these days is for what is known as inclusion, that is, including special education students in regular classrooms. We've always included them; but, the movement has picked up a real head of steam since the early 1990s with several states encouraging more inclusive education by way of providing training and grants to increase the number of courses into which students with disabilities can be integrated with their nondisabled counterparts.

Current research demonstrates that students with disabilities who are involved in integrated classrooms make greater advancements in academics and self-concept. They are more likely to be perceived as a member of the school community, and be afforded the opportunity to develop social relationships with nondisabled students. Also, LD students who spend more time in traditional classes are likely to do better in the job market.

Despite long-standing federal law, landmark court decisions, and the tireless efforts of advocacy groups to ensure the established rights of individuals with disabilities, a large number of students with disabilities continue to be educated in segregated settings.

One aspect of the problem is the manner in which various persons interpret the federal statutes: such phrases as "equal educational opportunities for all of its children" or "right to a free and appropriate education in the least restrictive environment."

"Inclusion is a right, and not a privilege for a select few," wrote a panel of judges from the U.S. Court of Appeals for the Third Circuit. Among other statements, the panel said that disabled students who are placed in regular classrooms should be given whatever supports are necessary.

Another aspect of the problem is that a number of schools do not have integrated programs in place, or students may be determined to be in need of services that are more readily available in restrictive settings. More than a few teachers are reluctant to educate students with disabilities in their classrooms, and those same teachers as well as special education teachers, may not be knowledgeable regarding implementation strategies for inclusive education programs. Thus, school systems find segregated, self-contained placements to be more expedient and convenient.

## ONCE IN THE MAINSTREAM: SKILLS FOR SUCCESS

There are certain fundamental skills that professionals in the field of special education agree upon and that, once mastered, should enable a handicapped youngster to more fully and quickly experience educational achievement. It's kind of like David Letterman's top ten list, only in reverse order. Note that none of the ten have a direct tie to academic matters. The top one on the list is as you would have expected.

1. Listening skills
2. Skill in following written directions
3. Being able to stay on task
4. Having the wherewithal to ask for help
5. Capability of getting started
6. Completing work on time
7. Ability to work independently
8. Organizational skills
9. Social skills
10. Study skills

## SOCIAL CONSIDERATIONS AND THE LEARNING DISABLED

Even though professionals agree that social adjustment factors are very much a problem with the learning disabled, the issue has heretofore received little attention. The focus of a learning disability is usually centered on the learning situation, yet the consequences of any disability are rarely confined to the school setting. Other areas of life are affected, including the role of LD youngsters in their relationships with their family, friends, and social activities, e.g. athletics, church, and assorted school functions.

Some LD students may internalize and perceive less in their social environment, and may not learn so easily from various life experiences as their more normal counterparts do. Some LD students display an immaturity and social ineptness because of their particular learning disability. As a school counselor you can work with your disabled counselees on social adjustment issues. Just like all of us, the learning disabled person hungers for acceptance, but such eagerness can cause him or her to try too hard and/or to make the effort in inappropriate ways.

# TWO DISABLING CONDITIONS

## *Dyslexia*

Dyslexia, or Specific Language Difficulties, are terms used to describe those youngsters and adults with average or above-average intelligence who have severe difficulty in reading, writing, spelling, and, on occasion, mathematics. At each phase of learning a language, whether it be related to speech, spelling, reading, or writing, these people can experience serious problems and require specialized instruction appropriate to their individual needs in order to develop their intellectual ability to its fullest.

Some of the more noticeable characteristics of dyslexia are any combination of the following:

- Genuine difficulty in learning and committing to memory the printed word or symbol
- Reversals of letters or improper letter sequencing, e.g., letter b for the letter d; the word was for saw
- Bizarre spelling errors
- Illegible handwriting
- Poorly constructed compositions

Very few people exhibit all of the characteristics, but there is enough similarity to distinguish them as a definitive group with special educational needs. Many professionals now employ the term "dyslexic" as an all-encompassing term to cover any specific language difficulty.

There is little doubt that the dyslexic experiences serious language difficulties, sometimes involving the inability of a young child to differentiate the meaning of certain sounds. Computer games are being developed to help that youngster learn the appropriate sounds, which should help them learn to read and write more accurately. With proper diagnosis and treatment, dyslexics can learn and learn well.

## *Attention Deficit Disorder*

The American School Counselor Association (ASCA) in its 1994 position statement cites the fact that Attention Deficit Disorder (ADD) affects from 5 to 10 percent of all school-age children, and that the cause of ADD is thought to be genetic or hereditary; it is one of the most common childhood disorders. Barkley (1990) favored a conservative prevalence rate of 3% to 5%; Hosie and Erk (1993) cited 5 % to 10 %. Males are on the average six times more frequently identified in ADD clinic samples than are females. Females might be under identified because they do not tend to be so disruptive in school and at home as are males.

Evidently there is an imbalance of neurochemicals that act as triggers, transmitters, and receptors within the brain. Attention deficit disorder is not considered to be caused by brain damage, birth trauma, poor parenting, inadequate discipline, nutritional deficiencies, allergies, or family separation. Nonetheless, it may severely affect family relations, cause problems with teachers, impede learning and consequent achievement, impact on peer relationships, and result in a poor self-image.

A diagnosis of ADD can be made as early as age three. Unfortunately, many children are not diagnosed until third grade or later. The difficulty in altering the course of ADD is exponentially increased for each year that the child or adolescent remains undiagnosed or untreated. The three most important components of a thorough ADD evaluation are (1) the clinical interview, (2) the medical examination, and (3) the completion and scoring of ADD behavior scales.

As a school counselor, you are likely to be the first professional to be consulted. Here are five "you can's" for your consideration:

1. You can observe and informally evaluate suspected counselees. Such action can pave the way for eventual formal identification.

2. Once identified, you can take the lead in implementing a multidisciplinary-multidimensional treatment program. Here you might make a commitment to help your students by voluntarily serving as an on-site coordinator in any treatment plan.

3. You can be a provider of feedback on the social and academic performance of an ADD student to the multidisciplinary treatment team.

4. You can help organize ADD workshops for teachers, parents, and community advocates for the disorder.

5. You can act as a consultant to teachers, other school personnel, lay community members, and parents on the characteristics and problems of ADD.

### "H" STANDS FOR HYPERACTIVITY

ADHD stands for Attention Deficit/Hyperactivity Disorder, and it is one of the fastest growing ADD categories for children and adults. Less than a decade ago, specialists believed that symptoms of ADHD faded toward the end of adolescence, but more recent research shows that ADHD often continues into adulthood. In fact, about two thirds of ADHD kids continue to have symptoms as adults, according to Howard Baker, M.D., senior attending psychiatrist at The Institute of Pennsylvania Hospital.

What are the characteristics of ADHD? The disorder is usually marked by the inability to sit still, a poor scholastic record, and a propensity for general irritability and temper tantrums. While children and adults with ADHD may have a short fuse and exhibit high energy levels, more likely than not the disorder manifests itself in not being able to sustain attention. Attention shifts involuntarily and without warning. Dr. Baker says, "It can feel like standing in a strobe light." Because students with ADHD seek novel and intense activities, they find themselves creating crises in order to get their work done. Their attention shifts from the relevant to the irrelevant as they search out novelty. Since ADHD persons have a tendency to act impulsively, they set themselves up for trouble by taking on too much responsibility and not setting proper limits. Time management is not one of their strengths.

While low self-esteem and anti-social behavior are frequent consequences of ADHD, the number one problem facing therapists is how to keep their patient's attention focused long enough to work on problem-solving skills.

## ROLE OF THE SCHOOL COUNSELOR IN ADHD

Management of the environment is critical in helping youngsters with ADHD. These youngsters require clear, specific regulations; frequent, immediate, and consistent consequences. They have difficulty bringing internal control and external situations into harmony; therefore, the external situation has to be manipulated. A combination of treatment options is usually the way to go, and, as a counselor, you *can* be a most helpful professional. Here are a few guidelines.

- Behavior therapy might be a beneficial approach as you work with your counselee on developing better coping mechanisms. Behavior therapy teaches students how to set up a reward system for successfully staying on task. Rewards should be changed frequently, and they should be important to the student.

- Teaching time-management skills can help the ADHD student set priorities and organize tasks. Mechanical aids such as alarms and timers are useful, as well as several of the more sophisticated datebook organizers that are now on the market.

- Any established rules should be made simple and clear.

- Your counselee needs to release his or her energy. He or she should be offered periodic breaks, recess, etc.

- Lengthy assignments should be divided into smaller components. Course content should be simplified until the student can handle the assigned material sufficiently, and then it should gradually increase in complexity.

- Always build on strengths rather than magnify weaknesses!

## FEDERAL STATUTES ON ADD

With the issuance of its 1991 policy statement, the U.S. Department of Education confirmed what parents and professionals serving youngsters with ADD had been battling about for some time: ADD children were potentially eligible for services under both the Individuals with Disabilities Education Act (IDEA) and Section 504 of the Rehabilitation Act of 1973. The IDEA requires, however, that the child be in need of special education and related services; whereas Section 504 regulations do not speak of special education *and* related services, but rather of special education *or* related services. Therefore, while your ADD students might not qualify under the IDEA, they do qualify under 504. Also, the eligibility criteria under Section 504 are broader than those contained in the IDEA.

So, with all the attention ADD has commanded, especially since the early 1990s, Section 504 has taken on new life.

### Section 504 Defined

Section 504 is an Act that prohibits discrimination against persons with a handicap in any program receiving federal financial assistance. It is one of several sections of the Federal Rehabilitation Act of 1973. The Act defines a person with a handicap as anyone who:

1. Has a mental or physical impairment that substantially limits one or more major life activities, e.g., caring for one's self, performing manual tasks, walking, seeing, hearing, speaking, breathing, *learning*, and working.
2. Has a record of such impairment, or
3. Is regarded as having an impairment.

In order to fulfill its obligation under Section 504, a school receiving federal monies of any kind must recognize its responsibility to assure that no discrimination against any person with a disability is knowingly permitted in any of the programs and practices of that particular school system.

School districts have specific responsibilities under the Act, which extend to identifying, evaluating, and—if the student is determined to be eligible under Section 504—to afford access to appropriate educational services. If the parent or guardian disagrees with the determination made by the professional staff of a given school district, he or she has a right to a hearing with an impartial hearing officer.

Working with the learning disabled can be a very gratifying experience for the school counselor. The term "individualism" can take on new and heightened meaning.

## SUGGESTED READINGS

Barkley, R. A. (1990), Attention-Deficit Hyperactivity Disorder: A Handbook for Diagnosis and Treatment. New York: Guilford.

Hosie, T. W., and Erk, R. R. (1993, January), American Counseling Association Reading Program: "Attention-Deficit Disorder," *Guidepost*, Vol. 35.

# CHAPTER 8

# ORIENTATION PROGRAMS AND WORKSHOPS

Timing can be everything in producing a quality orientation program: time of day, time of year; a morning in September for giving seniors in-house college admission procedures; late August for a freshman orientation program; mid-February for parental perspectives on how the freshmen have been doing; April to assist families of juniors with the college selection process. Different districts have different needs, of course; perhaps one of the following would be appropriate for you.

## THREE FRESHMAN ORIENTATION PROGRAMS

A late August freshman orientation program, such as the one that follows, has the advantage of your tapping into a high level of student/parent interest as families look forward to a new facility and a brand new educational experience. The first two programs presuppose that counselors are on duty during the summer—or, at the very least, are available ten days prior to the opening of school. For each program, we first offer the letter of invitation, then the syllabus of the main points to be presented. Program #1 is conducted over several days to allow for small group presentations.

## *# 1: Counselors Lead Small Groups*

Counselors are asked to speak to the families of prospective freshmen. The invitation shown in Figure 8-1 specifies the date, time, and location.

**FIGURE 8-1**

July 199X

Dear Parents:

As parents of an incoming freshman, you are cordially invited to visit the High School in August. The Counseling Department will be conducting a program designed to orient both you and your youngster to available guidance and counseling services.

It is preferable that your son/daughter attend this program with you. You will be meeting in a small group session with a number of other families. The session will last approximately one hour. A brief tour of the school will also be included.

I look forward to seeing you at the time and date listed below.

Sincerely,

Nancy Kashen

Counselor

MEETING TIME: 9:00 A.M.

DATE: August 20

ROOM: ___134___

An outline of the appropriate topics (see Figure 8-2) is given to each presenter well before the presentation.

## *#2: Parents Remain at Home*

Another late August program has a twist—parents are requested to remain at home, while students attend the sessions. Upper-class students are invited to assist school counselors with the presentation. The program is spread over a three-day period to ensure that content sessions are small in size (about 25 students). In this particular school, counselor caseloads number some 70 ninth graders, with counselors orienting their own counselees in the content sessions. One or two upper-class students help with *each* counselor presentation. (See Figures 8-3 and 8-4 for sample invitation and schedules.)

FIGURE 8-2

FRESHMAN SUMMER ORIENTATION PROGRAM

Suggested Topics

*Handouts:* mock transcripts, course guides, rank/grade-point-average computation sheets, and detailed maps of physical plant.

I. **Introduction**

Introduce yourself to the group and briefly highlight some of the topics you will be covering. You might inquire as to whether any of the parents have previously had children attend the high school. If so, you might want to informally enlist their support as resource people during your presentation.

II. **Graduation Requirements**

   A. Review all graduation requirements. (Use course guide as reference.)

   B. Review mock transcript. Discuss course levels, including honors and advanced placement programs.

   C. Discuss class rank and grade-point-average, including the extra weighting of honors and AP courses. (Use rank/grade-point-average calculation sheet where appropriate.)

III. **Drop Versus Change**

Discuss the dropping of courses and the changing of course levels. Describe the difference between a *drop* and a *level change*. Highlight all applicable deadlines and remind families that the deadlines appear in the Student/Parent Handbook that they should have received in the mail in mid-August.

IV. **Standardized Testing**

Describe the district's standardized testing program as it applies to grades 9–12. Mention that the school district considers the PSAT an integral part of its comprehensive standardized testing program and has underwritten the cost of testing all tenth and eleventh graders in October.

V. **College & Career Center**

Describe the purpose of the center as well as the role and function of the two specialist counselors and the two paraprofessionals who staff the center.

FIGURE 8-2 *CONTINUED*

VI.  **Student Assistance Program**

Highlight the role of the Student Assistance Coordinator. Describe the Peer Helper program. Discuss the function of the Core Team, including team involvement.

VII.  **Child Study Team**

Discuss the CST role and when intervention is warranted. Also highlight 504 and when the development of a 504 Plan might be appropriate.

VIII.  **High School Adjustment**

A.  Hold up the Student/Parent Handbook for viewing. Briefly highlight contents, including attendance policies, disciplinary procedures, student appeal process, etc.

B.  Encourage the students to participate in co-curricular activities. Review minimum academic requirements for such participation.

C.  Discuss the bell schedule and the flexibility of the system during the first several days of school, especially as it affects entering freshmen.

IX.  **Student/Counselor Relations**

A.  Discuss reasons for seeing a counselor. Highlight the role and function of the counselor generalist, including the advocacy role.

B.  Describe how appointments can be made. Also, what constitutes an emergency and how to handle such an emergency.

C.  Explore the issue of teacher contact, including the arrangement of a case conference, if necessary. Mention the availability of voice mail for teachers. Discuss what the counseling department can and cannot do.

D.  Review departmental policy on the obtaining of homework once a student is ill. Describe the Home Instruction program. Also review procedures for Home Instruction.

FIGURE 8-3

---

**Brandywine High School**

**Starksburg, Maryland**

To the Class of 19XX

Welcome! As a member of the Class of 19XX, we invite you to attend a meaningful orientation program conducted by both the Counseling Department and upper-class students. We would like to make your transition from the middle school to the high school as smooth as possible.

Please bring the previously mailed schedules, locker assignments and combinations with you to the orientation. You will be given time to locate and open your locker, as well as locate all of your classrooms.

Bus transportation will be provided for any student who lives farther than two miles from the high school. Pick-up time will be at approximately 9:00 A.M. (See back of letter for designated bus routes.) The activity will begin at 9:45 and end at 11:30.

This particular program will be conducted on August 28, 29, and 30. Note that the class has been divided into three sections. Please check the enclosed alphabetical breakdown to determine your proper day of attendance.

As this will be the first activity for the Class of 19XX, we request that you dress appropriately.

Enjoy the remainder of the summer, and we look forward to seeing you here at the high school on one of the three designated days.

---

FIGURE 8-4

---

**Program**

*(Time Approximate)*

9:45 A.M.: *High School Auditorium*

Welcoming Remarks by:

Dr. John Stafford, Principal

Dr. Dorothy Starnov, Assistant Principal for Freshmen

Dr. Matthew Goldman, Counseling Chair

Barry Steckler, Student Government President

10:15 A.M.: *Content Sessions—Classrooms*

Counselor and Student Presentation

Scheduled Building "Walk Through"

Question & Answer Period

*#3: An April Evening Affair*

It was a scene reminiscent of the baggage area at any major airport. But instead of limousine drivers holding placards high for their patrons, it was honor society students holding up alphabet cards in the Hightstown High School Commons, as parents and students exited the auditorium through one of four designated doorways to follow a typical student schedule. For this New Jersey school, it was the beginning of yet another well-executed eighth-grade orientation program held in April for students moving from the middle school to the high school the following September. Figure 8-5 shows the invitation.

FIGURE 8-5

8TH GRADE PARENT ORIENTATION
HIGHTSTOWN HIGH SCHOOL AUDITORIUM
MARCH 22, 199X
7:30 P.M.

An Invitation to All Parents/Guardians:

You are cordially invited to a special presentation for parents/guardians of 8th grade students. The orientation will include:

—a visit with each content area supervisor or coordinator to hear a brief overview of courses

—a complete and up-to-date Program of Studies with required and elective courses

—a tour of the facility

The information you receive at this orientation will outline the requirements for graduation and will also include the numerous opportunities available to HHS students in academic, artistic, and athletic areas. In addition, the information presented at this meeting will be necessary for you and your child to make wise course selections, as well as help you become familiar with such topics as: academic units, attendance policies, class rank, supervised study, resource centers, etc. Guidance Counselors and Administrators will be available throughout the evening to answer your questions.

It is important that parents and students learn about the great number of curricular and co-curricular opportunities available at Highstown High School. My staff and I welcome and encourage your attendance at this important meeting.

Sincerely,

Martin Barlow
Principal

The high school had obtained the names of prospective students from the public middle school and local parochial schools, and had assigned each family to a "letter"; each student was handed a packet that included a course book—with the student's name attached. Families attended a brief welcoming session in the auditorium, then began their trek through a *fourteen-period* day (to touch base with all curricular areas). Each "letter" group started at a designated room, then proceeded to the next room at the change of period. Periods were of five-minute duration, with two minutes allotted for passing time. The rooms were obviously chosen to provide a "one way" flow of traffic. A portion of the schedule is given in Figures 8-6 and 8-7.

**FIGURE 8-6**

8th GRADE PARENT ORIENTATION

199X

SUBJECT AREA ORIENTATION

| Group # | Starts with: | Subject | Room |
|---|---|---|---|
| A | | Music | Commons |
| B | | English | 308 |
| C | | Business | 310 |
| . . . | | | |
| M | | Home Economics and TV | 601 |
| N | | Humanities | 706 |
| All, after last period: | | Athletics/Clubs | Gym |

Representatives from the Special Education Department and the Child Study Team will be available in Room 404.

FIGURE 8-7

8th GRADE PARENT ORIENTATION
199X
TIME SCHEDULE

| Period | Begin | End |
|--------|-------|-----|
| 1 | 7:30 | 7:35 |
| 2 | 7:37 | 7:42 |
| 3 | 7:44 | 7:49 |
| . . . | | |
| 14 | 9:01 | 9:06 |
| Athletics/Clubs | 9:08 | 9:30 |

Could there be a direct correlation between orientation program quality and the extent to which a school is concerned about its families? In compassionate districts, parents feel more locked-in than locked-out of the school district's educational effort. Hightstown High School is an example of the many caring environments in the nation. Some of that caring is reflected in the quality—the substance and creativity—of the school's student and parent orientation programs.

Instead of just having department chairpersons describe curriculum offerings to parents seated in an auditorium, many Hightstown faculty members did the explaining in their classrooms; they were very visible at that evening affair, and that's what makes this event work so well. From the band director's signaling band members to march down the auditorium aisles and mount the stage, to the final gathering of families in the gymnasium to sign up at *student-manned* tables for next year's co-curricular activities, the orientation program is a stunning example of cooperation among students, faculty, administrators, supervisors, and parents. No question that parental feet had to keep moving—five minutes go by quickly—but it is an evening of substance and exhilaration.

## LONG-RANGE PLANNING

Quality orientation programs call for quality planning, which translates into allowing sufficient time to develop the event. Note how one school district took the requisite time in their development of a Parent Academy program. Here, too, parents were asked to keep their offspring at home. It starts with a letter to the parents, as shown in Figure 8-8.

FIGURE 8-8

## OCEAN VIEW SCHOOL DISTRICT
## PARENT ACADEMY

May 10, 199X

The Guidance Advisory Committee of the Ocean View School District is planning to offer a "Parent Academy" for middle and high school parents/guardians. The academy would be held at Ocean View High School on Wednesday, November 22, 199X during American Education Week. The program would be free of charge, but would require preregistration. Various topics that pertain to student growth and development would be offered. Tentative program design calls for two one-hour sessions, with a twenty minute break between sessions.

The Parent Academy should provide you with an opportunity to acquire information about your specific areas of interest. Furthermore, you will meet other parents who may share your same interests or concerns. Our major thrust is to increase communication between home and school. Listed below are possible topics:

| | |
|---|---|
| Cruising the Information Highway | Surviving the Middle School Years |
| Financing That College Education | What Musical Instrument Should I Play? |
| Selecting a Computer for Your Youngster | ADHD: What Is It? |
| Homework/Study Tips for Parents | Eating Disorders: An Unending Problem |

In order to properly plan this activity, the committee requests your help on two fronts: participant and/or instructor. Please give thought to both roles.

-------------------------------------------------------------------------------

### Parent Academy Survey

1. My child/children attend(s): __ the Middle School __ the High School

2. I would probably: __attend the academy __not attend the academy __ not certain

3. Best program hours for me would be: __ 7:00 to 9:30 P.M. __7:30 to 10:00 P.M.

4. I would be interested in teaching a course at the academy. __Yes __No

   Name: _____    Telephone: _____

   Topic: _____

5. Please mention below some of your areas of concern so that topics can be offered that will be of interest to a large number of parents:

   _____

   _____

   _____

   Additional Comments/Suggestions: _____

   _____

   _____

# FURTHER TIPS ON DEVELOPING ORIENTATION PROGRAMS/WORKSHOPS

Each community is a unique entity. There are a number of "little touches" that can help you with a warmer, more welcoming approach. Here are just a few thoughts:

- Any letter of invitation to the home should be sent by the new counselor, not the department chairperson. The more personal the invitation, the more positive the response.

- Programs are always scored high where families are afforded the opportunity to ask plenty of questions.

- Assure your families that no question is too mundane. What you don't need is parents sitting on their hands and not asking questions for fear of looking foolish.

- If preregistration is required, provide your families with enough lead-time to register. Too much lead-time, though, can lead to a registration form being misplaced or forgotten altogether.

# CHAPTER 9

# MULTICULTURAL COUNSELING

Ours is very much an immigrant society, and multiculturalism is a dynamic component of the society that cannot be ignored. The impact is most experienced in the school environment where ethnic differences naturally create diversity in perceptions, behaviors, relationships, learning mastery, and attitudes. Linguistic variance is but a minor aspect of a major problem. The methods by which different cultures use semantics to communicate life experiences to the general population within their respective cultures offers by far the greatest challenge.

Much of America is an easily recognizable melting pot of various ethnic and cultural backgrounds; individuals struggle to live together as one people, while at the same time attempting to honor the many evident and not-so-evident differences. It's a tall order. And how this country manages this present and future reality will ultimately determine whether we will be a nation of warring subcultures, continuously afraid of differences, or a society that reflects peaceful coexistence and embraces diversity.

A good deal of the "management" falls squarely on the shoulders of educators—educators who receive impressionable children at age five, and who have considerable influence over their growth and development until age seventeen or eighteen. Learning to accept should *begin* at home, of course, but it *continues* in the school.

The secondary school counselor is in the forefront of the "influence" end of it. A counselor should be able to provide *all* of his or her counselees with *appropriate* services. In order to render such services, the counselor needs to be *multiculturally competent* (an interesting phrase). We need to see a Caucasian counselor serving well the needs of an African-American counselee and vice versa—and any other cross-cultural combinations of counselors and counselees that might be present within a particular school setting.

Of course, the responsibility that demands competency also demands skills training, an open mind and attitude, confrontation with one's own ethnicity, and a broad school-based curriculum that includes the historical contributions of various ethnic groups. A school's culture emanates in part from the staff, who in turn bring with them their own cultural attributes. School counselors are no exception here. It's critical that the counselor understand this fact, since there must be both awareness of one's own culture and recognition and acceptance of the individual student's culture to avoid a biased selection and presentation of thoughts, ideas, and program materials.

Counseling is a human relations profession. Counselor and client relating well to one another through cultural similarities, and in spite of cultural differences, creates a nonthreatening environment that in turn sets the stage for solid rapport building, along with the optimal transfer of knowledge, both in the broader social setting and in the instructional domain.

Culture can be defined as a shared set of behaviors, values, and attributes that differentiates a certain segment of a total population. The school counselor, promoting the aforementioned climate, allows for the creation and existence of a legitimate school culture and successful assimilation. Since behaviors are learned primarily from example, it is the school's duty, including that of the counselor, to model and foster tolerance of cultural differences among staff and students. School and society *can* accommodate cultural diversity, and at the same time allow for assimilation without compromising individual cultural identity. For example, and on a more mundane note, a school with a "no hat" policy can accommodate those young women of specific cultural and religious backgrounds who wish to cover their heads.

Counselors from all ethnic and cultural groups need continuing assistance in enhancing the delivery of their skills. Unfortunately, graduate training programs, and much of what is being written in the literature, are long on raising the consciousness of counselors, especially those of Euro-American descent, and short on practical strategies and techniques.

## LONG ON THE PRACTICAL

An exception to that point is discussed in an article entitled, "Enhancing Multicultural Relations: Intervention Strategies for the School Counselor," which appeared in the November 1995 issue of ASCA's The School Counselor. Author Laurie Sheperd Johnson reminds the reader that school counselors are in a "pivotal position to lead the way in promoting multicultural relations within the school community." With this supposition in mind, Johnson sent an inquiry to 100 local guidance and counseling directors in the State of New York in an effort to discover what initiatives, if any, their departments were undertaking to address the increasing diversity in the schools, including the enhancement of multicultural relations.

What the author found was that the schools shared a sense of accomplishment in the activities and programs they had begun to institute, but readily admitted that their efforts were barely adequate to address the burgeoning needs in their respective schools. Many of the activities were single event, stand-alone types, typically sponsored by subject area departments and engaging only a small segment of the total school population. There was little indication from the directors that multicultural awareness activities were incorporated into the broader curriculum as part of an ongoing, programmatic initiative.

If the schools really want to promote multicultural awareness and acceptance, then Johnson believes that they need to "embrace the thesis that for meaningful and long-term benefits to be harvested, any initiative must be multifaceted (entailing varied activity and service approaches); inclusionary (engaging students, teachers, pupil personnel, administrators, parents, and community members); developmental (proactive rather than reactive in nature); continuous (featuring ongoing and successive efforts); and district-supported (if not districtwide)."

In her article, Johnson presents a four-phase process: 1. Formulate an integrated plan; 2. Conduct a needs assessment; 3. Design and implement program interventions; 4. Conduct ongoing assessment. It includes the identification of interventions that can be implemented by school counselors who are interested in developing a *comprehensive* multicultural relations initiative in their schools. The author also outlines the resources for each of the interventions described. Well worth reading!

# CULTURAL FACTORS AND THE COUNSELING PROCESS

For years, the responsibility for emotional problems fell on the shoulders of the individual. Cultural factors were considered irrelevant to the counseling process. Such an ideology would be acceptable today if there were not considerable evidence to suggest that ethnicity, gender, and social class have something to do with the severity of a given situation, types of referrals, and the rate at which clients drop out of offered treatment. If a person is the primary source of his or her emotional problem, why do certain groups of individuals experience more emotional problems than others? Furthermore, the concept that counselees fail in counseling because they are unsuitable for counseling, incapable of attaining insight or lack proper motivation, is now a dead issue as well. Findings now indicate that membership in certain groups does not render certain people poor candidates for counseling assistance.

Our counselees live in a social environment that directly impacts on their behavior. Certain social traits of a person—ethnicity, gender, and social class—can lead the social environment to treat the person in a particular fashion, and such treatment can contribute to the counselee's behavior in the counseling session. Thus, you cannot afford to be class or color blind and expect to provide appropriate and competent help to your students.

You also need to understand that the variables of ethnicity, gender, or social class will not determine the outcome of a session. You cannot and should not predict the outcome of a counseling relationship based on those factors as they apply to you or your counselee. There is considerable variance within ethnic or social groups, including a wide distribution of characteristics among all members of a group. Additionally, emotional upset is not a function of one's group membership.

Your charge, and it's a big one, is to know enough about the cultural backgrounds of your counselees so as to comprehend how these cultural factors affect them, and then employ *culturally sensitive interventions* to bring those students into the counseling process.

For you to be optimally effective, then, you will need to be familiar with those techniques that are suitable for various ethnic groups. For example, a directive approach might be the way to go with certain ethnic groups, whereas other groups might be repulsed by such an approach and/or regard you as incompetent. The same care needs to be taken in body language and physical contact, where touching a counselee might be an offensive gesture.

Little research has been done on cultural variables and the capability of the counselee to trust the counselor. But there is some evidence to show that certain minorities and low-income families of *all* ethnic groups do not fare well in the counseling process as, say, Caucasian Euro-Americans. Perhaps one of your best moves might be to study how you and your counselee use ethnicity, gender, or social class in your interaction together. It is suggested that cultural factors and dispositional factors, like emotional trauma, become most meaningful when used by participants within a social interaction context. More precisely, the primary skill of a multiculturally competent counselor is to have the capability to recognize that issues of ethnicity, gender, or social class might be interfering with the progress of a particular session, and then have the wherewithal to be able to address those issues in a manner that will allow the counselor to once again move the process forward.

There is no question that cultural considerations can both support and constrain a person's behavior. Such considerations can be the root of a person's desire to change or resist change. It's easy for your counselee to resist and maintain the status quo, to keep the self intact within his or her cultural context. As a counselor, you have been trained to challenge that sense of self; although, again, many of your counselees will call upon that sense of self to resist change, even when they know that such change would be good for them.

With a minority counselee, you have even a tougher nut to crack because often the sense of self is partly derived from membership in a group—a group that does not share the value system of the mainstream culture. We see this so often as we work with our underachieving students where to be smart is not at all "cool." Loyalty to group can sometimes be an impediment to positive growth and development. Also, resistance can take many forms within the counseling session; and, where there is resistance, you will want to take the time to explore the reasons for it, remembering that the problem could be ethnic or class issues with which the counselee—or even you as the counselor—is wrestling.

Finally, we believe that differences in ethnicity, social class, or gender will not inhibit the development of a sound relationship between counselor and counselee. Your primary focus should be on the problem at hand, with the primary goal being the resolving of the problem to the counselee's satisfaction. You will be looking at the problem as it exists within your client, and as it is part of the social environment. Your goal will be to get your student to arrive at his or her own understanding of the problem at both personal and social levels. Once the understanding has taken place, then the two of you can develop strategies for change. If the problem is centered mainly with your counselee, then any strategies need to focus on personal change. If, however, the problem is derived from the family, community, or economic condition, then any interventions need to focus on these entities.

# MINORITY HIGHER EDUCATION ENROLLMENT ON THE UPSWING

Since 1982, growth in minority enrollment has significantly outpaced increases in the enrollment of Caucasians in the nation's colleges and universities, so states a report from the United States Department of Education entitled *Trends in Enrollment in Higher Education by Racial/Ethnic Category*. Between 1982 and 1992, the time period surveyed, enrollment in institutions of higher education grew some 17 percent overall, with an increase of only 8.7 percent for Caucasian Euro-Americans. On the other hand, minority enrollment rose profoundly. The number of African-Americans enrolled in college increased by 26.6 percent during the time period. Other minority groups followed suit, with the enrollment of Native Americans and Alaskan Natives rising 35.1 percent; Hispanic enrollment climbed 83.9 percent, and Asian and Pacific Islander numbers jumped 98.5 percent.

The student demographics described in the report underline the importance of multicultural issues as they pertain to college counseling at the secondary level, including the very serious and continuing problem of student retention. It's not enough just to open doors to all kinds of minority students—it's keeping them there once they've arrived on campus. Some of this can be accomplished through *appropriate* student-to-campus matches.

Although more African-Americans are graduating from high school than previously, and black-white test-score gaps are narrowing, blacks who enter college are graduating in lower rates than they did in 1965. This statistic was garnered from an American College Testing (ACT) report entitled *Equity of Higher Educational Opportunity for Women, Black, Hispanic, and Low Income Students*. ACT examined retention progress since 1965—the year the federal government committed itself to improving access to education through the Higher Education Act. Regrettably, educational gains made by blacks in high school completion and college entrance rates has been offset by problems with retention. In 1965, 45 percent of blacks who entered college completed four or more years of study; but by 1987, the rate had slipped to 32 percent. To explain the retention problem, Thomas Mortensen, author of the ACT study, cites research which indicates that students do not succeed unless they are academically and *socially integrated* into a campus community. Leaders in the area of support and consequent retention have historically been Vassar College, New York; Ohio State University; and Williams College, Massachusetts.

## *Self-Segregation: A Campus Myth*

Self-segregation is evidently a campus myth—at least for certain minority students. A 1995 University of Michigan study found that minority college students are more likely to study, dine, and go out with members of other racial and ethnic groups than their white counterparts.

About 69 percent of Asian-Americans and 78 percent of Mexican-Americans reported frequently dining with someone of a different racial or ethnic background. For the same groups, 60 and 72 percent reported studying often with members of other groups. About 55 percent of African-American students often dine across racial and ethnic lines and 49 percent study with individuals outside their group. But only 21 percent of whites dine with students from other ethnic groups and 15 percent study with students from other groups.

Dating outside the groups occurs less frequently, with 42 percent of Asian-Americans, 13 percent of African-Americans, and 4 percent of whites frequently going out with students outside their group.

Sylvia Hurtado, assistant professor of education at the University of Michigan and author of the study, said the findings debunk a common perception that minority students segregate themselves on campus. In fact, states Hurtado, "students of color are crossing ethnic/racial lines the most, while white students seem to be segregating themselves."

What, if any, are the implications for school counselors as they counsel their students?

## *Williams College*

There has been a definitive effort to do something about the retention rates of students of color since 1987. Not only are secondary school counselors looking at the appropriate applicant/campus match more closely, but the colleges themselves have developed more comprehensive sophisticated support services, especially concerning social adjustment. It has not been a question so much of academic achievement of students of color that has driven many from a given campus as it has been of social and emotional comfort.

Williams College in Massachusetts well exemplifies what is transpiring on a host of college and university campuses today in the way of support services. One of the most pronounced changes in Williams since 1990 has been the diversification of its student body. Whereas freshman classes entering in the early 1980s included about 65 people who described themselves as other than Caucasian (13%), that number has risen steadily to a point where Americans of color make up about a quarter of all entering first-year students. During the same period, new student cultural organizations have arisen at a rate of about one per year.

There are other signs of diversification, as well, at this prestigious school. In 1989 Williams constructed a new Multicultural Center that houses a large meeting area, library, kitchen, and organizational offices for several campus groups. A member of the college's professional staff is assigned full-time to the Center to assist student groups housed there, and to help develop and implement activities and engage performers and speakers of multicultural interest. The mission of the Center, therefore, is to encourage recognition and respect for the cultural diversity and pluralism of the Williams College community.

More than a few entering freshmen are surprised to find out just how pluralistic some college campuses can be. School counselors become privy to some of this through feedback forms or at feedback sessions. Actually, it can be a breath of fresh air for some young people who, once in college, find themselves more free to mix and mingle with all ethnic types without fear of being labeled or taunted. Young people who hail from high schools where there are few if any minority students can be taken back by the potpourri of ethnic and cultural diversification. Even students who come from affable school systems where the predominant minority population might be Asian-Pacific Islanders and "India" Indians, can be surprised at the extent of the diversification.

When it comes to expectation versus reality of this or any other related issue, you are in an excellent position to help provide for a smooth transition from secondary school to college by knowing your colleges and universities *and* by knowing your students.

## TIPS FOR COUNSELORS FROM ESL TEACHERS

With ESL students, language can often be a counselor's first obstacle. ESL teachers are most cooperative in working with any "new" students. These same teachers can also be most cooperative in working with school counselors. Figure 9-1 gives a bit of advice:

### FIGURE 9-1

---

**How to Communicate with Your Beginning/Intermediate ESL Students**

1.  Speak slowly. Enunciate clearly and emphasize key words.
2.  Use simple sentences.
3.  Attach meaning through actions, gestures, pictures, real objects, and drawings.
4.  Avoid contracted forms, the passive voice, and embedded clauses.
5.  Watch your use of *he, she*, or *they*. Instead, use the names of people.
6.  Employ high frequency words where appropriate. Example: *mother* and *father* rather than *parents*.
7.  Repeat words and phrases in a cheerful tone of voice.
8.  Use extended pauses between ideas.
9.  Speak in a normal tone. A loud voice sounds angry and can be ineffectual.
10. Smile a lot. Humor helps. Eye contact helps, too.
11. Body language is not universal. For example, Vietnamese and other Southeast Asians do not appreciate having their hair tousled or their heads patted. Such actions border on the sacrilegious.
12. Encourage your counselees to use their bilingual dictionaries.

The following is a little something from an unknown source that should bring a smile to your face.

**Hints on English Pronunciation for Foreigners**

I take it you already know
of tough and bough and cough and dough?
Others may stumble but not you,
on hiccough, thorough, laugh, and through.
Well done! And now you wish perhaps,
to learn of less familiar traps?

Beware of heard, a dreadful word
that looks like beard but sounds like bird.
And dead: it's said like bed, not bead
For goodness' sake don't call it 'deed'!
Watch out for meat and great and threat
(They rhyme with suite and straight and debt.)
A moth is not a moth in mother
Nor both in bother, broth in brother,
And here is not a match for there,
Nor dear and fear for bear and pear.

Now work on what you've come to know,
Now like bow, and know like bow;
English is a tricky tongue,
So learn it well, while you're still young.

# SUGGESTED READINGS

Atkinson, Donald R., Morten, George, and Sue, Wing Derald (1989), third edition, *Counseling American Minorities: A Cross Cultural Perspective*, William C. Brown Publishers (A wealth of information and practical techniques for working with cross-cultural populations.)

Hurtado. Sylvia (1995), University of Michigan study "Self-Segregation: A Campus Myth," Ann Arbor, MI.

Johnson, Laurie S. (1995), "Enhancing Multicultural Relations: Intervention Strategies for the School Counselor," *The School Counselor*, Vol. 43 No. 2, American School Counselor Association, Alexandria, VA 22304-3300.

# CHAPTER 10

# HUMAN RELATIONS AND COMMUNICATIONS

School counselors are increasingly being recognized as educators in a strong position to influence people, programs, activities, and institutions for the good of the individual *and* the whole of society. The school counselor has a professional responsibility to bring his or her influence to bear on a school system's efforts to promote *maximum* student growth. Even Daniel Arbuckle touted this message back in 1975: "It is the professional responsibility of the school counselor to do something about those conditions which are harming students . . ." Counselors are slowly but steadily getting the message that they *are* more influential than they think. Unfortunately, too many of them are experiencing on-the-job frustration because they are unaware that they have such influence, and/or are not knowledgeable as to how to use it ethically and appropriately.

Terms like "power" and "influence" can smack of manipulation for self-aggrandizement, or even conjure up a picture of underhandedness. Nothing could be further from the truth. School counselors are trained to focus on the needs and welfare of students and their families; and to sharpen that focus, they must use a bit of influence in their personal relationships now and then.

The whole concept of using influence, even in a limited fashion, has been working its way into counseling literature through social-influence theory and research. The fact that counselors have the capability and the wherewithal to exert influence to bring about desired changes has been gaining wider recognition by educational theorists.

Social-influence theory has led to the identification of three elements of interpersonal power in the counselor/counselee relationship: (1) attractiveness, (2) expertise, and (3) trustworthiness. Atkinson and Wampole (1982) wrote that attractiveness is the degree to which a counselee perceives his or her counselor as approachable and friendly; expertise is characterized by the counselee's view of the counselor as having specialized training and skill; and trustworthiness is the degree to which the counselee sees his or her counselor as open, honest, stable, and dependable.

## COMMUNICATING WITH THE ADMINISTRATION

The three elements of interpersonal power must be present as school counselors work side by side with administrators, above all with school principals. Both parties communicate with students, teachers, parents, and the community-at-large, and they do so across the entire school spectrum. The two parties have separate and joint responsibilities that cause schools to be successful learning environments.

On the flip side, the two professional roles differ sufficiently to make a certain amount of conflict inevitable. More to the point, it could be said that counselors and administrators come from two different frames of reference. At the cost of stereotyping and oversimplification, there *are* a number of ways whereby each profession views the school world differently; at the same time, each has something to offer the other.

Administrators' responsibilities are all-inclusive, from bringing the school's philosophy and its administrative policy alive, translating them into action, to ensuring that the school has enough substitute teachers on any given day. Administrators *can* be leaders (though in our judgment the two terms are not synonymous), and in that role provide leadership to people and programs. They supervise curriculum and instruction; hire, fire, and evaluate staff personnel; prepare and oversee budgets; help create master schedules; and get their hands muddied with student disciplinary problems. Let's also throw in building maintenance, school busing, and co-curricular programs for good measure. All of this hopefully amounts to the improvement of learning and the accompanying scholastic achievement for *all* students by means of a safe, secure, and caring environment. It's a tall order!

At the same time, counselors view school counseling as an *integral* part of the educational endeavor, an important process that engages students in problem solving and decision making that pertain to personal, social, and educational issues. School counselors believe that until students are capable of identifying and solving the problems that block effective learning, they will not be able to devote their full attention to the learning process. For counselors, students' mental health is "where it's at"; that is, mental health is a valid end in itself as well as an avenue toward enhancing student decision-making skills.

Of course, numerous administrators see all of these tasks as an ancillary phenomenon that indirectly supports student learning. Administrators would like to see counselors directly supporting school learning and achievement by working with students in skill-building activities that have an immediate and practical impact on the school environment. In addition, many principals like to see counselors acting as consultants to teachers and families in order to effect positive change in the learning process. To put it another way, principals are sometimes short on patience—they want action. For them, individual and group counseling activity should lead directly and rapidly to improved classroom behavior and academic progress. Conversely, counselors can be content with short-term or long-term payoffs when it comes to individual student personal, social, and educational gains.

The picture is changing, however. Administrators are becoming less restless as they see in action what school counselors have known for the past twenty or so years: individual learning styles play a large role in the eventual success or failure of a good many secondary students.

# COMMUNICATION AND PROBLEM SOLVING

Communication is a vital element in problem solving. To resolve a difficult situation, a principal usually summons all involved parties; does a lot of listening, questioning, and verifying; and generally engages the parties in conflict resolution and problem solving. But principals see confidentiality, a huge building block of the school counseling movement, as an impediment to expeditious problem solving. Confidentiality does limit the information that counselors can share with teachers, parents, and administrators. The counselor assures his or her counselee that his or her comments are safe. The principal, on the other hand, has the need to know in order to pull all of the information together, and act on what is taking place in the building. Deciding on just what information to share with their principals, or for that matter, any staff member, can be a significant and perplexing communications dilemma for counselors. Revelation demands mutual respect and trust between two professionals.

Student advocacy is another issue about which counselors and administrators have differing viewpoints. For the counselor, the individual reigns supreme. Each unique student has his or her own special needs. Counselors strive to make the total learning experience as profitable and supportive as possible for *each* student. For example, the counselor might choose a specific teacher who he or she believes will work best with a specific counselee; or the counselor might comment, even explain away, a troubled counselee's inappropriate behavior by referencing his or her more overriding personal and social problems. Much to the chagrin of some administrators, to the counselor *every* student is an exception.

Principals, on the other hand, are student body advocates who strive to promote the entire student body or a particular group's interests by ensuring an orderly and productive learning environment. Administrators always take into account the impact of any decision on the other students in a classroom or school as a whole. What administrators are justifiably prepared to do for one, they must be prepared to justifiably do for everyone.

That is why principals sometimes see counselors as too passive in their dealings with students and parents, afraid to take the hard line. This is especially true when it comes to placing a student in a particular course or course level. In an attempt to raise educational standards, many secondary schools now have course and course grade prerequisites, which to some extent limit the choices a counselor and client have to make. At any time you feel that there should be a variance from the accepted norm, you should be prepared to state, and if necessary place in writing, your position on the matter. Conversely, if your principal grants you "power of placement," then *your* decisions must be supported by him or her.

Students should be on a constant well-charted course of learning new material and acceptable behaviors. Significant deviation (unacceptable behavior) from the course, however, does not deny the need for realistic and appropriate consequences for the given student.

*Quality Counseling Programs*

Administrators who are blessed with quality counseling programs possess the wherewithal to continually laud the counselors, encourage their growth, and most of all *defend* them. Most do. Some don't. To sustain a hard-earned positive image, it helps to have a solid working relationship among four key individuals within a school system: (1) district superintendent, (2) building principal, (3) director of student services, and (4) the building chairperson of counseling and guidance. Here are a few tips that might help foster such a relationship:

- Be aware that next to counselors, administrators are probably the most maligned group of educators. A little empathy can go a long way.

- Administrators need to continually sense that you are using your special skills to make their job easier, as they plug away at running a smooth and efficient operation in the face of monetary restraints and all kinds of public reaction.

- Convince your administrators that there must be chain-of-command procedures for dealing with those community members who have counseling complaints. Superintendents and principals should channel irate parent phone calls to the affected counselor first, or to the department chairperson if the parent has already contacted the counselor. When administration does not follow chain-of-command procedures, there is a consequent lowering of staff morale, which undermines efforts to improve image.

- It is possible to hide behind powerlessness, thereby blaming your condition on someone else. Don't get caught up in the "dumping" that continues to go on in education. You need to make a concerted effort to improve your own condition. On the other hand, don't allow your publics to step all over you, either—which will soon bring us to the whole issue of privatization.

# INFLUENCE AND CONSULTATION

To get from point A to point B, you might well need to influence a person or organization toward your way of thinking. As you exert your influence, you are probably working in your consultation mode; the two overlap more often than not. Remember that consultation is the process by which a first party (consultant) helps a second party (consultee) solve a problem that concerns a third party (client). Consultation demands that the influence exercised be of a more subtle nature. Consultees generally know what is best from their point of view. You cannot *impose* solutions. Work together *toward* solutions. (See the more complete treatment of consultation in Chapter 1.)

# SCHOOL COUNSELING AND PRIVATIZATION

It's hard to hit a moving target. Don't stand still for too long, then, or you're likely to be privatized. Parts or wholes of public school systems are being privatized: for-profit companies are being invited to run public schools in various sections of the country.

When an entire school district, or even a single school building, "goes private," professional staff, including school counselors, can go as well. A case in point is an elementary school in Wilkinsburg, Pennsylvania, an eastern suburb of Pittsburgh. Wilkinsburg became the first school district in the country to give a company the authority to replace *all* professional staff. So in September of 1995, the school system became yet another flash point in the national debate over privatization and public schools.

The privatization movement in public school education has been emerging from a number of economic, demographic, and social changes that are currently taking place in the country, but the movement has actually been with us for some time. For years, schools have hired outside corporations to run their food services and transportation programs. A more recent phenomenon has been an expansion into custodial services. It's only been in the past several years that we are seeing boards of education contracting private firms to operate entire systems or individual buildings. With that license goes control over the destinies of a school's professional staff. Alas, in a number of instances, school counselors have become privatized.

Although the movement has been growing steadily (120 school districts serving nearly 80,000 students), there is no definitive research to date as to how privatization is impacting school counseling programs. Cass Dykeman explores the topic in the September 1995 issue of ASCA's *The School Counselor*. Through a questionnaire mailed to selected school superintendents, Dykeman learned that counselor privatization is significantly more common in small districts than in medium or large districts. The author's accumulated data reveals that 20% of all public school counseling in the state of Washington is contracted out. We should be careful not to generalize any findings to the school counseling movement nationwide, however; Washington continues to experience a shortage of counselors.

Similarly, if that state is locating its counselors through private means, one can't help but wonder to what extent these so-called counselors are credentialed. Dykeman answers some of that. "I am aware of many counselors who work for the contracted agencies who do not even possess an Associate of Arts degree." The fact that a school district can save a buck with such hiring practices is quite evident. What is not so evident is the nature of the impact these noncredentialed nondegreed individuals are having on the lives of young people.

We must not lose sight of the real purpose of improving our counseling skills: to better help those young people assigned to our care. On the other hand, the best defense is a good offense. These improvements will prove that you are necessary, and will reduce the risk of your position becoming privatized.

- Continuous self-assessment and departmental assessment is critical.

- Having an active Guidance Advisory Committee can be most helpful. This overseeing body, which normally meets during the evening hours, should include students, teachers, administrators, and parents.

- Strong but democratic department leadership on the part of the chairperson is crucial. All counselors need to *join together* as they employ common practices and common terminology in their everyday activities.

- A meaningful staff development program for counselors is needed whereby there is in-house opportunity to improve one's counseling skills. Also important is the freedom to attend *worthwhile* out-of-district workshops to enhance those same skills.

# COMMUNICATING WITH PARENTS

There is nothing like a solid triangle of communication: student, counselor, and family—much like the heralded tie of communications in athletics: coach, counselor, and family. The trick is to pull parents *back* into the picture; for one reason or another, they have absented themselves since elementary school days. School counselors may be in a strong position to influence, but it's difficult to influence when the parents aren't participating.

In the early seventies, Rutgers University in New Jersey offered a graduate course with the propitious title, "The Role of the School in American Society." My, oh my, have society and the role changed since that time. Both harried and savvy parents have been one of the driving forces of such change: harried, as in their conspicuous absence from the schools; savvy, as in their sometimes overbearing and persistent presence.

Thomas French, in a *New York Times* article of August 22, 1993, remarks that whenever parents ask him what's gone wrong with the public schools, his instinct is to hand them a mirror. French, who has intimate knowledge of Floridian public education (and has written a book about it) attended the "age-old ritual known as back-to-school night" at Largo High School in Largo, Florida. The author was surprised to see but 500 parents in attendance; Largo has an enrollment of some 1800 students.

In the annual Metropolitan Life Survey of the American Teacher, conducted by Louis Harris and Associates, a majority of teachers polled agreed that the No.1 priority in education policy should be to find a way to strengthen parents' roles in their children's education. Perhaps the most pressing problem in education has more to do with parents than with students: in the 1992 MetLife survey, 40 percent of the teachers who had completed just two years of teaching, and who stated that they were likely to leave education, cited uncooperative parents as a major factor.

Of course it's simplistic to lay all the problems of education at the feet of mothers and fathers—there are a number of others involved in the educative process who can shoulder some of the blame—but, according to French, "none of these problems compares with the disappearance and disarray of parents . . . parents who never set foot on school grounds; parents who don't show up for conferences; parents who insult and sometimes threaten teachers; parents who show little interest in what's happening to their children; parents who don't seem to care if their kids are actually going to school."

As a counselor, you know that parental involvement is, for the most part, a prerequisite for academic success. And have you noticed that when you do get parents in your office, some of them have little chance of talking about their children's problems because they're too busy talking about their own? A good number consumed with holding their own lives together, some trying to cope with everything from divorce to substance abuse, have almost no time or energy left for their children.

Pulitzer Prize-winning critic William Henry sees schools as rehabilitation centers "obliged to make up for the social and psychological deficiencies of some parents, the ignorance and bone idleness of others, the economic privations of others still, and the myriad unkindness of nature. Where schools of the fifties, particularly post-Sputnik, focused on stimulating the brightest, schools of today focus on bringing the backward up to speed . . . In fifties educational parlance, a 'special' child meant a gifted one. Now it usually means one who is severely handicapped."

Henry, in his splendid but nonetheless controversial work, *In Defense of Elitism*, goes on to state: "the debate continues to rage about why the decline [in student performance] has happened . . . Some of the reasons are obvious. Parents no longer teach reverence for authority and learning. Many of them arrive at teacher conferences loaded for bear, prepared to treat any shortcoming of their child's as exclusively the fault of the school—if they come at all, which is anecdotally reported to be less and less likely, as more mothers work outside the home. Students reared on Sesame Street expect learning to be chirpy, funny, swift-paced, and full of entertainment. They have far less patience than their forebears with such wearisome but necessary tasks as memorization."

Who knows better than you that parents need *special* assistance and support! And the location of your school district might just dictate the complexity and extensiveness of any assistance and support. Here are a few things worth considering as you work with families:

- Most parents do perceive you as experienced and competent, but have you made them aware that you are also responsive and caring, that you will go the extra mile if need be? They'd like that, because research continues to indicate that when it comes to school counseling, one-on-one is a high priority with most parents.

- An evening program can be a fine opportunity to assure parents that you are indeed their child's advocate, and that you will be keeping a watchful eye on all aspects of the child's growth and development.

- The word "enjoy" is not used nearly enough. Use it! Parents enjoy hearing that you are enjoying their children.

- Don't hesitate to be creative as you plan your annual schedule of evening programs. Avoid trying to cover too much territory in one evening; it's much better to focus on one or two issues. Plan programs around grade levels and the need to know. Timing is everything in effective programming, from time management and study habits for freshmen to college application procedures for seniors.

- Never hesitate to frankly but tactfully convey to parents what your role is and is not. Of course, the best way to communicate your role is to perform it.

- Be accepting of parental differences. Just as you unconditionally accept each of your counselees, do the same thing with parents. Grit your teeth, if necessary. At the same time, you can offer sound advice on *specific* problems.

- When parental involvement becomes excessive, *you* should take control in order to return more control to your counselee.

- A number of parents satisfy their own selfish needs through their children. Work to break through some or all of this as you advocate for your affected students. Assuming a take-charge attitude in your counseling sessions can play well here. Any meeting with dominating parents should be tightly structured, with little or no time wasted on being defensive. Once parents have had their say, you might make a statement such as, "In my *professional* opinion, this is the direction I think we should take"; or "This *depart-ment* supports the idea of students not taking an endless number of college admission tests." Remember: it's not so much what you say, but *how* you say it. School counselors are criticized as much for their tone of voice as they are for what the voice produces. So holding the line is fine, but do it with grace and diplomacy.

- Tread lightly with certain ethnic and religious families. Sometimes a parent assumes that the counselor shares his or her values, or vice versa. As you know, such is not always the case. There will also be occasions where your client will reject parental values; a value-compromise will then have to be struck before any forward movement can be experienced. Or you might run the risk of pulling back and not offering direct advice because you perceive that it's not in agreement with family values. *But your job is to advise.* You *can* render advice and still honor the true values of the entire family.

## Communication and the Single Parent

In some sections of the country, every fifth youngster under the age of eighteen lives with one parent—some twelve million with mothers, some one million with fathers. Although divorce might be the first thing that comes to mind when we think of a single-parent home, widowhood, single-parent adoption, separation, desertion, or unwed parenthood all result in single-parent situations as well. Add to this a family scene where one parent is seriously or continuously ill, or where a parent is constantly absent from the household for business reasons, and you have a vast number of families where you can find a parent "going it alone."

Whether they assumed the role by happenstance or by choice, single parents have much the same concerns as their counterparts from two-parent households, but with single parents, there are gaps to be filled, and you can do some of that filling. Certainly an important first step is to know which of your counselees come from single-parent households. The benefits of this shared knowledge are reciprocal. You become sensitized to your counselee's special situation. He or she feels better in knowing that you know, and consequently might more readily seek your advice and services. Understand that some youngsters resent the absence of a parent, and are embarrassed to have other people aware of it. Yet in your position you can make some inroads—at the very least, for your professional self.

Youngsters need time to assimilate all that has happened to them, and to acknowledge their sadness, loneliness, and resentment. You can help your counselees sort out their feelings. Incidentally, a youngster from a single-parent situation might benefit from having a counselor of a particular sex.

Single parents especially welcome assistance from the school. Middle school is a great time for the school counselor to reach out by way of the telephone or a written note to help keep these individuals informed. Most single parents hold full-time jobs. Most have answering machines. A message on an answering machine *is* appreciated. A good job of single parenting *can* be done, and in many instances, *is* being done. In fact, there are those people who believe that a child is better off in a stable single-parent environment than in a two-parent setting that is seriously dysfunctional.

# SUGGESTED READINGS

Arbuckle, Daniel S. (1975), *Counseling and Psychotherapy* (2nd ed.). Boston: Allyn & Bacon.

Atkinson, Donald and Wampole, Barbara (1982). "A Comparison of the Counselor Rating Form and the Counselor Effectiveness Rating Scale," *Counselor Education and Supervision*, Vol. 22.

Dykeman, Cass (1995), "The Privatization of School Counseling," *The School Counselor*, Vol. 43. American School Counselor Association, Alexandria, VA.

Henry, William A., *In Defense of Elitism* (1994), Bantam Doubleday Dell Publishing Group, New York, NY 10036.

# CHAPTER 11

# IT'S MORE THAN LAW

The American School Counselor Association (ASCA), the national organization for school counselors, long ago established tenets or ethical standards for the profession. More specifically, the document that you will want to procure from ASCA is the *Ethical Standards for School Counselors*, the most recent revision being in 1992. Periodic revisions are necessary because the perception of what is ethical changes as societal values and the counseling profession itself change.

In the four-page document, ASCA clearly spells out the principles of ethical behavior necessary to maintain high standards of integrity and leadership among its members. The organization offers a series of the school counselor's responsibilities to students, parents, counseling colleagues and other professional associates, school and community, and—most importantly—to self.

As you examine the list of responsibilities that follow, note that all appear to be applicable to any school counselor in the nation, whether an ASCA member or not. (Incidentally, ASCA has separated from the American Counselor Association [ACA], and it is now possible to join ASCA without having to join ACA.) Here is some material to ponder that pertains to students and to self.

### Ethical and Other Responsibilities to Ponder

1. Act in the best interest of your counselees at all times. Advocate in good faith. Remember that you are counseling a truly unique individual. As a school counselor you must be concerned about your counselees' educational, vocational, personal, and social development, and encourage optimum growth in these areas.

2. Communicate to your counselees any possible limitations on the counseling relationship at the *outset* of the relationship. Such notice could include confidentiality issues, such as the possible necessity for consulting with other professionals, privileged communication, and legal or authoritative restraints. The *meaning* and *limits* of confidentiality should be openly and clearly communicated.

3. Counsel to enhance your counselees' awareness of personal values, attitudes, and beliefs, and don't hesitate to inform them when personal characteristics might hinder effectiveness.

4. Counsel within the boundaries of personal competence. Be sensitive to your personal skill levels and limitations. Know when to refer!

5. Be able to communicate with your counselees about any of their specific behaviors, as well as the reason(s) for said behaviors. A theoretical rationale (framework) should always underpin your counseling strategies and interventions.

6. Encourage family involvement where possible, especially when working with minors in sensitive areas that could be controversial. Family systems counseling is the wave of the future.

7. Adhere to written job descriptions. Make certain that what you are doing is defined as an appropriate function in your setting.

8. Read and abide by the ethical standards of your profession. Keep a copy of ASCA's ethical standards on hand. Refer to it periodically, and act accordingly.

9. Consult with other professionals, e.g., colleagues, supervisors, and counselor educators, so as to have a ready, accessible network of professionals.

10. Join appropriate professional associations. Read their publications and participate in professional development opportunities. Remember that with the school counselor professional and personal growth is a continuous process.

11. Stay current with laws and court rulings, particularly those that pertain to the counseling of minors.

12. Take care not to encourage your counselees to accept values, lifestyles, plans, decisions, and beliefs that represent only your personal orientation. In short, be sensitive to the potential effects your own personal characteristics can have on your clients.

13. Protect the confidentiality of your counselees' records, and release personal data only according to prescribed law and local school policies. Any information maintained through electronic data storage methods should be treated with the same care as that of traditional student records.

Interest in seminars and workshops devoted to ethical and legal issues in school counseling has been steadily rising. Some of this is due to a society more sensitive to litigation, and to the fact that so many of today's school counselor functions have ethical and legal overtones. Ethical standards act as a kind of road map, but they are by no means solutions to the numerous dilemmas that professional counselors face.

Ethics and law are not synonymous terms, even though there is a relationship between the two principles. *Counseling Minor Clients* (Salo & Sumate, 1993) is an excellent source book and should be required reading for all school counselors during—or after—graduate training.

## SUGGESTED READINGS

Huey, Wayne C. & Remley, T. P. Jr., (1988) *Ethical & Legal Issues in School Counseling*, American School Counselor Association (ASCA), Alexandria, VA 22304.

Salo, M.M., & Shumate, S.G. (1993) *Counseling Minor Clients*, American School Counselor Association (ASCA), Alexandria, VA 22304.

# SECTION II

# PERSONAL AND SOCIAL DEVELOPMENT OF THE SECONDARY STUDENT

◆ ◆ ◆ ◆ ◆

"Individuality" is a significant word in a counselor's vocabulary. There is something beautiful about a person being a "one of a kind," the only one on the planet; unless you believe in absolute doubles, that is. Of course it would be easier for school counselors to work with kids if they were all cut from the same cloth—but they're not. The unique youngster in front of you might have problems *similar* to those of his or her friends; the student might have a similar home life, live in a similar neighborhood, and take similar courses—but the combination is *the student's*. This is the only life *he* or *she* has lived.

That life comes replete with *unique* personal and social problems that can have their origins in the school setting and then extend into the community, or vice-versa. The enhancement of personal and social skills is a key factor in students being able to live with themselves and with others in adolescent years *and* in adulthood. Affected skills include decision-making, interpersonal relations, communications, self-concept, self-assessment, valuing, accepting individual differences, respecting the rights of others, and conflict resolution. Section II addresses many of these topics.

Peer relations is certainly a big area of concern for today's adolescents. If one youngster is having relationship difficulties, he or she can now turn to another youngster for advice. The extraordinary power of positive peer influence, whereby students assist students to make healthy informed decisions, has taken firm hold in the past decade. Peer helping is

93

everywhere—program titles may vary from school to school, but the basic concept is the same: students helping other students in subject area tutoring, buddy programs, school orientation that includes the welcoming of transfer students, peer group discussion sessions, and hotline staffing.

Sometimes a personal problem can escalate into a crisis situation. Counselors have always had to deal with crises; and with schools continuing to be awash in drugs and alcohol, and with adolescent suicide on the increase, the word "crises" is still very much in the school counselor's lexicon.

A crisis situation is a set of affairs that will set in motion precipitous change. A suicide attempt is a crisis; long-term chemical abuse is a crisis; so are the life-threatening diseases of bulimia and anorexia: change set each in motion, changes will occur within it, and a change will be required to get out of it.

A personal crisis is an emotional state within which a person reacts to a hazardous event. If people in crisis are able to cope with the given situation effectively, they can strengthen their position in life. As a counselor, you can use this often overlooked characteristic of a crisis in helping your clients further enrich their characters and personalities.

Before you engage in any kind of counseling activity with crises issues, you should have a working knowledge of state laws, as well as state and local boards of education policies that govern the handling of such issues. Regulations vary considerably from state to state. *Special* attention must also be paid to any ethical and/or legal guidelines pertaining to child abuse and neglect, suicide, and substance abuse.

Personal and Social Development is the major developmental area that pertains to the life skills youngsters will need to succeed in the twenty-first century. As a school counselor, you are *the* most appropriate professional in the school to promote positive student growth and development, and to help students and staff make necessary adjustments to any life events that might stand in the way of students achieving their potential.

# CHAPTER 12

# SELF-CONCEPT, SELF-ASSESSMENT, AND VALUING

*"An individual's self-concept is the core of his personality. It affects every aspect of human behavior: the ability to learn, the capacity to grow and change, the choice of friends, mates, and careers. It's no exaggeration to say that a strong positive self-image is the best possible preparation for success in life."*

—Dr. Joyce Brothers
(Say Yes to Your Potential *by Skip Ross*)

If this is the case, and it certainly seems to be, then it is vital that the counselor make a valiant effort to help each counselee have a positive self-image.

Terminology is interesting here. "Self-concept" refers to those ideas and attitudes one has about oneself at any given moment. And while "self-concept" is cognitive, "self-esteem" is affective: it refers to the extent to which one values oneself. "Self-image," then, might be considered to be the sum total of the attitudes, facts, and feelings a person has accumulated about him- or herself.

The self-image of most students is a vague, nebulous feeling about their status, but if they can pay some attention to the idea, quality growth can occur. Don Hamachek states in his book, *Encounters with the Self,* "Acquiring a self-concept involves a slow process of differentiation as a person gradually emerges into focus out of his total world of awareness and defines progressively more clearly just what and who he is."

# SELF-ASSESSMENT

Being aware of what he or she *is* and *has* is vital to enable each student to decide what he or she wants to *be* and *do*; that process is called—not surprisingly—"self-assessment." Self-assessment is the acknowledgment of one's *abilities, interests, aspirations, and values—as they are now.*

In order to be able to *see* themselves better, your counselees should take the time to sit with pencil and paper and *list* their abilities and interests, and note their aspirations and values. They will find many more positives than negatives.

### *Abilities*

Even though students have been tested to death, few of them understand their *actual* achievement and aptitude scores well enough to fully assess specific strengths and weaknesses, and their positioning both locally and nationally. Because they are secondary school *students*, the most evident of their abilities are academic, but other talents must be documented, as well. Does your counselee like to draw, paint, and design? Have a natural aptitude for creative expression? How about the performing arts, or athletics, or woodworking, or using sign language? If he or she answers with even a hesitant "yes," then it is important to seriously evaluate the depth and range of the ability. The list might look like Figure 12-1.

### FIGURE 12-1

| Ability | How Good? | Evidence? |
|---------|-----------|-----------|
| Math | Very good | SAT = 740 |
| Verbal | Not so good | SAT = 420, but took reading course this semester |
| Tennis | Pretty good | Varsity team two years |
| Work with kids | Good | Tutored kids in math |

### *Interests*

Since activities are motivated by interests, your students should start by listing *all* of their activities, in school and out of school, and study them to find commonalities. Remember that a student spends but one third of the day in school; out-of-school activities are extremely important in analyzing one's interests. When writing the list, several points should be kept in mind:

1. Start by making two lists: in-school and out-of-school.
2. List all interests, large and small.
3. Consider work experience as indicative of interest.

4. Bring together related or similar activities.

5. Prioritize the interests in importance to you.

6. Examine for the unusual.

7. Keep the final list brief.

### Aspirations

"What do I really want out of life?" For most youngsters, it is "What do I want today?" It seems that young people have a hard time realistically considering the future; their concerns are more involved with the present. They are much more likely to decide at six o'clock what they are going to do at nine then to make plans for the following weekend. At the same time, it is quite common to hear, "I'm going to be rich someday," or "I'll be a famous lawyer," or "I want to own a Porsche." It is more reassuring to hear, "I want to take care of sick children," or "I want to be a *good* lawyer."

Are we more materialistic than before? Probably. Has the immediacy of television eaten away at long-range planning? Probably. Has the increase in our generation's financial well-being caused our children to want more? Quite probably. In years gone by, a father would build a wagon for his child; today he writes a check—or signs a credit card slip—to buy one.

What does this have to do with hopes and plans? Everything takes less time than it used to; things come and go in an instant; we seldom grow our own food or build our own tools. Young people, then, are less likely to *think* that they have to plan ahead—or that they have to sit quietly and decide what they really want.

Start with the simple for your counselees, but start early. Let them tell you what they really want to be doing when they graduate from high school; is it work or college or the military? Then you can do some career planning, remembering that the actual choice of a career path is not due for a few years: young people should be learning enough about themselves to at least know the area in which to start. For some of them, it will be liberal arts. That's fine, especially if the youngster can say, for example, that he or she leans toward the sciences, so the college he or she chooses should have a strong science department.

Other aspirations are important, too: studying in a city; moving to another part of the country; to own and run a ranch; to "go international." No aspiration is definitive; all will change and meld and develop. Of course, knowing what you really want makes many decisions easier: "If I really want to be a nuclear physicist, I'll choose the appropriate college." Or, "If I have to choose between ski country and playing soccer, I'll choose soccer."

### Values

By this time, the youngster has considered his or her abilities, interests, plans; now he or she must ask, "Why am I doing this, anyway? What is *important* to me? What do I *value?*"

A long time ago, St. John's University in New York advertised: "Learn to use your mind; acquire greater appreciation for the world of culture; receive training in self-discipline; prepare for living a fuller, more useful life; attain greater perspective into the world around you; cultivate a greater awareness of social problems; and become better equipped to handle your obligations to society."

Great goals based on great values, aren't they? But where did they come from? Parents, educators, religious leaders, and politicians think that at least part of their role is to transmit *their* standards to "their" young people. True, but for those young people to *have* values, to act according to values, they must *develop their values themselves*. Valuing is an active process of *choosing* beliefs and behavior, *prizing* the same, and *acting* on one's beliefs. Young people are great at this. It's important to remind them, though, that like any educational process, one learns from the masters—in this case, especially from those whose qualities they admire.

Values are located in the specifics that indicate value. Your counselees have thought about—and listed —their interests and aspirations; now the question is, "Why is this important to me? What am I really trying to be?"

Incidentally, no one should be discouraged by faults or lack of growth: it is always good to be "unfinished"!

## GROWTH IN VALUES AND . . .

In the beginning of the chapter, we referred to assessment in terms of "as we are *now*." The "now" is even more important in valuing. Dr. Brian Hall, in his book *The Genesis Effect*, has verbalized what he feels is a pattern of growth in values based on maturation as a human person. Discussing his findings so briefly is, of course, an injustice; but some aspects of his "growth" theory have great implications in understanding—and dealing with—our counselees. An outline of Hall's theory is given in Figure 12-2.

The point is this: every person grows from self-centeredness for survival to social interaction; the interaction grows from coping to participation. If a person is in a bad situation, e.g., poverty, homelessness, lack of parenting, ghetto living, etc., he or she might well be in Phase I. The values, then, will be to simply survive. Most of our secondary students seem to be in Phase II—they always seem to be coping with a course or a teacher or friends or parents, don't they? What we want to do is help them move from seeing the world as a *problem* to accepting a world in which they can *participate*.

## . . . BELONGING TO A GROUP

Which brings us to another point: succeeding and belonging in a social world means "membership" in many groups. A youngster is male or female; belongs to a religious group or not; is a particular color; is of a particular ethnic group; is a "nerd" or a "geek" or a "jock," is an athlete, musician, or club member; is in the "honors" group or the "standard"; has two parents or one or none; is rich or poor or "regular."

Sometimes membership in a group has a great impact on the way a person sees him- or herself. It is not only how strongly he or she identifies with that group, but also how that group fares in the local society. For example: a child not only has to really accept—and hopefully be proud of—his religious heritage; he must then fit his "group" into his planning, i.e., does he want to attend a "Catholic college?" Or a youngster with homosexuality in his background: he not only must deal with it on a personal level, but must also deal with its social acceptance.

FIGURE 12-2

| ELEMENTS IN CONSCIOUSNESS | PHASE I | PHASE II | PHASE III | PHASE IV |
|---|---|---|---|---|
| How the world is perceived by the individual: | The world is a MYSTERY over which I have NO CONTROL. | The world is a PROBLEM with which I must COPE. | The world is a PROJECT in which I must PARTICIPATE. | The world is a MYSTERY for which WE must CARE. |
| How the individual perceives SELF-FUNCTION in the world: | The self EXISTS at the center of a HOSTILE WORLD and struggles to SURVIVE. | The self DOES THINGS to succeed in a SOCIAL WORLD and seeks to BELONG and BE APPROVED BY SIGNIFICANT PERSONS. | The self ACTS on the CREATED WORLD with conscience and independence, and strives to RESHAPE the ENVIRONMENTS. | Selves GIVE LIFE to the GLOBAL WORLD through INTIMACY and SOLITUDE within and HARMONY without. |
| What HUMAN NEEDS the self needs to satisfy: | PHYSICAL NEED for food, pleasure, warmth and shelter. | SOCIAL NEED for acceptance, affirmation, approval, and achievement. | PERSONAL NEED to express creative insights, be oneself, direct one's life, and own one's ideas. | COMMUNAL NEED for global harmony by nurturing persons and communities. |
| TYPES OF VALUES | STAGE I A & B | STAGE II A & B | STAGE III A & B | STAGE IV A & B |
| Primary GOAL values: | Self-preservation; Security | Family/Belonging Self-worth; Self-competence/ confidence. | Self-actualization Service, Vocation; Human Dignity. | Intimacy, solitude; Beauty, transcendence. |
| MEANS values: | Safety/Survival | Instrumentality; Education. | Empathy, Independence; Accountability. | Interdependence; Intermediate technology. |

One "group" that is subject to great social pressure is that of womanhood. Women have been fighting for equal educational opportunities for centuries, and haven't gotten them yet. It's not that they are not offered the same academic courses—for the most part—or sports or transportation; it's the subtle differences that hamper growth into a self-confident capable adult. Just as "society" presumes that the rich are better off than the poor, or that minorities don't work as well, or that tall people play basketball, so "society" assumes that women aren't good in math, or don't really want a career, or don't want to be a plumber. It's called "prejudice"—which means pre-judging.

Much has been written about the apparent change in many young women from independence and confidence in grade school to reticence and lack of competitiveness in middle school. Myra and David Sadker, in their book *Failing at Fairness: How America's Schools Cheat Girls*, correlate the stress of "moving up" with changes in the adolescent's physiology. For most girls, these changes happen concurrently; with boys, the physical changes happen later. Athletic activity is a prime example: boys tend to grow stronger, taller, and more confident; the changes in a girl's shape make relearning a necessity.

That factor of which the counselor should be most aware is the subtle pressure of the educator—teacher and counselor alike—to pay more attention to boys than to girls: to give them more time to answer a question; to be more positive about their response; to be more imaginative in suggestions for their future. It's not that young men should be denied these advantages; it's that young women should get them, too.

In order to know themselves well, young people should list the "groups" to which they belong, and think about the effect each "membership" has in their lives. To know the *whole* person, you have to know him or her inside-out: the abilities, interests, aspirations, and values—and the relationships to society, as well.

# SUGGESTED READINGS

American Association of University Women (1992), *How Schools Shortchange Girls*, 1111 16th St., N.W., Washington DC 20036.

Hall, Brian P. (1986), *The Genesis Effect*. Mahwah, NJ: Paulist Press.

Hamachek, Don E. (1978), *Encounters with the Self*. New York: Holt, Rinehart, and Winston.

Ross, Skip, with Carole C. Carlson (1983), *Say Yes to Your Potential*. Waco, TX: Woerd Books.

Sadker, Myra & David. (1994), *Failing at Fairness: How America's Schools Cheat Girls*. New York: Charles Scribner's Sons.

# CHAPTER 13

# COMMITMENT, RESPONSIBILITY, AND REALITY THERAPY

When we invited our neighbor's son Robert to a Saturday Phillies game, he thanked us but turned us down, explaining that he had already agreed to work that day for his school's S.A.V.E. program. "Boy, I wish I could go," he remarked, "but I said I'd help pick up litter, and I guess I better do it." We were a bit surprised by the youngster's comment. "That's different," we thought. In a society where commitment means *maybe* and fidelity is caught somewhere between principle and expediency, it was a refreshing response. A good many youngsters would have dumped (no pun intended) their S.A.V.E. obligation in a minute and gone to the ball game. Robert was the exception.

Commitment and fidelity: what's the difference? Fidelity is the determination to hold to something or someone of value; it contains a large measure of "heart." Fidelity can be an inner need, a deep thirst in one's life for something of meaning, and it presupposes that values are personally accepted. Commitment is the decision to act, to follow the path that will realize that fidelity. When the principle of commitment is nurtured by parents in a youngster's formative years, it grows and flourishes and is not lost in the shifting sands of cultural fads and attitudes.

It has become important for the school to recognize the value of commitment; it is vital to the growth of each youngster. Counselors can—no, counselors *should*—teach commitment. We teach it when we hold the line on schedule changes, or when we instill in our students

101

the importance of selecting an extra-curricular activity and then *sticking with it*. We even teach it when we counsel a student to honor his or her college admission early-decision covenant.

But teaching commitment can be an uphill battle when young people come from homes where the principle is rendered little more than lip service by parents. Counselors and teachers are often called upon to draw from youngsters a value that parents themselves aren't experiencing or practicing.

Commitment is best taught when modeled! As school counselors, we model it when we perform any or all aspects of our job, whether it be reporting to work on time, the amount of energy expended in performing our role, and the seriousness of purpose displayed as we approach each task. So when young people observe our adult behavior, we are teaching by example—modeling. And youngsters are very good at detecting the difference between words and behavior.

Commitment is a decision of the mind, an intellectual exercise, not an emotional happening. To be committed, we first must want to be faithful to something—a job, a cause, doing well in school, marriage. One might wonder about the commitment of the young woman in *The New Yorker* cartoon who remarked to her boyfriend, "I'm not talking about a life-long relationship; I'm talking about marriage."

In *Habits of the Heart*, Robert Bellah concludes that most Americans prize commitment, but have difficulty in naming those things to which they are committed. If we value commitment to family, for instance, all too often it gets pushed to the back burner when it interferes with another value, our individual needs. So we should be honest with ourselves as we continuously engage in the process of examining our values and behavior. Such adult self-examination can be uncomfortable—downright painful at times; but it needs to be accomplished, especially if we're going to teach commitment to young people.

# RESPONSIBILITY

Even employers are concerned about commitment, as well as the related term *responsibility*. In the Career Development section we discuss the fact that corporate America has become increasingly concerned with the antisocial aspect of their employees' behavior. Corporations are looking to hire responsible young people who have the capability of being an effective member of a company. *Team play*: two big words with today's corporations.

One definition of responsibility pertains to personal accountability, the condition of being answerable for one's behavior. And so it might be said that once a person becomes obligated (committed) to something, he or she assumes a certain amount of responsibility in seeing the task through to completion.

When students commit to a S.A.V.E. program, for example, they shoulder the responsibility of lugging litter bags around into which the trash is deposited. Unfortunately, not enough of today's youth regard themselves as responsible; on the contrary, they believe they are owed something.

In a rather searing September 21, 1994 *Newsweek* magazine article entitled, "The Culture of Neglect," Richard Hersh, president of Hobart and William Smith Colleges, comments: "A generation has come to college quite fragile, not very secure about who it is, fearful of its lack of identity and without confidence in its future. . . . This diminished sense of self has caused a growth in racism, sexism, assault, date rape, attempted suicide, eating disorders, theft, property damage, and cheating on most campuses." (The president seems to have gotten them all.) Hersh believes that much of this can be attributed to a generation that has experienced few authentic connections with adults in its lifetime. "I call this the 'Culture of Neglect,' and we—parents, teachers, professors, and administrators—are the primary architects. It begins at home, where social and economic factors, such as declining wages and stagnating incomes requiring longer work hours, result in less family time. Young people have been permitted or must take part-time jobs rather than spending time in school, on homework, or with their families. More children and adolescents are being reared in a vacuum, with television (and America Online) as their only supervisor, and there is little expectation that they *learn* personal responsibility. Immersed in themselves, they're left to their peers. We have failed to teach an ethic of concern and to *model a culture of responsibility.*"

## REALITY THERAPY AND RESPONSIBILITY

Dr. William Glasser, a California psychiatrist and founder of Reality Therapy, defines responsibility as "the ability to fulfill one's needs, and to do so in a way that does not deprive others of the ability to fulfill their needs." Glasser points out in his 1965 work, *Reality Therapy: A New Approach to Psychiatry*, that responsibility is central to his developed approach. (He went on to write *The Quality School* in 1990.) Reality therapy is applicable to individuals with behavioral and emotional problems, as well as to any individual or group seeking to either gain a success identity for themselves and/or help others toward the same goal. According to Glasser:

"The first step in changing behavior is to find out what the behavior is that we are trying to correct. We must face reality and admit that we cannot rewrite a person's history. No matter how cruel and unusual are the circumstances that led to a person's behavior, we must make it clear to him that past events are not to be used as an excuse . . . No matter what 'happened' to him in the past, he must take full responsibility for what he does *now.*

"Until an individual accepts the fact that he is responsible for what he does, there can be no treatment . . . Individual responsibility is the goal of treatment and unhappiness is the result and not the cause of irresponsibility."

And so: responsible people do what gives them a feeling of self-worth and a feeling that they are worthwhile to others, while irresponsible people may or may not do what they say they will do, depending upon how they feel, the effort they have to put forth, and what's in it for them. Glasser believes that acquiring responsibility is a complicated, lifelong problem, and it is an ability that must be *learned.* It is not an easy task, but most people do "strive to create an environment in which both by example and direct teaching they communicate this knowledge to those they love."

The renowned psychiatrist, who has consulted with numerous teachers and school counselors across the nation, believes that the teaching of responsibility is "*the* most important task of all higher animals, man most certainly included." Humankind has worked hard to develop the intellectual capability of teaching responsibility.

Children learn from responsible parents, an involvement that includes both parental teaching and parental example; parents teach through the proper balance of love and discipline. Responsibility is also taught by the school, church, relatives, and peers. As with so many other things, the earlier someone is exposed to love and discipline, the better he or she will learn responsibility. And the trait can be taught to young and old alike; it's just easier to learn correctly the first time rather than to overcome bad experience. Learning how to study in college for example, is considerably more difficult than learning how to study in elementary or even secondary school.

Young people want to receive credit for being responsible—or, put another way, they want to make their own decisions and have their parents *accept* the fact they have done so. Parents want their children to be responsible, but have a hard time deciding how far the "independence" should go. Young people will not accept discipline and learn more appropriate behaviors unless they feel that the parents themselves care enough to demonstrate the responsible way to behave. Through discipline laced with love, parents *must* teach their children to become more and more responsible. "Parents who are willing to suffer the pain of the child's intense anger by firmly holding him to the responsible course are teaching him a lesson that will help him all his life . . . We learn responsibility through involvements with responsible fellow human beings, preferably loving parents who will love and discipline us properly, who are intelligent enough to allow us freedom to try out our newly acquired responsibility as soon as we show readiness to do so."

William Glasser's methods and teachings are embraced by more than a few school counselors in the country.

### Glasser in a Nutshell: Five Steps

Reality Therapy, as Glasser describes it, involves specific steps that *must be followed in sequence* if the healing process is to occur. When you first take your counselee through these steps, the process can seem simple—even superficial. But such simplicity and superficiality can be deceptive; counselors who continue to practice the system discover its complexities and build on them accordingly. You *can* become a most competent practitioner early on when you adhere to the basic principles and follow the steps in sequence.

#### STEP #1:

The first step asks you to make friends with your counselee. This approach differs from the rather cold, clinical detachment that characterizes many professionals. Carl Rogers thought of it as rapport building, an important facet of client-centered therapy. Accomplishing the first step might be just taking the time to throw your counselee a warm smile, extend a hand to him or her, or provide a few words of sincere welcome. Keep in mind that it can take several sessions to actually earn the friendship and trust from an apprehensive and guarded youngster. You really can't move forward until an atmosphere of warmth, friendship, and trust exists.

STEP #2:

This step requires your counselee—not you—to describe the problem clearly. You can, of course, raise questions to help clarify the problem; but for the system to be optimally effective, your counselee must describe his or her problem. Once the problem has been described, you will need to ask, "What are you doing now to solve this problem?" This is where the student, with your assistance, has to think through the problem, and clearly state what he or she is doing to improve the situation. After stalling, rationalizing, blaming, and feeling a little self-pity, your counselee will most likely reply, "Nothing."

STEP #3:

It is at this point that your patience will indeed be tested: the student is going to develop a plan to solve the problem. He or she is going to create the plan, but you can guide him or her through the developmental process by asking clarifying questions. The plan should be both practical and achievable, and your counselee must assume ownership for the plan. In other words, he or she has got to look upon it as his/her own creation! Such ownership is critical because it provides an impetus for the client to move to the next step.

STEP #4:

The fourth step requires the student to commit to taking action on the proposed plan. You can encourage action by posing questions such as "How do you plan to do this?" or "Where can you do this?" or "When are you going to do this?" or "Can you get back to me first thing tomorrow and let me know how you made out?" This style of question is intended to get the student to commit to action at a specific time and place. The commitment is further solidified when the student agrees to *report any results* to the counselor.

If the plan works, you might want to shift the direction of your counseling to other related problems in your counselee's life. If the plan doesn't work, and that is often the case, a new plan must be developed and a new commitment must be obtained. In constructing a new plan, you will need to help your counselee evaluate the old one to acquire an understanding of what is worth repeating and what needs to be discarded. Of course you will want to encourage *any* movement your counselee makes toward taking action and assuming responsibility.

STEP #5:

Never quit! This step demands your total dedication to the matter at hand. As you know, some students require months, even years of counseling. They need support and friendship when things are not going well in their lives. Some of these same youngsters provide counselors with all kinds of opportunities to give up on them—they even tease their counselors about it: "I'm a real problem for you, aren't I?"

The demands of employing reality therapy are daunting. At the same time, the rewards are great and gratifying, both for counselors who utilize the system and for young people who benefit from its principles.

The case history presented below should provide you with a practical understanding of how Glasser's system works:

| | |
|---|---|
| Counselor: | "Hi, Meg. How can I help you?" |
| Megan: | "It's my father. He's the duke of dork—a real jerk. I can't stand him." |
| Counselor: | "You're having a problem communicating with your father?" |
| Megan: | "That's putting it mildly. I can't stand him." |
| Counselor: | (Thoughtfully and almost to himself.) "I know. You said that before." |
| Megan: | "Well, I'm saying it again. I hate being around him." |
| Counselor: | "What are you doing to improve the situation—you know, to solve your problem?" |
| Megan: | "My problem? How 'bout my father's problem? He's making my life a living hell." |
| Counselor: | (Warmly) "I understand where you're coming from. But what are *you* doing to solve the problem?" |
| Megan: | "Well, uh, I don't know what to do. That's why I'm here. What should I do?" |
| Counselor: | "I'm glad you came in, Meg." ( Turning it back to her again.) "But what have *you* done to improve your relationship with your father?" |
| Megan: | "I—I guess nothing. I don't know what to do." |
| Counselor: | "What is it that you want from your father?" |
| Megan: | "Money. I've got car insurance to pay—I don't have enough clothes—my allowance isn't enough—I'm broke. All my father will say is that I should go get a job 'cause it's not his problem." |
| Counselor: | "Is there any way your father would lend you some money?" |
| Megan: | "I don't think so." (Then reflecting for a moment.) "Maybe if I agreed to get a job." |
| Counselor: | "How could you best approach your father to find out?" |
| Megan: | "Well, maybe if I could keep my cool when I talk to him—if I tell him that I only want a loan, and that I'll get a job to pay him back." |
| Counselor: | "That sounds like a good plan. When are you going to talk to your father?" |
| Megan: | "He'll be home tonight. I guess I could talk to him tonight." |
| Counselor: | (Smiling.) "And you're going to keep your cool, right?" |
| Megan: | (Returning the smile.) "Right." |
| Counselor: | "Sounds good. Will you let me know tomorrow how you made out?" |
| Megan: | "Yeah. And thanks." |

In contrast to other methodologies, Reality Therapy can be learned and effectively practiced by virtually any professional willing to apply its principles in a precise and systematic sequence. Renowned therapists such as Carl Jung, Albert Ellis, and Carl Rogers probably would have been successful no matter what system they employed; their formidable insights and personality strengths would have been sufficient to help their clients understand and cope with their problems. (Actually, Albert Ellis' Rational Emotive Therapy, although maintaining its differences, is probably the closest thing to Reality Therapy. Both systems focus on finding practical solutions in the present. Ellis is still very much alive and continuing to conduct seminars in New York City.) School counselors, on the other hand, often need more practical models—such as Reality Therapy.

Many counselors are eclectic in their approach, even to the point of shifting from one methodology to another as they work with an individual counselee. That's okay, too; the trick is to recognize what methodology you're employing at any given moment. Easier said than done, but an important process to master, nonetheless.

As young people pick their way through the mine fields of frustration and disappointments, it is important not to further penalize them with unnecessary criticisms of their behavior. Similarly, we should not interfere with the natural consequences of their behavior. This means we should not be rescuing, enabling, or excusing them. When natural consequences are blocked, a student's growth and development is impaired.

## PARENTS AND RESPONSIBILITY

Success—both in school and in life—depends as much on responsible attitudes and a positive self-image as it does on native intelligence. Just look at successful adults: they feel confident in their strengths, they see themselves as valuable to society, and they're capable of taking charge of their lives. To help build these same attributes in today's teenagers, Figure 13-1 is a two-page handout usable with parents, both on an individual and group basis.

FIGURE 13-1

---

**Responsible Teenagers**

Dear Parent:

Teenagers who go on to become successful adults feel secure within themselves, respect themselves, know how to establish and work toward accomplishing both short- and long-range goals, and are willing to accept responsibility for their behavior. As a parent you can help your youngster develop these skills and attitudes. For example, school and homework *can* become a high priority. Good students are not necessarily more intelligent than their counterparts, but they are usually further along the road of self-direction. And successful students *do* tend to have responsible attitudes as to school attendance and homework.

Here are a few tips to help your teenager take his or her education seriously:

- **Set attainable goals:** Babies crawl before they walk. Understand that course grades might need to be pulled up a little at a time. Be willing to settle for small gains. Other attainable goals could include making the honor roll or conquering procrastination regarding homework completion. Help your youngster break any established goals into achievable segments, for it's important not only to see the long-range picture, but the smaller steps along the way, as well.

- **Build on strengths:** Teenagers have their individual academic strengths and weaknesses. Some are good at reading and writing, while others are better at mathematics and science—or for that matter, art and music. Very few teenagers have it all. Regrettably, today's students are all too accustomed to having their weaknesses highlighted. As a parent you can accentuate the *positive*!

- **Make homework an important priority:** Provide your youngster with a private place to study, and make certain that homework supplies are readily available. Don't hesitate to remind your youngster that homework is *his or her* job. An occasional offer of assistance is fine, but don't do the work for them. Cooperative learning with siblings and friends should be encouraged but not overdone.

- **"Prime time" study time can vary with each youngster:** There is no any single best time for homework. And learning rates vary. Some students need more time to complete assignments—the same students can need more time on tests. Some students like to "get with their homework" right after school. Others prefer to study mid- to late evening.

- **Celebrate successes:** Refrigerator doors can be for secondary school students, too. Create a display of your youngster's best work.

- **Become involved:** It's interesting that as children grow older, their parents become less involved in their school lives. In elementary school, there is almost day-to-day involvement, but as the child progresses through the grades, it's like the line from *September Song*: "And it all dwindles down to a precious few." Don't let this happen to you! Get to know your youngster's teachers and school counselor. Make the effort to attend back-to-school nights and parent conferences.

Good luck!

# SUGGESTED READINGS

Bellah, Robert N. (1985), *Habits of the Heart: Individualism & Commitment in American Life.* New York, NY 10022: HarperCollins.

Glasser, William (1965), *Reality Therapy: A New Approach to Psychiatry.* New York, NY 10022: HarperCollins.

Glasser, William (1990), *The Quality School.* New York, NY 10022: HarperCollins.

Goleman, Daniel (1995), *Emotional Intelligence.* New York, NY 10036: Bantam Books ("Must Reading.")

Hayes, E. Kent (1989), *Why Good Parents Have Bad Kids.* New York, NY 10103: Doubleday, Inc.

# Chapter 14

# Harassment

Harassment is defined as a repeated pattern of unprovoked aggressive behaviors of a physical and/or psychological nature carried out by an individual or group against an individual or group with the intent of causing harm or hurt. Harassing behaviors are those behaviors that are unwelcome, unwanted, and uncomfortable in the view of the recipient. Such behaviors have the effect of creating a hostile environment. Harassment can be blatant, subtle, or shades thereof.

We have long been familiar with many *raisons d'être* of harassment: religion, ethnicity, socio-economic scale, physical and/or mental condition. Sexual harassment is yet another genre, of which the public has become increasingly aware. We've known for some time that we should not "put down" a person of another color or religion or aptitude; what we must now pay close attention to is the "put down" given—often unwittingly—to a person of the other sex.

## SEXUAL HARASSMENT

In the 1986 case *Meritor State Bank vs. Vinson*, the United States Supreme Court identified two types of sexual harassment: "hostile environment" and "quid pro quo."

"Quid pro quo" is applicable in the school setting when a person in power, such as a teacher, supervisor, or administrator, renders decisions that affect the student's education based on whether or not the student complies with the power person's sexual demands.

"Hostile environment" is applicable when someone's harassing behavior, including that of a student, causes the school setting to become hostile or intimidating, and unreasonably interferes with the educative process and/or the student's general welfare.

Another way to express the issue: sexual harassment within the school setting is defined as unwanted and unwelcome sexual advances; requests for sexual favors and other inappropriate conduct; or communication of a sexual nature when made by a staff member to a student, by any student to another student, or by any student to a staff member when:

1. Submission to such conduct is made either explicitly or implicitly a condition of a student's evaluation, promotion, opportunities, privileges, and any other benefits related to the educative process;

2. Submission to or rejection of such conduct by a student is employed as a basis for decisions affecting the student;

3. Such conduct is intended to interfere with a student's academic performance, or to create a hostile educational environment.

A school administration should oversee the development of procedures regarding the implementation of a school's harassment policy that include sanctions, protection of individual rights to confidentiality and due process, and notification procedures. It can be left to either the building administration and/or to the counseling department to ensure that all staff and students are thoroughly informed about policy, and are educated as to what sexual harassment is all about.

The main thrust for teaching about sexual harassment in the schools should be that of bringing people together in a *cooperative non-threatening manner* to explore and understand the reasons for, and consequences of, this widespread social problem. Various components of the program can be successfully presented in middle and junior high school, as well as in high school. Courses such as psychology, sociology, and human sexuality are perfect arenas for such presentations. So, too, are counseling and guidance programs. Studying sexual harassment in the school can be beneficial to the student in that such study can be accomplished in a stable and controlled environment. We must remember that young people have the wherewithal to learn early and quickly. For many youngsters all it takes is a little education to effect positive change.

Since so much sexual harassment takes place in grades 6 through 8, the middle and junior high school are the perfect settings for this instructional activity. In a *few* school districts, counselors can be seen conducting special group sessions or doing classroom presentations on the topic.

The following materials and information should be helpful to you as you attempt to further enlighten your counselees on the topic.

## *Where Sexual Harassment Occurs in the School*

Of incidents reported, the following percentages were due to "sexual harassment":

| | |
|---|---|
| In the classroom | 71% |
| In the hallways | 67% |
| In the cafeteria | 17% |
| In the auditorium | 10% |
| Other | 19% |

## *Subtle and Not So Subtle Sexually Harassing Behaviors in High School*

- "Rating." Some students enjoy hanging out in the hallways while rating their peers on a scale of 1 to 10 as they pass by.
- Sexual gestures with the hands and body.
- Spreading rumors of a sexual nature.
- Obscene T-shirts or any other clothing paraphernalia, such as hats, pins, and jewelry.
- Graffiti. It continues to be everywhere.
- Touching oneself sexually in front of others.
- "Spiking." Some students enjoy pulling down other people's pants.
- Mooning.
- Name-calling, from "honey" to "lesbo" to "bitch" or worse.
- "Hard-hat" stuff. (whistling, catcalls, or howling)
- "Making out" in the hallway. Large numbers of students in a given hallway can rapidly create a "hostile environment."
- Pornographic pictures, films, and cartoons.
- Dirty jokes.
- Rape.
- Attempted or completed sexual assault.
- Touching or stroking another person on the arm, face, breast, or buttock.
- "Slam books" that contain lists of names complete with derogatory sexual comments.
- Stalking, cornering, blocking, or standing too close.
- "Wedgies" (grabbing someone else's underwear and pulling it up).

You can probably think of more. Discussing these behaviors with your students should be a most revealing exercise, in that you will hear differing opinions as to what constitutes sexually harassing behavior. Each school system has its own personality, with its own set of acceptabilities.

*A note:* One young lady looked at the list and said that the "wedgie" harassment was physical, not sexual. It is important to realize that many sexual behaviors have physical overtones, and many physical abuses have sexual overtones.

You can use the true or false quiz (see Figure 14-1) in a group presentation. We have provided facilitator notes in the answer key that can be used for discussion purposes after the students have taken the quiz.

Here is yet another group activity that can be therapeutic: students brainstorm terms that might be considered sexually harassing, placing the terms under the categories of *plant, animal, food,* and *other.* Female and male students can be in the same group, but they should construct separate lists. If you are working with a large number of students, break them into smaller groups. Once the list has been derived, students should score each term as either complimentary (C) or derogatory (D). When all is complete, you might find that female students usually come up with more derogatory terms that pertain to male students and male students come up with more derogatory terms that pertain to female students. Note that we have suggested a few terms in each category to get you started.

| **Plant** | **Animal** | **Food** | **Other** |
|-----------|-----------|----------|-----------|
| Rose | Chick | Honey | Babe |
| Violet | Cow | Muffin (stud) | Hunk |
| Pansy | Pig | String bean | Dirt bag |
| Sweet pea | Dog | Fruit cake | Wimp |

There *are* those students who believe that the entire issue of sexual harassment is "much ado about nothing." Hopefully for them that's true. Yet when we hear student #1 exclaim to student #2, "Get out of my face!" we know that student #1 is taking the offending action most seriously. So many students don't realize that much offensive behavior is indeed sexual harassment.

- "Boys will be boys" has been around for a long time. A good deal of the "boys will be boys" behavior is heavier in nature than in previous times, and more publicly displayed than previously.

- Sexually harassing behavior is more likely to transpire in schools where the administration fails to implement policy, and thereby fails to send a strong message that such behaviors won't be tolerated.

- One principal would not allow sexual harassment sensitivity sessions to be conducted in his building because he didn't want students to know their rights. His thinking: "They might sue us."

Sensitizing students without sensitizing adults makes no sense. It starts at the top: administrators, teachers, counselors—all staff—should look long and hard at the *prevention* of sexual harassment. Continuing change cannot be attained until we change the awareness of the adults who work with our young people.

FIGURE 14-1

## The Truth and Falseness of Sexual Harassment

Read each statement carefully.

Circle *T* for *True* if you believe the statement to be generally true.

Circle *F* for *False* if you believe the statement to be generally false.

T   F   1.   Men and boys can be the receivers of sexual harassment.

T   F   2.   Sexual harassment is a decided problem in American schools.

T   F   3.   Sexual harassment can occur between people of the same sex.

T   F   4.   Saying no is usually sufficient to stop any action.

T   F   5.   Women engaged in professional jobs such as teaching, medicine, and law are not so likely to experience sexual harassment as those in blue-collar positions, e.g. truck drivers, secretaries, and factory workers.

T   F   6.   Women and girls rarely file charges once the harassment has taken place.

T   F   7.   Most men and boys enjoy getting sexual attention on the job or in the school setting.

T   F   8.   Women and girls use their sex appeal to get what they want at work and at school.

T   F   9.   Probably the best method of dealing with sexual harassment is to ignore it.

T   F   10.   Women of color are harassed more often than are Caucasian women.

T   F   11.   Most victims of harassment report it to their employer or school administrator.

T   F   12.   Flirting and teasing are not all that serious. They can cause work and school to be much more enjoyable.

T   F   13.   Schools and workplaces need to know if sexual harassment is occurring.

T   F   14.   If a student does not like sexual attention, but the giver means it only as a joke, then it's not really sexually harassing behavior.

T   F   15.   The only people who are permitted to harass are those in positions of authority such as teachers, employers, and administrators.

T   F   16.   Most women and girls enjoy getting sexual attention at work and at school.

T   F   17.   If harassment occurs in school between students, it is illegal and the school system can be held liable.

T   F   18.   If a woman or girl dresses in a provocative fashion and/or behaves in a sexual way, she is sending a signal that she wants to be sexually harassed.

*ANSWER KEY* with Facilitator Notes

1. T
2. T (50% of girls report it)
3. T (20% male, 80% female)
4. F
5. F
6. T
7. T, F (goes both ways)
8. F
9. F

10. T (women of color are more vulnerable)
11. F
12. F
13. T
14. F (it's in the eye of the beholder)
15. F
16. F
17. T
18. F

# SUGGESTED READING

Strauss, Susan (1992), *Sexual Harassment and Teens*, Free Spirit Publishing, Inc., Minneapolis, MN 55401. (An excellent manual that can be used by school personnel for counseling on an individual basis or as the centerpiece for group activity.)

# CHAPTER 15

# CHILD ABUSE AND NEGLECT

People have been beating on one another since the dawn of history. Children are an especially favored target by many abusers: children have been traumatized, abused sexually, locked in basements, submerged in bathtubs, beaten about the face, and abandoned altogether. Because we now hear so much about abuse, we tend to think it's a phenomenon born in the 20th century, but it's not. What is new, however, is that the topic has been formally identified and categorized, and its rather complex forms of pathology intensely studied.

Thanks to Dr. C. Henry Kempe and his colleagues at the University of Colorado Medical Center, the nation has come to recognize child abuse for what it is: a most serious and widespread threat to children's lives, a problem that crosses all socio-economic levels and all ethnic and racial boundary lines. It is a troubling issue that Kempe first titled "battered child syndrome." The doctor and his associates defined the term to mean a non-accidental physical injury to a child. There has been an expansion of the term, in that it now encompasses emotional abuse, physical neglect, and sexual abuse along with physical abuse.

By 1970, all fifty states had some sort of statute in place, based on a model child reporting law that had been previously prepared and disseminated by a bureau of the federal government. The National Committee to Prevent Child Abuse (NCPCA) was founded in 1972 to enlist concerned people in an all-out effort to prevent child abuse through advocacy, education, and research. NCPCA has chapters in all fifty states and the District of Columbia.

Since the enactment of state legislation and the work of NCPCA, the number of *reported* cases of abuse has increased dramatically. All states now mandate that individuals in the helping professions who suspect or are aware that a child is suffering serious physical or psychological injury must report this fact to the appropriate authorities. Some states even impose penalties for failing to report.

The school counselor is a mandated reporter. For the counselor, however, it is both a legal responsibility *and* a moral and ethical one. Historically, most counselors have taken proper action when they have suspected abuse; such action has not been limited to the reporting of an incident, but has also meant an offer of help to parents and youngsters caught up in this nightmare.

Many in the public see the abuse problem as symptomatic of violence out of control in a society. That is but one reason; there are other underlying causes for the problem. The National Center on Child Abuse and Neglect, an agency within the United States Department of Health and Human Services, reports that some one million children are badly mistreated by parents each year. An exact figure is difficult to obtain because occurrences more often than not take place behind closed doors. It is also not uncommon for incidents to be covered up by professionals, including physicians.

Now that the issue is more apparent to everyone, you as a school counselor should be well versed on local and state policy, referral procedures and agencies, as well as the entire dynamics of child abuse. You are in an excellent position to identify possible or actual cases of abuse. This ugliness is by no means restricted to the home. At times, it can be found— unbelievably— within the confines of the school; for example: corporal punishment, and sexual or emotional abuse by school officials.

# EMOTIONAL ABUSE

Emotional abuse is a continuous attempt to destroy a person's self-worth. The abuser accomplishes this through both words and actions; it takes the form of chronic belittling, humiliation, and ridicule. It also happens in the "best of families," so keep an eye out for the symptoms.

## *Physical Indicators of Emotional Abuse*

- Substance abuse
- Speech impediments
- Retarded physical development
- Ulcers, asthma, severe allergies, etc.

## *Behavioral Indicators of Emotional Abuse*

- Inappropriate habits in older children, e.g., biting, thumb sucking, rocking
- Delinquent behavior, especially in adolescents

- Antisocial behavior
- Neurotic symptoms, e.g., sleep impairment, incapability of normal play, etc.
- Self-destructive behavior
- Inappropriate adult-like behavior, such as acting like a parent to younger children
- Inappropriate infantile behavior

# PHYSICAL ABUSE

Physical abuse is any act that purposefully inflicts or intends to inflict bodily harm. It is a non-accidental injury or threat of injury to a child, and it includes both internal- and external-type injuries. One isolated incident alone will probably not prove that a child is being abused. A combination or pattern should send up a flag to you.

## *Physical Indicators of Physical Abuse*

- Unexplained bruises in various stages of healing, such as welts, black eyes, bite marks, bald spots. Or patterns of bruises caused by a particular instrument, e.g., belt buckle, coat hanger, whip, etc.
- Unexplained burns, especially of the cigarette, electric iron, or immersion variety. Look for a distinct line where the burn ends.
- Unexplained bone fractures, lacerations, or abrasions.
- Any type of injury that doesn't match the explanation offered.

## *Behavioral Indicators of Physical Abuse*

- Little or no self-discipline
- A shying away from physical contact
- Extremes of withdrawn or aggressive behavior
- Arriving at school early and/or staying late, due to fear of being home
- Chronic running away from home
- Complaints of soreness or uncomfortable movement
- Wearing of inappropriate clothing for particular weather conditions
- Refusing to change clothes in physical education class
- Sudden alteration of behavior and/or academic achievement
- Signs of depression
- Unexplained rage

# PHYSICAL NEGLECT

Physical neglect is the failure or refusal of parents/guardians to provide their offspring with adequate food, clothing, shelter, medical or dental attention, and/or the general supervision they need in order for said offspring to remain healthy and safe. Physical neglect also extends to abandonment, expulsion from home, failure to enroll a child in school, and the encouragement of chronic truancy. A combination of physical indicators, as well as parent/guardian behaviors, should alert you to the possibility of physical neglect.

## *Physical Indicators of Physical Neglect*

- Unattended medical or dental needs
- Abandonment
- Continuing lack of supervision
- Prolonged hunger, improper dress, poor hygiene
- Presence of lice, distended stomach, emaciated appearance
- Malnourishment, filth, inadequate shelter
- Emotional disturbance due to constant friction at home
- Marital discord, mentally ill parents
- Cruel and inhuman treatment of child

## *Behavioral Indicators of Physical Neglect*

- Regular display of fatigue or listlessness
- Continually falling asleep in class
- Frequent absence or tardiness
- Self-destructive behavior
- Dropping out of school
- Stealing food or begging from classmates
- Shows exploitation and/or overwork
- Remains away from home for extended periods of time
- Extreme behavioral signs: overly aggressive or extremely affectionate
- Incapable of making and keeping friends
- Frequently occurring accidents, e.g. burns and falls

# SEXUAL ABUSE

Sexual abuse is any form of sexual activity forced upon a person without his or her consent. In the case of a child, it includes any act of sexual exploitation or assault by an adult person. More specifically, sexual abuse includes fondling genitals, intercourse, incest, rape, sodomy, exhibitionism, and sexual exploitation. It might be accomplished through the use of words, gestures, or physical sexual touch.

## *Physical Indicators of Sexual Abuse*

- Tattered, stained, or bloody clothing
- Pain or severe itching in the genital area
- Difficulty in normal walking or sitting
- Bruises or bleeding in the external genitalia
- Signs of venereal disease
- Frequent urinary, yeast, or other related infections

## *Behavioral Indicators of Sexual Abuse*

- Role reversal, as exemplified by an inordinate amount of concern for siblings
- Low self-esteem, self-disparagement, or general lack of self-confidence
- Problems with peer relations, including lack of involvement
- Reluctance to dress for physical education class
- Seductiveness carried to the extreme
- Large change in weight
- Suicidal behavior
- Inappropriate sex play and/or a premature understanding of sexuality
- Regressive or pseudo-mature behavior
- Refusing to go to a particular place, or be near a particular person
- Hysteria: inability to control emotions
- Unexplained acquisition of money or gifts
- Threatened by physical closeness or actual contact

# COUNSELOR RESPONSE WHEN ABUSE IS SUSPECTED

What should you do if you suspect that your counselee is being abused?

- Remain calm and believe the child.

- Gather basic facts, but do not interrogate the child.

- Reassure the child that it was proper and courageous for him or her to inform a responsible adult. It is always correct for a child to tell about an abuse. It is never the child's fault when an abuse occurs.

- Seek help for the child.

- Immediately report the situation to your department chair and/or student assistance coordinator. Assure the child that you will help him/her by informing others who will know better what to do.

Research seems to indicate that a good deal of child abuse is done by normal people who find themselves in a crisis state, such as a parent who becomes overwhelmed by certain living conditions and reacts with uncontrollable anger. Such reactions can stem from marital discord, financial insolvency, and mental health problems. Abuse and neglect often occur in families that have no support network of friends or relatives. It can occur, as well, when the intelligence level of the parents or guardians is such that they lack the understanding of their child's basic physical and emotional needs. Ninety percent of abuse and neglect cases occur in alcoholic homes.

Some origins of the abuse problem are evident in "community neglect," where the local community makes little or no provision for adequate medical assistance, housing, and reasonably-priced day care facilities for the children of working parents who need such supervision.

While most of the abuse is initiated by fathers, both sexes are guilty, sometimes sequentially: fathers beat mothers, who in turn beat their children; or one parent abuses and the other fails to report it. Abusers can be: people obsessed with disciplinary procedures; the short-in-stature napoleons; the alcoholic mothers; the distant stepfathers; or the love-starved, emotionally crippled people who "went through hell" in their own childhood. Some of these same people were foster children continually shuttled from one foster home to another. Abuse *does* beget abuse.

On rare occasions, children claim abuse as they attempt to take control of a household. Move cautiously; assess the situation as best you can, and if you suspect abuse/neglect, follow established local and state guidelines.

### *Further Advice*

- You can't fight child abuse by yourself: you will have to work closely with a number of colleagues, including school nurses. Remember that help for children implies help for parents.

- Provide in-service training to assist school personnel to understand the Child Abuse and Neglect Law, the characteristics of abused and neglected children, and the procedures for reporting suspected cases.

- Conduct parent-training programs to help parents be more effective in the raising of their children.
- Get in touch with your own feelings, but keep in mind that you are a professional. Avoid being judgmental.
- Know that your responses may have an effect on both the child and the parents.
- Remain firm in your approach. On the one hand, you might recognize the difficulties of being a parent; on the other, your role as an advocate of the child demands that you not condone or excuse any sort of abuse. You might sympathize with parental distress, but you and the school are legally obligated to report any suspected incidents of abuse.
- Be tactful and polite. Treat the suspected offending parents as you would any other parents.
- Assure them of confidentiality and grant them such. Remember that any stigma is likely to remain with the child as well as with the parents.

## SUGGESTED CONTACTS

Child Welfare League of America
67 Irving Place
New York, NY 10003
(212) 254-7410

Kids Peace: The National Center for Kids in Crisis
Bethlehem, PA 18015
(800) 25-PEACE

National Center for the Prevention of Child Abuse and Neglect
Department of Pediatrics
University of Colorado Medical Center
1205 Oneida Street
Denver, CO 80220
(303) 321-3963

National Center on Child Abuse and Neglect
Department of Health and Human Services
PO Box 1182
Washington, DC 20013
(202) 245-2860

National Committee for Prevention of Child Abuse
332 South Michigan Avenue
Chicago, IL 60604
(312) 663-3520

# CHAPTER 16

# DEPRESSION AND SUICIDE

"Stress" has no universal definition. Selye, in his 1976 work, *The Stress of Life*, defined stress as the "non-specific response of the body to any demand," and he made a logical distinction between "eustress" (positive force that is akin to finding excitement and challenge in life) and "distress" (the negative destructive form of stress). Most people see stress as a negative factor, but that is not always so.

Most of the stress research in secondary education has been directed toward staff personnel. There has been limited study conducted on student stress—an interesting piece of information, considering that most reports indicate that a good deal of adolescent negative stress occurs in the school setting. At the same time, schools *can* function as stress-reduction organizations. To do so, however, means being knowledgeable of the factors that cause stress and what is required to eliminate, or at least minimize, any sources of negative stress, all the while strengthening and enlarging any processes that are positive stressors.

In 1967, a social readjustment rating scale was developed that included some forty major life events. The scale was modified in 1972 for use by school students at all levels. Unfortunately, the weights utilized in that particular instrument were assigned by adults. 1980 witnessed the development of the Adolescent Life Change Event Scale with 31 items of importance to adolescents in all environments. A breakthrough in research came in 1983 when Patricia Smith further narrowed the focus to only events occurring within the school environment. She developed a Best School Life Events and a Worst School Life Events scale in order to examine for variances among secondary school student sectors, e.g., urban, rural, gender differences, and academic performance. Smith discovered significant differences among certain sectors on selected scale items.

About 50% of American students handle stress well. Some 10% don't seem to handle it at all. Capability of handling stress seems to improve as students progress from grade nine to grade twelve. Generally speaking, males tend to handle stress better than females.

If the school is to serve as a stress-reduction organization, then a simple survey of the student body to see where the problems lie can be an effective means of identifying potential sources of stress. The survey *does* work. In the process you'll uncover such stressors as performance grouping, fear of assault, fear of theft, job acquisition and retention, racial tensions, and faculty accessibility. These factors have been popping up on survey forms of the relatively few schools that are proactively addressing the issue. Identifying sources of student negative stress in a school could be a joint venture of administration and counseling.

Severe depression and suicidal behavior comes from reoccurring stressful situations with which the student feels unable to cope. High levels of stress can lead to depression—just ask any or all of the 10% who report they can't handle stress very well.

## DEPRESSION

Depression ranks high as a symptom of suicidal attempts. Several writers, including Holden in 1986, reported that depression is the most common ingredient in most suicides. Adolescents who make an attempt to take their lives often offer clear, overt signs of depression, including sleep disturbance, appetite reduction, and sudden and unwarranted unhappiness. Some of these findings have come from psychological autopsies that demonstrated that 3 of every 4 adolescents who committed suicide were depressed. And so it behooves the school counselor to have a working knowledge of the symptoms of depression. In addition to the three mentioned above, the following signs can be present:

- social withdrawal
- complaints of boredom
- comments about fatigue
- downward spiral in academic performance
- mood swings or a definite mood change that lasts for at least one month
- unexplainable feelings of guilt
- a disinterest in normally pleasurable events.

It is probably wise to screen all moderately to heavily depressed students for suicide ideation, and more than wise to err on the side of caution. In one study, fully half of the adolescents who attempted to take their lives displayed *masked* depression: hidden activity such as sexual promiscuity, anorexia/bulimia, or substance abuse. Incidentally, drugs and alcohol on the part of teenagers can be a method of self-medicating oneself against severe depression.

## *On the Practical Side*

You can enter the picture on the practical side. Shortly after his friend died, a counselor had a grieving and depressed student add up all of his losses of the past year. The counselor had the student list on paper numerous happenings he would never have thought of, such as plummeting grades following the death, loss of self-respect over the manner in which the student had treated his girlfriend, etc. The two even delved into the long-term growing-up process with any accompanying losses. Seeing the list enabled the student to more readily accept his depression and begin to cope with it.

## *Family Can Be the Key*

The families of severely depressed youngsters have been studied by a number of research people. These families often have impaired communication structures. A good deal of the communication can be unproductive and marked by regular conflict: a lack of problem-solving capability is common. And, most important, Hart and Keidel in 1979 reported that with families of severely depressed adolescents, negative as opposed to positive comments often abound.

Studies show that depression occurs more often in children and teenagers where one or more parents has a history of such depression. Further, it now appears that the tendencies to become depressed pass along through the genes. That might sound rather fatalistic and discouraging, but it could be most helpful to know that certain individuals *are* susceptible to depression so that the school could cope more effectively with the issue. Youngsters with a genetic predisposition could be educated to live positive and enjoyable lives.

Problematic communication can extend beyond the adolescent's home. Lack of productive dialogue can exist in an adolescent's other relationships, as well. For the teenager, suicide is an often-employed means of communication, a desperate call for assistance; a special cry for help that the teenager believes cannot be expressed in any other way.

# SUICIDE: A PERMANENT SOLUTION TO A TEMPORARY PROBLEM

In fiction, teen suicide is often treated romantically: the parental rejection of a Romeo and Juliet; love-gone-wrong between two young people through betrayal or misunderstanding; a life or world that no longer has meaning. In reality, however, the picture is very different. The self-inflicted death of a young person is a tawdry and messy affair, so full of uncertainty. And friends and loved ones left behind don't respond with epic prose, but rather with guilt, rage, confusion, emptiness, and loneliness.

First comes the shock, then the search. Invariably survivors will ask, "Why?" Usually there are no answers. Or at least none with which a family can be content to live. For as psychiatrist Andrew Slaby states in his book, *No One Saw My Pain: Why Teens Kill Themselves*, a family can never be free from such an event. "Truthfully, I don't believe any family ever really heals completely after the death of a child," Slaby writes. "Healing and coping—they're two different things entirely." On the other hand, the author argues that the survivors should not feel guilty because they failed to prevent a suicide: "Some people kill themselves no matter what intervention takes place."

Suicide can jolt society out of its day-to-day routine, making it take another all-too-infrequent pause to examine life and its importance. In schools all over the nation, jolts are more frequently being experienced; schools are very much a part of society. The problem is of frightening magnitude: according to national statistics, nearly 2,200 children under the age of 20 committed suicide in 1992, the latest year for which numbers are available. The suicide rate is greatest among white males between ages 14 and 20. What is especially alarming is the fact that the rate for young people has increased 22 percent since 1980. And for every suicide, there are some 350 failed attempts. The number of attempts has not risen, but the death rate has, with children now choosing more lethal ways to attempt to die. Sixty-five percent of the deaths in 1992 were caused by guns. Slaby points out that 55 percent of the teenage boys who take their lives do so with a firearm. Accurate statistics are hard to come by, as self-inflicted injury is still so stigmatized in the United States that many families and physicians are reluctant to acknowledge its presence in death.

Schools and other agencies are beginning to look at the pattern of self-destructive behavior in car accidents (autocide), drunk driving, and fights, some of which could be suicidal acts. And youngsters are engaging in self-mutilating pursuits, burning and cutting themselves to try to reduce pain or tension, the lethality of which must be assessed as well.

The ever-increasing number of jolts has caused school officials to become much more proficient in mobilizing recovery efforts following a tragedy. But the strongest effort must be for counselors, teachers, parents, and students to try to recognize the signs of a life-and-death struggle *before* it culminates in tragedy. Bringing suicide out into the open is probably the most important step toward reducing death by suicide. Interestingly, the slogan for the 1995 National Suicide Prevention Week campaign was "Stop the whispers . . . suicidal persons can be helped."

Of course, we educators should heed all warning signs: any sudden behavioral change, including withdrawal symptoms; evidence of substance abuse; parental abuse and/or neglect; insomnia; eating disorders; sexuality problems. We must also be aware that losses and changes, even positive ones, can significantly increase the stress in an adolescent's life. Here is a list of the top thirteen events that can trigger depression or thoughts of suicide.

| Rank | Life-Changing Event |
|------|---------------------|
| 1. | Death of a parent |
| 2. | Death of a sibling |
| 3. | Death of a close friend |
| 4. | Divorce or separation of parents |
| 5. | Failing one or more subjects In school |
| 6. | Being arrested by police |
| 7. | Being retained in school |
| 8. | Family member having an alcohol problem |
| 9. | Personal use of drugs and alcohol |

10.     Loss of a favorite pet
11.     Serious illness of parent or relative
12.     Losing a job
13.     Breaking up with a close boyfriend or girlfriend

### Loss and Disappointment

In addition to the top thirteen, life can be loaded with all kinds of losses and disappointments. Such losses and disappointments can trigger short-term depression that might eventually lead to prolonged or severe clinical depression. These losses and disappointments include:

- an important person moves away
- changing school systems
- broken friendship or romance
- deterioration of one's parents' relationship
- serious illness or injury to self or to another important person
- family hardship: heavy debt, job loss, property loss, etc.
- loss of virginity
- chemical dependency
- lag in physical development
- peer ridicule or rejection
- certain school-related problems
- failure to realize goal
- realizing a goal
- constant anxiety
- anxiety involved in growing up

# THE EISEL CASE

On November 8, 1988, Nicole Eisel, a middle school student in Montgomery County, Maryland, died in a murder-suicide pact consummated with another 13-year-old girl. There are those, including Nicole's father, who believe that the school counselors could have prevented the tragedy from happening. The father, a single parent, brought suit against the two involved counselors as well as against the school system. On October 29, 1991, the Court of Appeals, Maryland's highest court, disagreed with previous rulings that had rendered school counselors immune from liability for counselee suicide, and ordered the case heard.

As a school counselor, your comprehending the resulting implications of the Maryland decision is *most* important.

It has previously been thought that school counselors are immune from any liability for student suicide outside of the school setting. The courts have always been reluctant to hold counselors liable for counselee suicide unless the counselor had assumed physical responsibility for the student. On the other hand, if parents *could demonstrate* that the counselor *knew or should have known* of the deceased student's likelihood of taking his or her life and failed to alert the parents, it was another matter.

Nicole Eisel had become involved in Satanism and possibly had informed two of her friends that she intended to take her life. The friends reported Nicole's thoughts to *their* counselor who in turn notified Nicole's counselor. Both counselors sat with Nicole as she vehemently denied the thought. At that juncture, the counselors took no action to notify Nicole's parents or, for that matter, the school administration. There *is* some lack of agreement as to whether or not the counselor who was approached by Nicole's friends was specifically told that the youngster was thinking of killing herself. Nicole later died in a murder-suicide pact in a public park with another 13-year-old from a neighboring school.

Nicole's parents brought suit against the counselors and the school system. A Maryland circuit court dismissed the suit on the basis that it was not the duty of the school and counselors to intervene in the situation. The decision was appealed, and the Maryland Court of Appeals ruled on October 29, 1991 that the circuit court was in error and the case could be tried.

What should be immediately apparent from the Court of Appeals ruling is that you do have a duty to try to prevent the suicide of any of your counselees if you foresee such a danger. The court prefaced its finding with, "We hold that school counselors have a duty to use reasonable means to attempt to prevent suicide when they are on notice of a child or adolescent student's suicidal intent."

The entire issue has become of great importance to school counselors because of the growing frequency of adolescent suicide and the potential for liability as a result of not alerting parents. Some believe that counselors must weigh their potential liability against the need of their counselees to have a confidential spot to unload their feelings. Not so! Most states today have well-defined laws that forbid school counselors to simply "sit" on this particular issue. Not only that, but in many school districts counselor training and competence in mental health problems have increased significantly. There is no reason to sit. Or is there?

With the Eisel finding that a school counselor could be held accountable for potential harm that has been reported by a third party, and then denied by the student, you have to consider whether or not to believe your troubled counselee. Furthermore, this case illustrates the importance of counseling departments strengthening their lines of communication with parents of minors—working toward helping family members to better communicate with each other. Contrary to what certain counselor educators and counselors in-the-field might believe, the student/counselor relationship is *not* damaged by involving parents in problem solving.

Counselors also need more training in informing their counselees of the limits of confidentiality, including *how* they can do so with minimal disruption of the trust that needs to exist in the client/counselor relationship. There's no question that the issue of confidentiality is a big component in the relationship. But there *are* limits. Confidentiality guidelines that pertain to child abuse, suicide, and drugs and alcohol need to be discussed early on with new clients. Take time and be up-front with your new counselees!

## *The Final Decision*

The Eisel case was finally heard on March 8, 1994, more than five years after Nicole Eisel's tragic death. According to the police, and as reported in the *Washington Post* newspaper of March 8, 1994, Nicole Eisel had a history of drug use. She also had a history of not doing well in school; that included a poor attendance record.

The father, Stephen Eisel, contended that school officials had been negligent in failing to intervene to prevent the death. He contended that the school officials were aware of Nicole's suicidal tendencies before her death. During the course of the proceedings, the two counselors contended that Nicole's friends had only mentioned that Nicole was "very upset" and that the friends had never mentioned suicide. The two-week civil trial culminated in a "not guilty" verdict for the two counselors and the school system.

## *Having Policy in Place*

Even aside from state regulations, all school systems should have reasonable health policies in place that will not only protect the rights of parents, but also protect the school and its employees from liability. Most teachers and counselors pay little or no attention to school district policy until they need it, which is usually when they've goofed. Such lack of attention often results from a lack of perusal time or the unavailability of the document. (Telephone directory-size policy manuals are often buried somewhere in the principal's office. It would be wonderful if school districts would produce a special volume that contains only those policies that *directly* impact on the counselor or teacher's job performance, with at least one copy available in all departmental offices.)

We tend to think of written policy as "heavy stuff," when in fact some of it can be interesting reading. More important, a policy statement can sometimes point directly to what is expected in a particular situation. Case in point: the school district policy on student welfare, an excerpt of which is given in Figure 16-1.

## *Comments That Relate to Eisel*

- Students can *indirectly* express suicidal thoughts. "Very upset" can be a signal.
- You need to be vigilant about body marks, abrasions, and lacerations.
- Take third-party notification seriously.
- Always consult with one of your colleagues when in doubt.
- Student Assistance people and Core Teams are there for the using.
- Parents should always be notified regardless of the degree of risk.
- Policy needs to be in place that excludes high-risk students from school until cleared for return by an outside agency. When in doubt, insist that the parents have their offspring screened.
- Never leave the high-risk student unattended.

FIGURE 16-1

---

**ELEMENTARY AND SECONDARY**

A. Suicide Intervention Techniques

  1. A staff member is concerned about a student engaging in a suicide attempt due to one or more of the following situations:

    a. The student has directly or *indirectly* expressed suicidal thoughts, either verbally or through writings or drawings.

    b. The staff member notices marks or cuts on the wrists, neck, or other parts of the body that might indicate a suicidal gesture.

    c. A third party, such as peer, family member, or other adult, contacts the staff member relative to his or her concern for a student that he or she feels is at risk for suicide.

    d. The staff member learns of a previous suicide attempt of which the school and/or parent/guardian is unaware.

    e. The student's behavior is reflective of a person at risk for suicide:

      (1) A sudden change in normal behavior.

      (2) A withdrawing from family and friends.

      (3) A giving away of cherished possessions.

      (4) A noticeable change in eating habits.

      (5) A neglect of personal appearance.

      (6 A breakdown of family structure due to death, divorce, or parental rejection.

      (7) A change in type of friends.

      (8) A use of drugs and/or alcohol.

  2. Intervention procedures:

    a. The staff member will *notify* the principal or his/her designee who will in turn contact appropriate and available school personnel, i.e. the student's counselor, a child study team member, and/or the student assistance specialist.

    b. Accompany (where appropriate) the student to the designated place of meeting with the staff member, who will herein be termed primary counselor.

FIGURE **16-1** *CONTINUED*

B. Notification Procedures

1. The primary counselor, upon receiving notification of a student at risk for suicide will:

    a. Perform an initial assessment for lethality (seriousness of intent; ability and means to perform the act).

    b. Ensure that the student is *not left unattended* throughout the process, or allowed to leave the room unaccompanied by an adult.

    c. Contact the parent/guardian *regardless* of the degree of risk assessed, informing them of the situation and advising them as to the action that needs to be taken.

2. In cases where the primary counselor has assessed a *high or questionable* degree of risk, the principal or his/her designees shall:

    a. Assemble the building's Core Team to assist the primary counselor to deal with the issue. Any Core Team member may provide coverage of the student while the primary counselor reports on the problem. Core Team members may help in placing telephone calls, assist the primary counselor with decision making, and respond to other students who might be affected by the circumstances.

    b. *Insist* that a parent/guardian come to the school for the student in question, and accompany him or her to an appropriate community agency or provider for the purpose of a more extensive suicide legality assessment.

    c. If the parent/guardian cannot be reached or refuses to come to the school, the principal *must not allow the student to return home unescorted*. The Core Team may consider several options: transport the student to the agency or provider; telephone the state Division of Youth and Family Services if the parent/guardian is uncooperative; or remain with the student until the parent/guardian can be contacted.

    d. Parents/guardians who refuse to adhere to Core Team recommendations will be reported to the Division of Youth and Family Services for suspicion of negligence.

3. In cases where the primary counselor assesses no degree of risk:

    a. The parents *are still notified* of the situation.

    b. The student is returned to class.

    c. The staff member is thanked for the referral and instructed to report any continued manifestations of the previously observed behavior.

C. Any attempted suicide shall be considered a "crisis." Professional staff personnel shall refer to the procedures outlined in the school district's *Crisis Response Plan* and follow stated procedures.

*In-service Training*

Participating in an in-house workshop, or even in an extended department meeting at which you and your colleagues can kick around a few case studies, can be beneficial in seeing the nuances, the subtle differences in the individual circumstances. You'll find yourself coming back to the theme, "when in doubt, share your findings."

*The Case of Brian*

In the quest for identity and autonomy, adolescents tend to encounter interpersonal conflicts more often than do younger or older persons, either within the family setting or with their own peers. When one of these relationships becomes troubled, the other relationships can serve as a support system to help the adolescent through the difficult times. In times of stress, an isolated youngster without either support is at high risk. A problematic romance or a perceived rejection may be all that is needed to push the adolescent to the brink of suicide. Take the case of Brian.

> *A school counselor is working with Brian, who appears to be somewhat depressed. He mentions that his girlfriend of one and a half years has just "dumped" him for another guy. Within the thirty-minute session, the counselor asks, "Have you ever thought of taking your life?" "Haven't most people at one time or another?" responds the young man. "Many have," states the counselor, in an attempt to assure the youngster that such reflection was normal. "No thanks," continues the young man, "I wouldn't do it." But he does. That night he takes his father's revolver and kills himself.*

What, if any, was the counselor's responsibility in this particular issue? Does this case differ from that of Eisel?

# THE ACADEMICALLY TALENTED AND SUICIDE

The academically talented will often display symptoms that warrant counseling intervention. Symptoms can be classified in a number of categories, including perfectionism, disappointments, insecurities, career planning, and depression.

Perfectionism is often self-imposed with the academically talented. A student who has a history of performing well in the academic arena might not fair so well in a course that requires physical skills. Even a "B" grade in a technology or physical education course can cause considerable stress, and repeated occurrences of this can lead to a negative self-image or to a sense of failure. What might be small stuff to the onlooker, can be a monumental problem to the academically talented student.

Since each academically talented student is unique, like any other student, each one handles life's disappointments differently. What can be a really stressful situation for one can be a piece of cake for another. Disappointments for this type of student can be related to having a lack of friends—or, for that matter, even acquaintances. Many academically talented students feel out of sync with their environment; students with IQs of over 150 are likely to experience difficulty fitting in anywhere and must endure the accompanying stress. Feeling out of place with one's environment can not only create stress, but a daily dosage of such a problem can trigger depression.

Insecurities for adolescents are often related to parental values. Academically talented students find it a struggle to formulate an appropriate set of values and aspirations and to reconcile them with parental expectations and demands. This is really no different from other youngsters, except that the thinking processes of the academically talented reflect the same confidence that adults exhibit in their thinking. Yet these students are quick to reject parental advice, regardless of merit.

Career planning is an area where academically talented students close doors too readily—they tend to play it safe, and are more likely to come up with options that are within their control. You can be influential here. Being the third-party person you are, they *will* listen. For example, with something as big—or small—as applying to a particular college, they might not listen to their parents, but they will listen to you. First, you must offer help in understanding the options; then you might explore together his or her capabilities, and finally, you could work together to comprehend the possible consequences of various decisions.

You should also know that academically talented students are big doubters—they often doubt the wisdom of their decisions. They are also less likely to seek your help than other kinds of students, so you need to be sensitive to their special needs, both from a preventative viewpoint and when a negative stressor has kicked in. This is all the more reason for having a proactive counseling curriculum in place, whereby you *must see all* of your counselees a set number of times each year. Since they're too busy or too self-directed to come to you, you need to send for them.

In college, suicide attempts happen more often with students who are highly creative, have above-average grades, attend highly selective colleges and universities, and whose grade-point averages have taken a sudden nose dive. Could this be another illustration of the perfectionism problem, a genuine block for the person who continues to struggle to form a fragile identity? The symptoms of disappointment and insecurity come in to play here, as well. Most academically talented students worry about disappointing their parents in regard to the educational endeavor. Many of these self-motivated, independent thinkers are insecure as they constantly search to balance their own values and morals with those of the family, church, and society as a whole.

It is hard for young people to be different; they can't yet see that "difference" is vital for society, that there is a special place where they belong. The following poem was written by a high school senior in Alton, Illinois, two weeks before he took his own life:

### On Education

He always wanted to explain things
But no one cared
So he drew

. . . .

And it would be only him and the sky and
The things inside him that needed saying.
It was after that he drew the picture.
It was a beautiful picture.
He kept it under his pillow
And would let no one see it.

. . . .

When he started school,
He brought it with him,
Not to show to anyone,
Just to have along as a friend.

. . . .

The teacher came and spoke to him.
She told him to wear a tie like all the other boys.
He said he didn't like them.
She said it didn't matter!

. . . .

After that his mother bought him a tie,
And he always drew airplanes and rocketships
Like everyone else.
And he threw the old picture away.
And when he lay alone looking at the sky,
It was big and blue and all of everything,
But he wasn't anymore.

. . . .

He was like everyone else.
The things inside that needed saying
Didn't need it anymore.
It had stopped pushing.
It was crushed.
Stiff.
Like everything else.

# SUGGESTED READINGS

Hart, N., and Keidel, G. (1979) "The Suicidal Adolescent," *American Journal of Nursing*, 79, (1), pp. 80-84.

Holden, C. (1986), "Youth Suicide: New Research Focuses on a Growing Social Problem," *Science*, 233, pp. 839-841.

Selye, H. (1976), *The Stress of Life*. New York: McGraw-Hill.

Slaby, Andrew (1994), *No One Saw My Pain: Why Teens Kill Themselves*. New York: W. W. Norton & Company.

Smith, Patricia (1983), *A Study of Selected Stressors for Secondary Students*. Unpublished doctoral dissertation, Memphis Tennessee State University.

# CHAPTER 17

# SUBSTANCE ABUSE

Experimenting with and/or profound use of readily available psychoactive substances, including alcohol, marijuana, and cocaine, has become a part of growing up for all too many young people in the United States. The National Institute on Drug Abuse indicates that 7 percent of young Americans between the ages of 12 and 21 have a drinking problem.

Although alcohol and drugs have been with us for a long time, in recent years they have become much more accessible to young people. Indeed, since the 1980s people have discovered the means of producing chemicals in makeshift home laboratories—a little like the production of bathtub gin in the 1920s, except that this more recent phenomenon should not be taken lightly. Some very powerful substances are now being put together in homes across the country.

## THE MICHIGAN SURVEY

The 1995 results of the University of Michigan's Institute for Social Research annual survey of American secondary school students in grades eight, ten, and twelve, indicate that the use of marijuana, stimulants, LSD, and inhalants continues to be on the upswing. Research scientists Lloyd Johnston, Patrick O'Malley, and Jerald Bachman also note an increase in cigarette smoking in all three grades.

The highly respected Michigan survey is funded through a series of grants from the National Institute on Drug Abuse (NIDA), once a separate entity but now a division of the National Institutes of Health in the U.S. Department of Health and Human Services. Among other things, the survey measures and explains changes in drug use among American young people. At the present time, approximately 50,000 students in more than 400 public and private schools are surveyed annually. Seniors have been completing self-administered questionnaires given to them in classrooms by University of Michigan personnel since 1975. The survey of eighth- and tenth-graders began in 1991. Together, the three groups constitute nationally representative samples of all eighth-, tenth-, and twelfth-grade students in the United States.

## *The Findings*

Here are some of the findings that should afford you some idea as to the extent of teenage drug involvement.

The proportion of 8th-graders taking any illicit drug in the 12 months prior to the 1995 survey has almost doubled since 1991 (from 11 percent to 21 percent). Since 1992 the proportion using any illicit drugs in the prior 12 months rose by nearly two-thirds among 10th-graders (from 20 percent to 33 percent) and by nearly half among 12th-graders (from 27 percent to 39 percent).

In 1995, marijuana use continued the strong resurgence that began in the early 1990s, with increased use at all three grade levels. Among 8th-graders, annual prevalence rose to two-and-one-half times its level in 1991, from 6 percent in 1991 to 16 percent in 1995. Among 10th-graders there's been a doubling effect—from the low point in use in 1992 of 15 percent to 29 percent in 1995; among 12th-graders annual prevalence increased by more than half, from the low point of 22 percent in 1992 to 35 percent in 1995.

"Of particular concern is the continuing rise in daily marijuana use," observes Lloyd Johnston. Nearly one in 20 of today's high school seniors is a current daily marijuana user.

The investigators found that while marijuana use has shown the sharpest increase, the use of a number of other illicit drugs, including LSD, hallucinogens other than LSD, amphetamines, stimulants, and inhalants, has also continued to drift upwards. The use of cocaine in any form continued a gradual upward climb, though most of the one-year changes did not reach statistical significance. The same was true for crack cocaine. The annual prevalence rates for use of cocaine in any form was 2.6 percent, 3.5 percent, and 4 percent for grades 8, 10, and 12 respectively; while for crack use they were 1.6 percent, 1.8 percent, and 2.1 percent.

"While these levels of illicit drug use are certainly reason for concern," remarks Johnston," it should be noted that they are still well below the peak levels attained in the late 1970s.

According to the survey, alcohol use among secondary students has remained rather stable in the past few years, though at rates at which most adults would probably consider to be unacceptably high. In 1995 the proportions of students having five or more drinks in a row during the two weeks preceding the survey were 15 percent, 24 percent, and 30 percent for the 8th, 10th, and 12th graders respectively.

## *Perceived Risks*

Beliefs about the harmfulness of the various drugs have proven to be very important determinants of use. The proportions of students seeing drugs as dangerous continued to decline in 1995. There was a sharp decline in the perceived risk of using marijuana—a decline that generally began after 1991 at all three grade levels. There was also a decline in the perceived dangers of using crack cocaine at all three grade levels. The perceived dangers of LSD use also continued to decline in 1995, a decline that began after 1991.

## *Peer Norms*

Peer disapproval of drug use is considered to be an important deterrent to use; unfortunately, the norms against using illicit drugs have been softening since 1991. Still, the great majority of American youth disapprove of even trying any illicit drugs other than marijuana. Even for marijuana, the researchers found that 71 percent of 8th-graders in 1995 disapproved of trying it, 60 percent of 10th-graders, and 57 percent of 12th-graders.

"As long as we see erosion in the dangers youngsters believe to be associated with these drugs, and erosion in the norms against their use, I expect that we will see a continuation of the increase in drug use," Johnston cautions.

# KEY WORDS IN WHY ADOLESCENTS USE DRUGS

Why *do* teenagers resort to using alcohol/drugs? Why do they seem to disregard adult warnings and medical findings; pay little or no heed to what they learn in school and from the media; and decide that they are somehow invulnerable to getting hooked? Let's focus on eleven critical words for a moment, often-heard words that succinctly describe why young people are more and more turning to alcohol and other related drugs. The terms and commentary should provide you with further background on the problem.

1. *Gratification*. And we mean instant! Relief is just a button away: computers, microwaves, and pills. As adults know well, things that really matter in life can take time to master. Today we have the "young and the restless." Alcohol and drugs work immediately—get them into your system and your feelings can change in no time flat, and with little or no effort on your part.

2. *Advertising*. "You should never have to feel bad about anything;" so say the television ads for over-the-counter drugs. The liquor industry spends millions of dollars yearly in convincing Americans that "you can be anything you want to be" by drinking something alcoholic.

3. *Passivity*. Television promotes passivity and thwarts creativity. The intake of drugs and alcohol is a passive self-centered happening, as well.

4. *Availability*. It's everywhere: hamlets, villages, towns, townships, and cities. Interestingly, alcohol, the drug of choice for adults, is also the #1 drug of abuse for teenagers. Three out of ten, or five million teenagers are experiencing problems with alcohol. The United States ranks sixth in the world in deaths due to alcoholism.

5. *Subculture.* Teenagers have no problem relating to particular music groups, including individual members within these groups. Lyrics of songs as well as television and film themes are sometimes biased toward substance abuse. Some baby-boomer parents remain stuck in the sixties drug culture, even to the point of smoking an occasional joint with their adolescent offspring.

6. *Genetics.* Genetic influence is a factor. Both brain wave activity and brain chemical studies of chemically dependent people point to a genetic link. Also, studies of twins provide ample evidence of genetic influence in the development of addiction. The studies reveal that when one twin is addicted, the other is as well, even when the twins are raised in separate homes or by separate families.

7. *Dysfunction.* Some adolescents are being raised in alcoholic or chemical-abusing families. Family characteristics and behavioral patterns related to chemical use can be significant influences in chemical abuse and addiction, e.g., if family members openly abuse certain substances, other family members may accept such abuse as normal and appropriate behavior. Other adolescents come from homes that are dysfunctional for other reasons, with parents drinking or using drugs as an escape from reality.

8. *Contribution.* You've heard the expression, "no contribution is too small," as it relates to charitable giving. It would also be a fitting expression to assign to those young people who would love to be more recognized for contributing to home and community. At one time in this country, as in other societies, kids went straight from childhood to adulthood without passing "Go." At age thirteen, they were considered young men and young women. These resourceful youngsters could be seen coming in from the fields after hours of laboring; marrying at an early age; and, for the most part, contributing rather significantly to the support of home and community. There was no stage called "adolescence." All of that has changed, with adolescents now expected to "act their age," whatever that means. You might say it's a situation of betwixt and between—no longer a child, but not yet an adult. Getting adolescents involved in productive work—not just tasks around the house, but work that contributes to the welfare of family and society—enhances their self-respect and self-esteem. Values are strengthened in the process. Regrettably, in our present society many adolescents feel undervalued, which in turn causes adolescent years to be those of confusion, frustration, and unhappiness. Drinking and using drugs offer a temporary escape, usually with devastating consequences.

9. *Acceptance.* Young people are becoming more accepting of drug use and less worried about its consequences. New classes of young people are replacing previous ones who knew more about drugs and their adverse effects. (Teens from a decade ago knew more about drugs because there were more people around them who were users, and they could observe the effects of drug use first hand.)

10. *Minimize.* Many public proponents of legalization try to minimize the consequences of drugs, in particular marijuana, in order to support their policy conclusions.

11. *Cigarettes.* Since cigarette smoking teaches youngsters how to take smoke into their lungs, that smoking is strongly correlated with the use of marijuana. The researchers suggest that the upturn in cigarette smoking since 1991 may well have contributed to the increase in marijuana use over the same period. (Since 1992, the smoking rate has

risen by more than one-fifth among high school seniors, with one in three stating that they smoked in the 30 days prior to the survey.)

# SYMPTOMS OF ABUSE

Youngsters who become involved in chemical abuse often come from dysfunctional families and demonstrate other underlying problems that may or may not be school-related. They can have an impaired self-image, as well. Yet the symptomology of drug and alcohol abuse is not always clear.

Business and industry have been quite successful in identifying these symptoms, however, and in supporting and working with their employees toward an effective recovery. From adults in treatment, therapists have come to recognize a simple guideline as to the progression of abuse: (1) alienation of family by abuser, (2) loss of job, and (3) deterioration of health. Middle-management supervisors monitor job performance. When there appears to be a dip in performance, such as lack of output or excessive absenteeism, then it might be determined that counseling is in order. The business and industry model could also be applicable to the public or private school setting. "Dip in performance" could be reduction in grades; "loss of job" could be dropping out.

While other variables can cause one or more of the characteristic symptoms, therapists who do extensive work in treating abusers find that there are some that constantly reoccur. For young people, the following symptoms might be present.

## *Educational Symptoms*

- Truancy
- Class cutting
- Lateness to school or to particular classes
- General loss of interest in learning
- Dropping out of co-curricular activities
- Changing friends
- Hostile behavior that might be accompanied by emotional outbursts
- Secretive telephone conversations
- Always going "nowhere special"
- Not sharing the identity of friends with parents
- Unexplained appearance of money
- Suddenly into the borrowing of money
- A slow or radical drop in course grades
- Minimizing the intake and/or effects of psychoactive substances
- Dropping out of school

## *Psychological Symptoms*

- Depressive behavior
- Hyperactive behavior
- Mood swings
- Anxiety; confusion
- Hallucinations
- Loss of, or increase in appetite
- Apathetic attitude
- Lack of ambition and drive

## *Physical Symptoms*

- Loss of coordination
- Changes related to vision
- Slurred speech
- Loss in memory functions
- Trembling movements
- Needle marks
- Dreamy or vapid facial expressions
- Unexplained appearance of drug substances and/or paraphernalia
- Disappearance of drugs from family medicine cabinet
- Altered physical appearance

# INTERVENTION TECHNIQUES AND STRATEGIES

As you work with youth and their families, you are presented with a real challenge to find solutions to drug and alcohol abuse. There will be times when, in order to have a decisive impact, school professionals and others from the community will need an approach and treatment design that includes the total family. School counselors are most often involved in the recognition and support phases of abuse, as opposed to its actual treatment. Counselors can be there for the support of any affected student during the course of the school day. At the same time, counselors need to be knowledgeable as to the gamut of possible intervention techniques and strategies.

- Take the drinking and any other drug usage seriously. Teenagers have a great penchant for underestimating how much alcohol or other substances they consume.

- Get the facts. Get descriptions, not feelings. Abusers are neither ready to nor capable of dealing with feelings. Drugs and alcohol are not "feeling" issues. They *can* become life-threatening! Besides, abusers have placed themselves emotionally "on hold." That is not to deny that they don't have other serious behavioral problems; however, the chief thrust should be to get rid of the chemicals; the air will then be clear to address any other issues.

- Avoid the role of passive listener, which is not effective with substance abusers and their families. Your approach should be directive.

- Know when and where to refer to an in-house specialist or outside practitioner or agency.

- When referring your counselee to an in-house specialist, it's how and what you say that counts. Arrange the meeting between counselee and specialist. Some determination might have to be made as to whether a Core Team or Crisis Intervention Team meeting is warranted.

- The school needs to involve *both* parents. If and when the student were to go into treatment, it would be crucial that the family go with the student. The family is usually the student's major support system. And if one parent appears more passive than the other, be sure to get him or her involved in the process. Put parents in control. Empower them. We need to strengthen them to take charge, not simply take charge for them. Therefore, we need to help them say no, set limits, and avoid unnecessary and wasteful confrontation with their child.

- Be familiar with any local school and state policies and procedures. With school counseling, confidentiality is a complex and controversial issue, both from the standpoint of federal and state statutes, and the subjective determination of just which situation is life-threatening. Most school systems now have clearly delineated policies and procedures in place that cover the topic of substance abuse.

# ABUSE IS NOT DEPENDENCY

What transpires when a youngster starts using? What then are the signs that he or she is in trouble—perhaps heading precipitously toward the realm of addiction?

We know now that chemical dependence is an incurable disease with certain describable characteristics. We also know that it proceeds according to clear and definable stages—and that it can be treated and arrested. We know, too, that chemical dependence in young people differs from that of adults. What might be considered signs of dependence in adults might be nothing more than common adolescent behaviors in certain teenagers.

As a school counselor, if you suspect that one of your counselees is abusing or even misusing alcohol/drugs, you will want to know two things: how far the usage has progressed, and the depth of the student's delusional state. When they tell you, "I only had one drink"—multiply by three.

There are numerous reasons for alcohol addiction, including the fact that some young people are genetically predisposed to alcoholism—especially those whose biological parents or grandparents are alcoholic.

In his 1987 book, *Choices & Consequences: What to Do When a Teenager Uses Alcohol/Drugs*, author and therapist Dick Schaefer states that we can tell if someone has the disease: ". . . his or her relationship with the chemical becomes more important than anything else in his or her life. Chemical dependence is a 'love affair' with the drug of choice." Using drugs becomes more important than relationships, doing well in school or on the job. In fact, as Schaefer points out, chemicals are not merely people substitutes, they are life substitutes. "Using becomes the reason to get up in the morning and go out at night."

Abuse is not dependency; the terms are by no means synonymous. A person can be chemically dependent and not abuse the substance, or abuse the substance and not have chemical dependence. Abuse, however, *can* lead to addiction through a loss of choice and control. Schaefer depicts some of this in terms of a valley chart, with non-addictive usage on the left and addiction on the right; it is adapted in Figure 17-1.

FIGURE 17-1

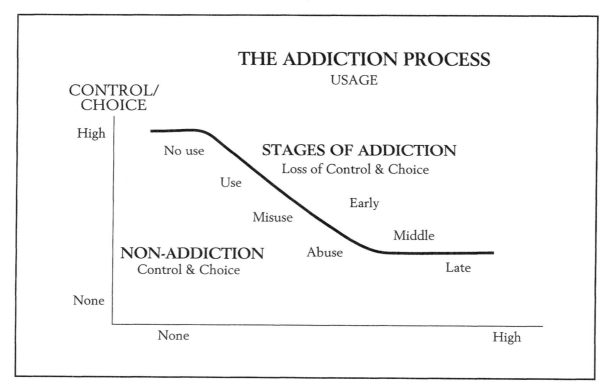

*Three Levels of Non-Addictive Involvement*

- Use: Chemical is used to enhance a pleasant event: an occasional or daily serving of wine at mealtime; a couple of beers at poolside; a cocktail or two before a special dinner.
- Misuse: Chemical has begun to interfere somewhat with daily routine, e.g. increased intake leads to occasional light hangovers, sporadic lateness to school or job.
- Abuse: Chemical consistently interferes with one or more areas, e.g. often drunk on weekends, or driving while intoxicated.

# CHILDREN OF ALCOHOLIC PARENTS

The statistics are awesome. One out of every nine Americans grows up with at least one alcoholic parent. Sixteen percent of the children of nonalcoholic parents are abused; while 56 percent of children of alcoholics (COAs) are abused. Children of alcoholics are four times more likely to become alcoholic than their counterparts from nonalcoholic families. Four out of every 25 of your students are children of alcoholics.

Less than half of the children of alcoholics ever discuss the situation with their parents. Seventy percent never tell a friend; 90 percent never tell a teacher or counselor. It's a problem—a big problem—but one never talks about it.

It's not much different with other chemical dependencies. The whole scenario places a large and improper burden on people far too young to be able to deal with the situation effectively.

Fortunately, with the advent of substance abuse specialists in the schools, and greater knowledge and awareness on the part of generalist counselors, a good many youngsters have been helped to cope with their own problemed lives.

# SUGGESTED READINGS/CONTACTS

Bell, Tammy (1990), *Preventing Adolescent Relapse: A Guide for Parents, Teachers, and Counselor*, Herald/House Independence Press, Independence, MO 64055.

Hazelden Publishing and Education, Pleasant Valley Road, Center City, Minnesota 55012. (A leader in the movement. Exceptional educational materials and programs. They now have a special educators catalog.)

National Institutes of Health, Bethesda, Maryland. Tel: 1-800-729-6686. (Umbrella organization of the National Institute on Drug Abuse.)

Schaefer, Dick (1987), *Choices and Consequences: What to Do When a Teenager Uses Alcohol/Drugs*. Minneapolis, MN 55439: Johnson Institute Books.

# CHAPTER 18

# ANOREXIA NERVOSA AND BULIMIA

The concept of the perfect body has been substantially modified throughout the ages. In the 1700s, such perfection was characterized by voluptuously rounded figures, albeit tiny waists. The physicians of the period complained that women who would be regarded as medically obese by today's standards refused to lose weight even when their health was at risk.

Even though the nation was in awe of Mae West whose figure made her the sex symbol of the 1930s, society was well on its way toward a slimmer figure. Indeed, since the 1800s "thin's been in." There was wartime pinup Betty Grable of the 1940s, and then Marilyn Monroe, the sex goddess of the 1950s. But it was the more drastic new image of Twiggy, the British fashion model of the late 1960s, that set things in motion, and led countless numbers of women to resort to anorexic behavior to control weight. To emulate Twiggy, the new ideal for women was to be thin, flat-chested, and curveless. The pursuit of the perfect body in the 1970s and 1980s found women resorting to bulimic behavior.

What *is* the difference between Anorexia Nervosa and Bulimia? Not much, according to some experts. Anorexia Nervosa is an eating disorder characterized by an intense fear of becoming fat. It includes an ongoing pattern of self-starvation and a preoccupation with food and losing weight. There is no known physical malady that accounts for this weight loss. Bulimia is an eating disorder characterized by that same intense fear, but has the added component of binge-eating (rapid consumption of large amounts of food in a short period of time) followed by purging (self-induced elimination). As with anorexia, bulimic behavior is not caused by any known physical illness.

In the 1980s, women not only had to be thin, but strong and athletic as well. People such as Cher, with her outrageous style, made sure of that. We became bombarded with Jack LaLanne commercials that inadvertently supported eating disorders and the obsession for weight reduction through fitness and exercise. And so a virtual epidemic of eating disorders has been sweeping the nation since the mid-seventies—much of this because of the intense social and cultural pressures on young people, especially women, to look thin.

In the case of Anorexia Nervosa, the relentless pursuit of thinness is hard to conceal. Nor is it often meant to be concealed: for many individuals, thinness means control, effectiveness, and mastery. Young people become skeletal in appearance, intolerant of the cold as they walk about dressed in layers of wool. And thinness can also translate into no menstrual period, dryness of skin, excess fine body hair, decreased body temperature, and a slowness of heart rate. Eating habits of anorexics are remarkable. Little food is consumed, especially if the food has any caloric value, and the time taken to complete a meal is often in inverse proportion to the number of calories consumed. The anorexic wears her abstention like a badge of honor.

In sharp contrast stands the guilt-ridden bulimic, less successful in her quest for thinness, which lack of success can be cause for dishonor. She can make an extraordinary effort to hide her abnormal eating behavior, and the behavior can be masked for a long time. Family and friends' concern might become elevated by a young woman's capability of eating large quantities of food, all the while gaining no weight as she makes frequent trips to the bathroom to purge herself. These same family members and friends might notice a deterioration in the young woman's social life, academic performance, or job performance. Or careful examination might reveal parotid (salivary) gland enlargement, tooth enamel loss, or scars on the dorsa (back) of the hands acquired from induced vomiting.

An estimated 100,000 people, mostly women, suffer from anorexia or bulimia. It is believed that eating disorders affect some 13 percent of college women, that 15 percent of girls in middle school and high school are dieting, and that 20 percent of women under the age of twenty vomit to control weight. Men are contained in the 100,000 count; but for them, the affliction most often goes undetected.

When one considers the social and personal (2000 die each year) consequences of these behaviors, as well as the sheer numbers of persons affected, it is imperative that school officials, including counselors, be sensitive to the possible existence of an eating disorder in virtually any youngster. But what *are* some of these consequences?

# MEDICAL CONSEQUENCES

The following are capsule descriptions of some of the medical complications associated with the two eating disorders.

## Anorexia Nervosa

- *Heart problems:* Starving oneself can lead to the shrinking of the heart muscle, rate slowdown, and rhythmic irregularity.
- *Kidneys:* Anorexic behavior can cause dehydration, kidney stones, and ultimate kidney failure.
- *Lanugo:* Lanugo is a fine body-hair condition that can develop on the arms and face of anorexics.
- *Muscle atrophy:* Muscle tissue can deteriorate because of significant weight loss.
- *Osteoporosis:* Bone density becomes a problem; the bones become brittle through a lack of calcium.
- *Digestive problems:* Restricted eating can result in delayed gastric emptying, causing bowel irritation and constipation.
- *Amenorrhea:* Menstruation often ceases in anorexics, even before extensive weight loss.
- *Fatigue:* Anorexics can experience not only periods of dizziness and lightheadedness, but also a generalized lack of energy.

## Bulimia

- *Dental problems:* The particular acids in vomit erode tooth enamel, leading to numerous cavities and other dental problems.
- *Electrolyte imbalance:* The body's electrolytes can become imbalanced and depleted. Vomiting and the use of laxatives and diuretics can cause sodium and potassium to be flushed from the body. This can lead to an alteration in the rhythm of the heart and even to sudden death.
- *Throat/esophagus/stomach:* Self-induced vomiting can cause irritation and tearing in the lining of the throat, esophagus, and stomach.
- *Gland swelling:* Vomit can irritate and thereby cause swelling of the glands around the face and neck.
- *Laxative dependence:* When bulimics abuse the use of laxatives, an inability to have normal bowel movements can occur.
- *Eyes:* Blood vessels can burst in the eyes of a bulimic.

Figure 18-1 is a handout that can be used with individuals or groups. Some school systems do joint informational programs utilizing the expertise of nurses and counselors.

FIGURE 18-1

## Sound Advice for Families

How you can effectively deal with an anorexic/bulimic son or daughter

**Don't:**

1. *Don't press your child to eat.* And don't hover over her while she eats. Leave the room if necessary. Your involvement with her eating is her way of manipulating you. Remove this tool from her hands.
2. Many parents ask, *"What have I done wrong?"* Nothing. You've done the best you could. Don't feel guilty. Once you've had a physician examine your child to begin counseling, getting well is her responsibility.
3. *Don't neglect your marriage partner or other siblings.* Too much focus on a sick child can perpetuate the illness and destroy the family. An anorexic needs to know that she is important to you, but no more important than any other family member.
4. *Do not make comparisons.* Don't put your child down by comparing her to her more "successful" siblings or friends. Her self-esteem can be reflective of your esteem for her.
5. *Do not be afraid of having your child separated from you.* If it becomes obvious that her continued presence and accompanying behavior is undermining the emotional health of the family, it might be necessary to have her housed separately, e.g., in an in-patient facility.
6. *The final separation is death.* Don't allow her possible threats of suicide to intimidate the family. Deal with that issue separately.

**Do:**

1. *Love your child as you should love yourself.* Love makes anyone feel welcome.
2. *Trust your child to find his/her own values, ideals, and standards,* rather than superimposing yours on hers. All ideals are just that, only ideals. In practice we often fall short, too; our own behavior can be adulterated with self-serving rewards.
3. *Do everything you can to encourage self-initiative, independence and autonomy.* Be aware, though, that anorexics tend to be perfectionists, so they are never satisfied with themselves. Perfectionism justifies their dissatisfaction with themselves.
4. *Get ready for a long-term illness.* Anorexics do get better. Many completely recover, very few die; but families must face months and sometimes years of treatment and anxiety. Each case is individual—ask any counselor or psychiatrist. A support group or parents' self-help group may make a significant difference to your family's survival: it helps you *deal with yourself* in relation to your anorexic/bulimic child. You must help your child understand that *your* life is as important as hers.

# WHEN AND TO WHOM TO REFER

Many states have center hotline numbers for this disease on both a county- and state-wide basis. You will want to have these "reach-out" numbers at your disposal. It appears that these centers are receiving their share of phone calls—many from teachers, counselors, and school nurses who are seeking general or particular information.

Another thrust might be to invite an expert to your school to address certain targeted student populations. Those experts who have done visitations report that after their presentations, many students have remained to talk personally about themselves, friends, or relatives. Some of the most effective presenters are those who have experienced the problem themselves. (When an "experienced" speaker gets personal, she projects her recognition that she's hooked into exactly the same feelings that some of the gathered students are feeling; the students in turn realize that they're not out there alone—that somebody else has gone through the process.)

Many teenagers will not seek treatment because they are afraid to tell their parents about their disorder. Some families just don't want to deal with the issue. There *are* a lot of resistant parents; nevertheless, as a professional, you can break through some of that resistance by broadening your knowledge base.

- Know that some schools are not receptive to having speakers. They are fearful of people glamorizing the disorder. Their theory: Talk about it and we'll get more eating disorders.

- Although it is one of the few psychiatric illnesses that left untreated might result in death, most sufferers can be cured.

- Some older women from 40 to 60 years of age suffer from anorexia. Some young girls of about 10 or 11 suffer from it, too.

- Perfectionism is big with the anorexic. There is often a frantic striving to achieve, propelled by an underlying guilt for failing to live up to the expectations of others.

- Because perfection is so elusive, feelings of inadequacy eventually set in that lead to a poor self-image.

- With the anorexic, the gender role is often rejected, in part because of a conflict between the afflicted and her mother. It can become an especially serious problem if the father does not support his daughter's growth toward womanhood.

- Heavy depression can set in whereby life becomes overwhelming and meaningless. Anorexic and bulimic behavior is the *result* of depression. Indeed, the disease can be thought of as a slow form of suicide, much like alcoholism. (See Chapter 16 on depression and suicide.)

- Perfect children make parents look perfect. Control can be an important factor with the parents of an anorexic; parents become glued to their child. Some parents try to control their children to the point of not permitting them to "fly" when the time is right. Conversely, the dominated anorexic exhibits little self-confidence and is ambivalent about her family—she wants to soar, yet is afraid to take flight.

- Look for deceptive practices with a practicing anorexic or bulimic: shoplifting, secretive eating, vomiting, and denial.

You will, of course, not have the requisite time or needed skills to deliver therapy to an anorexic or bulimic counselee. You might, however, find yourself working cooperatively with the school nurse and an outside agency or private practice specialist in supporting the recovery. There are several maxims that, although not endorsed by all professionals, in our judgment help underpin any recovery effort. You might want to internalize these maxims, making them part of your counseling methodology with *all* of your students:

**First:**    If an activity or exercise is worth doing, it is even worth doing poorly, because practice *will* enable the participant to do *better*, but not *perfectly*.

**Second:**  It's better to try and fail than to fail by not trying.

**Third:**    When we fail at some of the things we do in life, we can discover our limits. Putting oneself "on the line" can be a more difficult task for some adolescents than it can be for us adults, but it is a necessity for growth.

# CHAPTER 19

# COUNSELING YOUTH WITH DIFFERENT SEXUAL PREFERENCES

Gay and lesbian youth have one significant thing in common with their heterosexual counterparts: both groups are often taught to hate and fear homosexuality. The fact that many of these youngsters grow up to become that which they've been taught to hate and fear can have an overpowering impact on their sense of self. Even the youths who eventually "come out" and begin to identify themselves for who they really are, continue to incorporate this negative conditioning. For many individuals, the very difficult developmental process of coming out can be a traumatic experience—and one that may not even be completed well into the adult years. Some people are experts at hiding their homosexuality. They can be a picture of amiability on the outside, yet extremely resentful on the inside. More than a few teens and young adults spend years in self-loathing.

Cass (1979) identified the specific *developmental* stages in the coming-out process that lesbians and gays have to master: (1) identity confusion, (2) identity comparison, (3) identity tolerance, (4) identity acceptance, (5) identity pride, and (6) identity synthesis.

Pope and Jelly (1991) described coming out as a self-identity procedure and then compared the developmental stages in self-identity formation to those described by major developmental theorists, such as Freud, Erickson, Piaget, and Super.

Elliott (1990) mentions that coming out is a unique situation that differentiates gays and lesbians from other minority cultures, in that they're the only group in which the family of origin has to be told about an individual's membership status—evidently a powerful cohesive experience for gays and lesbians, a so-called right of passage. The passage can get downright rocky, though: there is a definite fear of ostracism and rejection by the family of origin.

And no matter how successful the process of coming out is for some of them, the effects of the earlier damaged self-concept can continue to take its toll on gays, lesbians, and bisexuals throughout their adult lives. Not only are these individuals faced with the hatred and hostility of society at large, including the possible rejection by loved ones, but they must also deal with what they have been taught: that this particular lifestyle is disgusting.

## ENTER THE ADOLESCENT

The damage to self caused by this self-hatred is a major contributing factor in the high rate of suicide and drug and/or alcohol abuse in this particular group of adolescents. In 1990, the United States government published a study highlighting the fact that gay and lesbian adolescents are two to three times more likely to attempt suicide than their heterosexual counterparts. That's heavy stuff. The same study estimated that gays, lesbians, and bisexuals make up about 30% of all completed suicide attempts. It's certainly a noteworthy percentage, and one of several issues with which psychiatrist Andrew Slaby deals in his extraordinary book, *No One Saw My Pain: Why Teens Kill Themselves.* The author writes that depression is often exacerbated when a youth feels shame over a subject that is taboo within the family: homosexuality, an unwanted pregnancy, or the family's unacknowledged history of mental illness. Severe depression, warns the psychiatrist, "should be considered as life-threatening as any other terminal medical condition." Of course, few if any would argue that depression and suicide are inexorably linked. (See Chapter 16.)

## WHAT IS THE SCHOOL COUNSELOR'S ROLE?

Various gay and lesbian support organizations have questioned young people as to how they perceived the role of teachers and counselors in the schools. The overwhelming response was that they (young people) do not feel safe confiding in adults at school. The prevailing attitude appears to be "much to lose and very little to gain." Evidently the fear of rejection and persecution is so pronounced that most of today's youth continue to feel the need to go it alone. It is an unfortunate scene, but a changing one, just like the dramatic change that has recently occurred in the demand for and time expended on personal counseling by school professionals.

Author Dan Woog addresses some of this in his provocative work, *School's Out: The Impact of Gay and Lesbian Issues on America's Schools.* Woog, himself a high school soccer coach, includes a "Help or Hindrance?" chapter on school counselors: "Welcome to the Gay Nineties," he writes. "Guidance counselors have become integral staff members of many buildings—right up there with once similarly shunned professionals like school nurses and health teachers—and they are indeed some of the first people to whom adolescents turn when they face problems like who am I, where do I fit in, uh-oh-I've-got-a-crush-on-a-guy-on-my-baseball-team." The author makes it quite clear that most school counselors—like most students and staff members—are not homosexuals, and that straight counselors *can* help lesbian, gay, bisexual, and questioning students. We certainly don't dispute that.

The reality that most students do not confide in teachers and counselors does not hide the fact that there are significant numbers of gay, lesbian, and bisexual youth in the school population, more so in certain sections of the country than in others. Nor does it hide the fact that several states, including New Jersey and Massachusetts, have recommendations and legislation in place to assist and protect sexual minority youth.

# PSYCHOSOCIAL ISSUES FOR SEXUAL MINORITY YOUTH

Undoubtedly the most critical psychosocial issue for those young people who have become known as sexual minority youth is the development of a positive and healthy sexual identity. The search for a positive and healthy sexual identity can occur, but it's usually accomplished *within the context of:*

## *Isolation*

1. Rejection of sexual minority youth by family and peers.
2. Social withdrawal of such youth.
3. Loneliness that includes the inability to meet others like themselves.

## *Lack of Support from Family, School, and Community*

1. As opposed to other minority youth, sexual minority youth are generally not raised in families that share in their oppression.
2. Sexual minority youth are socialized in a heterosexual society that does not support their efforts to establish a healthy lesbian/gay/bisexual identity.
3. Rejection of child due to sexual orientation can occur in a home.
4. Youngster's sexual orientation is sometimes viewed as incompatible with family's religious beliefs.
5. Lack of positive inclusion of related materials in the school curriculum.
6. Failure of the school to protect the safety and welfare of the individual.

## Lack of Information

1. Available media information is frequently inaccurate.
2. Appropriate and substantive materials are usually not available in places to which sexual minority youth have access.

## Violence, Abuse, and Harassment

1. Significant numbers of gays and lesbians report having been harassed, threatened with violence, or physically assaulted in middle school and high school because they were perceived to be lesbian or gay.
2. According to the American Psychological Association, sexual minority youth are one of the most targeted groups for youth violence.
3. A New York City public school survey highlights the fact that young people feel more justified in abusing sexual minority youth than other minority groups.

## Invisibility

1. Sexual minority youth are often not identified by visibility clues.
2. Such invisibility leads to the difficulty of identifying each other.
3. It leads in turn to the difficulty of adult service providers to identify such youth.

## Lack of Role Models

1. Images of lesbians and gays in the media and society-at-large are frequently negative stereotypes.
2. Positive role models are often not identified and therefore not present due to social stigmas.
3. Lack of positive adult role models is another contributing factor to the significant dropout and suicide rate in our schools. A model staff member can be there for students' questions, either definitive or hypothetical.

# ACCEPTANCE AND TOLERANCE

As a school counselor, you don't have to love them; you don't have to embrace their lifestyle, or agree with their philosophy and ideals. You simply have to accept them for who they are and be *tolerant* of their beliefs. That's a tall order for some educators—an even taller order for millions of Americans. But there's no way back. There is no denying that there are any number of extreme rightist and/or religious organizations that believe there *is* a way to "rid ourselves" of this group; but in our judgment there isn't, and never will be. Gays and lesbians exist; *as a multicultural entity* they are here to stay.

Which brings us to the next point: a great debate is going on among counseling leaders as to the scope of the term "multiculturalism." On one side of the debate are those individuals who favor a definition of multiculturalism that includes lesbians and gays in that (1) the identity-formation tasks that racial and ethnic minorities must accomplish are the same for sexual minorities; (2) the multicultural counseling skills required for dealing with racial and ethnic minorities are similar to those needed to effectively deal with sexual minorities; (3) there is a lesbian and gay culture; and (4) gay and lesbian oppression, along with the results of that oppression by the majority culture, is very real—with very real effects on real people's lives, including that of personal growth and development, and career choice and progression.

As Dan Woog indicated, school counseling in America has come a long way. Again, most counselors, like most students, are not homosexuals. That doesn't mean, however, that you cannot be responsive to the needs of gays, lesbians, or bisexuals. Regrettably, many professionals haven't kept abreast of the latest teachings on modern sexuality, including sexuality and its tie to self-image. In the graduate training of older counselors, the topic was never explored, and quite frankly, many of those same counselors don't care to know. We're creatures of habit and it disrupts our routine to learn, but at the very least it is our responsibility to know when and to whom to refer our counselees for the proper assistance.

There are states such as Michigan, Massachusetts, California, Connecticut, and New Jersey where local school districts are pressing the training issue by offering in-service programs to *all* counselors. A good deal of the forward movement, however, appears to be at state and national levels through professional *and* union-type organizations.

### As a School Counselor You Can:

- Counsel young people to respect individual differences.

- Challenge all prejudicial remarks, including homophobic ones, rendered by students and staff personnel.

- Examine your own prejudices, remembering that counselors can be as much victims of homophobia as anyone else. The American Counseling Association's multicultural counseling competencies and standards, along with the American Psychological Association guidelines on cultural sensitivity, recommend that counselors become aware of their own background and the values and biases that emanate from that.

- Provide an open, relaxed, and supportive environment so that your counselee might feel comfortable (key term) in talking with you. And you need to be comfortable with the differences that may exist between you and your counselee, and sensitive to specific circumstances that would indicate the need to refer your counselee to someone better suited to fulfill his or her needs.

- Take time to learn the facts. Understand that certain research now shows that homosexuality is genetically determined, and that gender orientation is established by age six. If you have lesbian and gay counselees, you need to be knowledgeable about that culture in order to be a knowledgeable facilitator of your counselee's growth and development process. Elliott (1990) stated that counselors should become aware of socio-political issues, specific knowledge, necessary information, and institutional barriers that confront gay and lesbian clients who are seeking career counseling. Such awareness might well extend to the generalist counselor who also needs to be knowledgeable as to the history, culture, ethics, jargon, and sense of community that define the gay and lesbian culture.

- Respect your counselee's confidentiality. This, of course, is a "goes without saying" axiom in the school counseling profession. If your counselee should entrust you with a secret part of him or her, breaching confidentiality could be devastating to that person.

- Never ask, "Are you sure?" No one ever asks a heterosexual that question.

- Again, know when and where to refer. If you're uncomfortable dealing with the issue, *don't* hesitate to refer your counselee to someone who is not. Your discomfort will be quickly recognized. Know what resources are available at the local, county, and state levels, and be willing to share this information with your counselee.

- Be empathetic. Similarly, don't be too quick to suggest professional counseling. For adolescents, being told that they need therapy can be akin to being told that they are "sick." A person's gender orientation is only *one* aspect of his or her personality.

- Be prepared for a great deal of emotion. You might be the first adult to whom the student has ever spoken.

- Never force the issue. No matter what you suspect about a student's gender orientation, never confront him or her about it. Everyone comes out in his or her own time, if at all. Support is the name of the game! A student needs to work through the problem at his or her own speed. Concealment may well be a student's only coping strategy. And no matter how maladaptive you might believe that to be, asking someone whether or not he or she is homosexual might be stripping that someone of his or her only coping mechanism.

- Understand that gay people need to be covered as an entity in the development and implementation of anti-harassment policies. (See Chapter 14 on harassment.)

- Understand that there is a big difference between homosexuality and pedophilia. For those persons who worry about gay/bisexual counselors counseling behind closed doors, we need to remember that 90 percent of child molestation is cross-gender.

- Know that the vast majority of highschoolers are certain as to their sexuality, yet about 10 percent are confused and searching. In some schools, having openly gay and bisexual faculty has evidently been beneficial in that students can pose both hypothetical and definitive questions to these faculty members.

Education will be the driving force for the eventual acceptance of individual sexual differences by the entire fabric of American society.

# SUGGESTED READINGS

Cass, V.C. (1979) "Homosexual Identity Formation: A Theoretical Model," *Journal of Homosexuality*, 4, pp. 219-235.

Elliott, J.E. (1990, August) *Career Development with Lesbian and Gay Clients*. Paper presented at the meeting of the American Psychological Association, Boston.

Pope, M. and Jelly, J. (1991) MBTI, *Sexual Orientation and Career Development* [Summary], Proceedings of the 9th Biennial Conference of the Association for Psychological Type, 9, pp. 231-238.

Slaby, Andrew (1994) *No One Saw My Pain: Why Teens Kill Themselves*. New York: W.W. Norton & Company.

Woog, Dan (1995) *School's Out: The Impact of Gay and Lesbian Issues on America's Schools*. Boston: Alyson Publications.

# SECTION III

# POST-SECONDARY EDUCATIONAL DEVELOPMENT

◆ ◆ ◆ ◆

We have "bottomed out." College enrollment figures began to dip in 1990, so for parents and students it's been a "buyer's market," certain public colleges and universities excepted. According to United States Department of Education projections, though, there will be an enrollment increase in 1997 (about 100,000 more applicants), and thereafter about 150,000 more students will enroll each year until 2005. Enrollment will rise from some 15 million in 1997 to 16 million in 2005. That's good news for those collegiate institutions who are struggling to survive. Throughout this time period we will continue to see about one and a half million more women in college than men.

Other than a continuing downtrend in enrollment figures and more families gravitating toward public institutions, there has been little change in the college admission scene in the past decade. Regrettably, some admission counselors have become salespersons and some admission directors, enrollment managers. The National Association for College Admission Counseling (NACAC) has experienced membership growth and a new name, and the fifty or so most competitive schools are just as difficult to get into as ever. Students are still writing essays and submitting graded papers; school counselors are still gridding and checking boxes on four-page secondary school report forms; and parents are still as prestige conscious as ever.

But in the next ten years, change will be more rapid and decisive. Hi-tech will be the name of the game. Modems will be everywhere. Admission officials will speak directly to applicants through the computer and/or the television set. Applications will be procured through Internet and submitted through e-mail. Fees will be paid by simply pressing a couple of buttons.

Although school counselors continue to push an inordinate amount of paper, they're becoming increasingly militant about doing so; they're demanding that more be done to streamline the admission process. Some secondary schools have stepped out and designed their own secondary school report forms. Others have dumped class rank or are in the process of doing so. A new SAT is with us, but so are the prep programs.

Running off to senior college isn't the only answer. The next ten years promise to be fascinating times. Community colleges are going to thrive as never before, as criticism mounts over the large numbers of students who attend senior colleges and fail to graduate; the argument being that many of these dropouts should have commenced their studies at a two-year institution. Career programs at community colleges will flourish. Several universities will downsize like Trenton State College and the University of Rochester, in an effort to enhance their academic reputations and meet the criticism that they are far more eager to admit students than they are to graduate them.

Much of this reshaping is due to the fact that our advance in technology has both limited the blue-collar field *and* made the possession of a college degree insufficient to claim many a career. Actually, having a B.S. or B.A. degree is no longer a guarantee of a job. The question, then, is what type of post-secondary educational training does the individual student need? Senior college? Community college? Technical or Business school? Apprenticeship?

One of the difficulties in searching out and responding to student need regarding post-secondary education is the fact that school counselors are being pressed—spread paper thin—as to their role and function. For example, personal counseling has been considerably more center stage in the 1990s. Counselors are reeling with responsibilities related to drug and alcohol factors, pregnancy issues, child abuse and neglect problems, broken home situations, eating disorder complications, and cases of depression and suicide.

School systems have got to come to grip with the fact that they can't have it both ways. Either they hire well and broadly trained *generalist* counselors, assigning them caseloads of no more than 100 students, or they hire an adequate number of specialists to deal with students' personal problems, and leave the all-important educational and career counseling to the same generalist counselors, providing them with reasonable caseloads of no more than 200 students.

Much of the material in this section addresses a variety of college admission issues on both the theoretical and practical level.

# CHAPTER 20

# TO GO OR NOT TO GO

Perhaps a more appropriate title for this chapter might be "To Stay or Not to Stay," considering what's occurring on college campuses these days. As you counsel your students toward higher education, two significant and continuing problems should command your attention: (1) rising attrition (dropout/transfer) rates, especially at public institutions; and (2) some of the students who stay are remaining forever.

"Colleges Begin to Nudge Their Longtime Students," announces the headline—front-page stuff in the September 14, 1994 issue of *The New York Times*; a food-for-thought article that highlights the fact that large numbers of students have discovered how pleasant and inexpensive life can be behind ivy-covered walls, as they put off facing the challenges of the real world by extending their college stay for as long as ten years. According to *Times* reporter Maria Newman, one 23-year-old had just started his sixth year as an undergraduate at the University of Texas at Austin. The young man had not experienced trouble choosing a major; he just loved working for the school newspaper and would often take as few as three courses a semester to ensure years of setting type.

The Texas case is typical of some 55 percent of college students in the country. They're taking more and more time to graduate. And, until recently, nobody cared—except the bill-paying moms and dads, that is. But, increasingly, college officials are getting nervous and are beginning to prod their perennial students, now that enrollments are on the upswing after years of decline.

According to the National Center for Education Statistics, which began tracking college graduation rates in 1977, less than one-third of the college class of 1990 had earned undergraduate degrees within four years. The *Times* article quotes Texas University president Dr. Robert Berdahl as saying, "Because we're so inexpensive, there is no penalty for students staying in school longer." Berdahl undoubtedly speaks the truth. $9000 for everything at the University of Alabama, where only 23 percent graduate in four years, and the same dollar amount at the University of Minnesota where the rate is 28 percent, can translate into cheap beds and grub for those who survive the freshman year and want to stretch out the collegiate experience. Harvard, like a good many other private schools, doesn't seem to have the problem, what with its comprehensive cost of $32,000: 95 percent of the students graduate within five years. Could it be that parents of Harvard students blow a louder whistle?

Then there's the reverse problem: how to keep them in college for a year—or, for that matter, even a semester. As school counselors, we're so caught up in examining the admission data of the "privates," such as Bucknell, Reed, Wake Forest, or Dartmouth, that we forget that most of our students attend public institutions, some of whom have pathetic retention rates. Why *are* our young people dropping out or transferring in record numbers? The following nine reasons can serve as a centerpiece for small- or large-group discussion. You and your counselees can undoubtedly add a few more.

### REASONS WHY FRESHMEN DON'T RETURN FOR THEIR SOPHOMORE YEAR

1. Academically too competitive. Removes self from scene.
2. Coursework not difficult; student has all of the materials, but isn't ready to "put up the building." Result: Drops out entirely, or transfers back home to a community college.
3. Unhappiness with social situation.
4. School doesn't offer new-found major.
5. Experiences financial difficulties.
6. School too large or too small, or too impersonal or too intimate.
7. Locale is too citified or too rural.
8. Campus is too far away, or too close to home.
9. Flunks out.

## ONCE ON CAMPUS

Who really wants to be among the 25 percent or so who don't return for the sophomore year? Probably very few, if any. So here's a handout (see Figure 20-1) you can give to your counselees, some good advice to help them hit the ground running on their first day—running toward success, not failure.

FIGURE 20-1

## Surviving 'Til Thanksgiving—Or Later

1. **Time management.** Learning to manage your time well is tip number 1. It's also the number 1 toughest challenge of college. Nobody is going to be on campus to set a schedule for you, unless you have a mother like World War II general Douglas MacArthur. (So that she could keep an eye on her son, MacArthur's mother took a hotel room overlooking the West Point campus.) A solid *eight-hour workday* of classtime and study is what you need to shoot for. Get used to using small blocks of time for studying, like the time between classes or any time you're standing in line. (Always carry something to work on.) Large blocks of time can lead to goofing off. Planning is important, but don't over-schedule yourself, either.

2. **Writing well.** Being able to present an informed opinion about an issue *on paper* is an important life skill. Reading and writing and college are synonymous terms. Students who do not write well are at a distinct disadvantage in college. Besides the plethora of papers you will have to write, many college examinations are in essay format. Vocabulary and reading also go hand in hand. The best writers are usually the best readers.

3. **Understanding versus memory.** Never mind the rote or the regurgitation—strive for understanding. Besides, it's easier and more satisfying to comprehend something than to repeat it by rote. Spend most of your study time trying to make sense of a given topic rather than trying to commit it to memory. Any information you need to remember can be crammed into your *short-term memory* just prior to an examination.

4. **Selecting friends.** As you hit the ground running, avoid the negabobs and the whiners like the plague. Seek out positive people, the upbeats—those who intend to make the most of the collegiate experience.

5. **It pays to show up!** Attend all lectures and, whatever you do, don't sit in the back of the room. Quizzes and tests in college are usually based on an assigned textbook *and* the professor's lecture notes. Also, remember the maxim: "Better late than never." Go to class even if you know you're going to be late. If you cut a class, *never* ask the professor, "Did I miss anything?"

6. **Reworking, not rereading.** Rereading lecture notes and/or underlined textbook passages can be a waste of valuable time. *Reworking* your notes is the name of the game. Paraphrasing, reorganizing, outlining, and summarizing are techniques you should employ. All of this is aimed at greater understanding. Watch the abbreviations you use in taking notes—days later, you might not remember what was intended.

7. **Computer literacy.** By all means, snuggle up to a personal computer. You'll need to be proficient at word processing, data base, and spreadsheet programs. If you're not self-taught, take a computer applications course in high school. Some high schools even require a certain amount of computer literacy for graduation.

8. **Those first few weeks.** Get ready for a rough first few weeks. Be patient with yourself, though, and know that things *will* mellow out—usually by Thanksgiving.

9. **The beginning and the end.** Remember that the beginning and the end are the most important aspects of anything: the opening and closing of a piece of writing, a speech, a book, etc. Don't slack off at the beginning of a semester and then try to do catch-up at the end. Get yourself involved from day one, then stay strong throughout the semester.

10. **Self-awareness.** Never lose sight of what *you* most enjoy doing. It can be a flashing signal to an eventual major. A college campus can be a great place for you to *continue* to learn about yourself. Take the time to listen!

What we have not addressed thus far is the title of the chapter. Some critics believe there are too many people in college these days. What these same critics might be alluding to is that there are too many people in unsuitable majors: for example, majors selected with little or no thought given to potential employability. Such students are sometimes viewed by the public as education wasters. Other critics believe there are not enough students in college. Where lies the truth? For wherein it lies can impact on the school counselor's efforts to do a thorough and competent job of advisement at the secondary level.

A 1993 Cornell University study, "The Worsening Shortage of College Graduate Workers," which draws from U.S. Department of Labor data to assess future employment trends, would have you believe that the picture is nothing but rosy for any youngster thinking of attending college. The Cornell study indicates that between 1992 and the year 2000, America will need to add nearly a half million college graduates yearly to its work force. The Cornell report not only encourages college admission, but *completion* as well.

Since World War II, going to college has been "the thing to do" in America. No matter what anyone believes, the right to this rite will be with us for some time to come. Since so many of our students will be attending, perhaps we need to do a better job of ensuring that once matriculated, they successfully complete their program of studies.

One way in which we can better assist is to encourage our young people to ask questions that can really make a difference once he or she arrives on campus: questions related to program quality; questions that can truly distinguish colleges on the basis of educational philosophy, teaching styles, and learning styles. Questions such as:

- Is there a special approach to learning that permeates much of the coursework at this particular institution?

- How do the goals of this institution relate to my development as a student?

- In what ways does this school expect me to be different by the time I graduate?

- How will my progress be measured? How often will I receive an evaluation of my progress? What role, if any, will I play in the evaluation process?

- Does the location of the institution influence the curriculum? If so, how?

- Does the size of the institution influence the curriculum? If so, how?

- If I start to lose direction (class cutting, poor performance, etc.), will anyone notice, *and* will they let me know that they've noticed?

These questions presuppose that the candidate has some knowledge of him- or herself and sees the collegiate experience as an educational process in which he or she is involved. Unfortunately, too many of our students are simply "going to college." Quite frankly, counselors cannot and do not spend enough time helping families explore college selection characteristics that are more substantive in nature. Families need to raise questions that range from the sublime to the inconsequential, and as counselors we need to influence families to focus less on the superficial.

Arranging questions categorically can be helpful in your work with individual counselees or families. Such categorizing can afford everyone involved a better sense of the selection process with all of its nuances and complications.

### General "Feel of the College" Questions

1. What is the history of the college or university? Is its history important to the college's overall philosophy and objectives?
2. How old is the school? Is it liberal, conservative, or middle-of-the-road in its political and social outlook? What is the mix of the student body in regard to this same question?
3. Where does the student body come from? To what extent, if any, is there racial, ethnic, religious, and geographic diversity?
4. What is the general campus atmosphere? Heavily intellectual? Normally intellectual? Collegiate? Nonconformist? Pseudo intellectual? Socially concerned? Experimental?
5. What weaknesses does the college or university admit to?

### "Life on Campus" Questions

6. What are the facilities for worship on campus? Off campus? What are the campus religious organizations?
7. Fraternities? Sororities? What percentage of the student body joins? How does this percentage relate to my social adjustment on the campus? What are living arrangements like? Are meals served in the fraternity/sorority houses?
8. How extensive are the health facilities? Who comprises the permanent medical staff? Is there a medical and/or dental plan for students?
9. Are there any hidden costs? If I do not qualify for financial aid, are there still jobs available on campus or in the community? What is the pay scale?
10. Are there academic support services available? If so, what are they? Are there support organizations for particular ethnic or racial groups? If so, which ones, and are they located on campus?

### "Educational" Questions

11. What are the honorary and professional societies?
12. What percentage of seniors directly enter graduate school? Does the school have a job placement office? How and where are graduates employed? What is the placement record of the graduates of the school's various departments?
13. Can an entering student change from one department or school to another without a lot of hassle? If not, what does it take to do so? How extensive and intimate is the freshman advisement program?
14. Will it be relatively easy to get into the courses of my choice? What is the largest freshman class? If the school is a consortium member, is inter-campus transportation available so that I can readily take coursework on other campuses?

### *"Physical" Questions*

15. How about the library? What is it like? What are the hours? What do the physical arrangements for quiet study look like? Is there an escort service for late-studying females?

16. What is the physical condition of the dormitories? What percentage of the students live in them? What are my housing options? Must all freshmen live in a dormitory? Is housing guaranteed for all four years? Dorm regulations? Dorm and campus security?

17. What are the dining facilities like? Quality of food? Are there eating clubs? Must freshmen enroll in a dining plan? Is there more than one dining plan? Accommodations for special diets, such as kosher or vegetarian?

18. Do campus facilities live up to the pictures in the view book?

Of course, loading families with questions and then leaving them stranded with little or no assistance to interpret possible answers should be avoided at all costs. All too many students and parents do not know how to *interpret* the answers to the questions they are told to consider asking. They need help in *understanding the implications of the different kinds of responses they receive*; responses that, once properly interpreted, can go a long way toward informing them about the commitment, character, and culture of a given institution.

Helping your families to interpret responses will demand a large commitment of time and energy on your part, especially when you consider the unique qualities of each of your counselees. On the other hand, a counseling department can take the 18 questions above and design a single workshop or series of student/parent workshops that are devoted to the elaboration and interpretation of each of the issues.

For example, with question #12 you might highlight the fact that if graduate school attendance is "in the cards," families might want to check out what graduate schools the college's graduates typically attend. Many collegiate institutions now track their graduates and even publish informative brochures on graduate-school attendance. Also, college admission officers in their presentations at times, give secondary students inflated ideas about the specific occupational utility of a particular major. Unfortunately, with certain colleges there continues to be little or no communication between admission people and the college placement office's personnel. It might become necessary for families to dig for substantive information as to the potential employability of a particular major. Similarly, they need to explore the intrinsic, social, personal, and professional advantages of acquiring a college degree.

As for question #13, you could expand on the fact that secondary students change a great deal during high school, and the chances are that the same thing will happen in college. Therefore, students should find a college or university that will *let* them change. One of the most important qualities to look for in a "marketplace" is flexibility. For example, switching one's major should not become a test of courage or endurance. Possibilities should exist for double majoring, creating one's own major, or pursuing a strong minor. A school should stand ready to respond positively to any early indecision and/or confusion on the part of your counselee. The freshman year in particular should be a year of exploration.

There you have it! These are just two examples of how you as a professional can expand upon any of the 18 questions. Families need to be shown the way. Again, they need help in understanding the implications of the different kinds of responses they receive to questions they pose.

# CHAPTER 21

# COLLEGE SELECTION DECISION-MAKING MODEL

Each year, thousands of freshmen wake up in their dormitories only to realize that they have matriculated at a school that is either too pastoral or too citified, too conservative or too liberal, too big or too small, too tough or too easy. It is a genuine dilemma, which is often solved by transferring schools—or dropping out altogether. In spite of advances in education regarding decision-making, many students continue to have little or no experience in making important decisions such as "Where do I matriculate for four years?" (See Chapter 12 on self-awareness.)

High school seniors must come to grips with the fact that selecting a place at which to spend their next four years is a *decision* that calls for a great deal of self-analysis. Deep inside, most students know that the less they know about themselves, the more difficult the selection process is going to be. No matter what their plans, it is critical that your counselees know who they are, and college choice can precipitate such awareness.

A workable decision-making model can help your students arrive at a *best possible solution* when faced with resolving substantive issues. You can employ the model on an individual or group basis. Our introductory example of purchasing an automobile will give you an idea of how the model works.

Note: As you work through the model, you will first need to make certain that your decision-making statement includes an object, an action term, and a descriptor. Your first step will be to develop a decision-making statement.

169

# STEP 1. DECISION-MAKING STATEMENT

| | | |
|---|---|---|
| Example #1: | Statement: | To purchase a new car. |
| | Object: | Car |
| | Action Term: | Purchase |
| | Descriptor: | New |
| Example #2: | Statement: | To select seven colleges and/or universities to which to apply. |
| | Object: | College/University |
| | Action Term: | Select |
| | Descriptor: | Seven |

# STEP 2. ESTABLISH OBJECTIVES

As you establish your objectives, ask yourself: "What do I want this decision to do for me?" Your objectives should be concrete and placed in writing. It is most important that you establish your objectives *before* you come up with a set of alternatives. In the process of establishing objectives, there are three aspects you will want to keep in the back of your mind:

1. Results
2. Materials and Resources
3. Limitations

Examples of those aspects as they pertain to objectives of college selection are:

1. *Results:* Coed school: What would happen if I were to live in a coed dormitory?
2. *Materials and resources:* finances, time, and space. How much money does my family have available? What is my general time frame within the application process? How much space will I need once on campus?
3. *Limitations:* Are there any built-in restrictions? Is chapel attendance required? Are there any curfews? What are the school's specific rules and regulations? Are there separate bathrooms for men and women in coed dormitories?

CAR EXAMPLE:

The purchaser of the car established the following objectives:

Budget restriction of $15,000
Should be reliable, trouble free
Servicing department within 15 miles from home
Adequate trunk space to carry my sales materials

Car should get good mileage, e.g., 20 miles around town

At least a five-passenger vehicle

Should have a good safety record

Should be fun to drive

Should have airbags for both driver and front-seat passenger

Tape deck and air conditioning

Automatic door locks for security and ease of operation

**COLLEGE EXAMPLE:**

The college applicant established the following objectives:

Should be a coeducational institution

Comprehensive school, not a specialized one

Needs to be small (500 to 5000) or medium (6000 to 15,000)

Near (not more than 1 hour away) a medium- or large-sized city

Have a strong biology department

Have a men's soccer team—Division II, III

Total cost not to exceed $27,000

Should be situated on at least 100 acres

Located in Middle Atlantic or New England region

Have coed dormitories

Be fully accredited

Library open on weekends

At least 60% of students remain on campus on weekends

At least 20% of students are Catholic

Have smoke-free buildings and dormitories

# STEP 3.  CLASSIFY ALL OBJECTIVES

Your next move is to classify objectives as to "definites" and "hopes." "Definites" (D) are mandatory. They should be *measurable*; they also need to be *realistic*. "Hopes" (H) are wish-list items. They would be nice to have, but you could live without them. Place a D or H in front of each objective; for example:

D    Comprehensive school as opposed to a specialized one

D    Have a strong biology department

H    Have coed dorms

D    At least 60% of students remain on campus on weekends

# STEP 4. GENERATE ALTERNATIVES

You are now at the point where you can begin to generate alternatives. Compile a list of colleges and universities that contain all of the "definites" and at least a few of the "hopes." Below is a brief sample list of schools that pertain to the student's search for a "strong aerospace engineering department."

### Schools with Twenty or More Aerospace Graduates in a Given Year

| Arizona, U. of | AZ | 47 | Florida, U. of | FL | 48 |
|---|---|---|---|---|---|
| Boston U. | MA | 41 | Notre Dame, U. of | IN | 56 |
| Colorado, U. of | CO | 111 | Rensselaer | NY | 39 |

Source: *Comparative Guide to American Colleges* (Sixteenth Edition), New York: HarperCollins, 1994.

*Rugg's Recommendations on the Colleges* would be another source. But keep in mind that the above data can also be uncovered through the school itself.

# STEP 5. ADVERSE CONSEQUENCES

We now come to the final step: the "if I do this, then this might happen" type of thinking. If I do "X," then "Y" might happen. In short, what could go wrong? Always keep in mind that you are a *one-of-a-kind person*. There is no one else quite like you in the world, unless you believe in absolute doubles. Therefore, what could be important to you might not be so important to someone else. *You* are the one who will be attending the particular college. As you examine for any adverse consequences with your listed "definites" and "hopes," you might discover that:

- University of Arizona is so far west that I would have trouble getting home on occasion. Besides, dry weather bothers me.

- Rensselaer is not a comprehensive enough school.

List all adverse consequences, then assess for two factors: (1) the probability of occurrence, and (2) the seriousness of the issue. Use the symbols H (High), M (Medium), L (Low) as you conduct your assessment. *You* are the one who determines the weight assigned.

### Adverse Consequences Form

| Consequence: | Probability: | Seriousness: |
|---|---|---|
| *Arizona—too far* | *H* | *M* |
| *Arizona—too dry* | *M* | *L* |
| *Rensselaer—too restricted as to curriculum* | *H* | *M* |

There's nothing like a little quiet self-analysis. Once your counselees understand themselves better, they will be able to make those worthwhile decisions. Some formal activities can be a monumental waste of time; others can be productive exercises. This decision-making model helps promote self-exploration.

## A NOTE ABOUT COMPUTERIZED SEARCHES

Much of what we have just spoken about pertains to computerized searches, as well. Before students engage in any kind of computerized search, however, two things should have been accomplished: (1) they should know themselves well as the result of self-assessment activity, and (2) they should have made tentative decisions on typical selection characteristics based on their knowledge of themselves. Discovery activity can take place by an individual or group working through a decision-making model.

# CHAPTER 22

# CONSTRUCTING A SIX-RUNG SELECTIVITY LADDER

Colleges and universities come in all shapes and sizes. They are far more diverse in structure and curriculum than public schools—even more diverse than parochial, independent, and public schools combined. Their competitiveness of admission can range from the mind-boggling selectivity of Harvard, Stanford, and Yale, which take some 17 percent of their applicants, to open admissions institutions, which will accept almost anyone.

Since the late 1980s, staying current with the college admission selectivity picture has been a bit of a nightmare for the school counselor. The situation has been anything but stable with the continuing decline in the adolescent population. A good number of private institutions in America are now "hurting" for students. At the same time, many of the public colleges and universities have been riding an unparalleled wave of popularity, with admission standards slowly increasing. But things will begin to turn around in 1997; the applicant pool is expected to increase by 150,000 applicants per year, with some one million more candidates applying to college by the year 2005.

When the topic of college selection arises, counselors sometimes find themselves dealing with "difficult" parents: the negative ("She'll never get in anywhere with grades like that."), or the unrealistic who won't heed professional advice, and who discover in April that they had reached too high. Deep-breathing counselors continually remind parents that, "Yes, she'll get in somewhere with her grades as they are," or for the unrealistic, "It is *imperative* that we include some safety schools."

What can be done? The chief objective for the family's engagement is empowerment; it *is* important that school counselors help families feel in control of the choices they make. Consequently, the *entire* family should be active participants in a structured process of college selection, which might begin with the construction of a six-rung selectivity ladder, a great approach for getting your families off the ground. It's one way to orient them on selectivity, a fine way to handle negativism or excessive optimism, and a wonderful way of ensuring that you'll get some sleep at night.

Not all admission decisions are rendered solely on the basis of grade point average, class rank, and SAT/ACT scores—not by a long shot! But families have to start somewhere, and "roughing-in" selectivity levels by making academic profile comparisons using raw data is an excellent *beginning point.* It can open your families' eyes to what selectivity levels are all about. Adjustment for quality of coursework and the high school attended can be factored in early as you construct the ladder.

## SELECTIVITY LEVEL ADJUSTMENTS

Once the ladder is constructed, you can really earn your stripes by advising a family on what is known as "selectivity level adjustments." Published guides and various writers like to call this phenomenon "hooks," a characteristic of an applicant that makes the application stand out. Such adjustments—or hooks—fall into four general categories: (1) parentage (legacy), (2) race and ethnicity, (3) adjustment for nonacademic factors, especially athletics, and (4) adjustment for achievement (SAT II) scores. The first three categories are often referred to as "special admissions." Debate over the fairness of hooks rages on, and will probably never cease. It is important for you to realize that challenges to the system are rarely won, and that you need to work with the system as best you can in the name of your *individual* counselees. College admission folk have always been rather tightlipped as to how they select their candidates. "Diverse" is the word most often heard.

Figure 22-1 shows a sample ladder.

Let's fill in the ladder. (See Figure 22-2.) Take Lisa as an example: we combine her SAT scores of 540 verbal and 610 math into a total of 1150. Her GPA is 3.70. This data is then placed on the *Target* rung of the ladder. Notice that we have designed a target zone as well: 50 points on either side of her 1150 SAT, and 0.2 on either side of her 3.70 GPA.

The next step is for Lisa to place her selected colleges and universities on the proper rungs. Before she can accomplish this task, she must understand "reach" and "safety." (Plus [+] symbols signify "more difficult yet.") Before this understanding can occur, however, she needs to understand the "target" concept. A target school is one where her profile is *similar* to the average (mean) profile of freshmen at a particular institution. Where there is a match, that school would be considered a target. "Similar" is defined as being within 50 points, higher and lower, of the combined SAT, and within two-tenths (0.2) of a percent on the GPA. For example, the average Drew freshman has *about* a 1150 combined SAT score, and *about* a 3.50 GPA. Lisa has a 1150 and a 3.70. Drew would then be considered a target

FIGURE **22-1**

## SIX-RUNG SELECTIVITY LADDER

| Code | | GPA | Odds |
|---|---|---|---|
| R+ | | | 2/10 |
| R | | | 3/10 |
| T+ | | | 5/10 |
| T | | | 6/10 |
| S+ | | | 8/10 |
| S | | | 9/10 |

Distribution:

| | |
|---|---|
| R = Reach | R |
| T = Target | T |
| S = Safety | S |

FIGURE **22-2**

| Code | | | GPA | Odds |
|---|---|---|---|---|
| R+ | 1300 | | | 2/10 |
| R | 1250 | | 4.10 | 3/10 |
| T+ | 1200 | | 3.90 | 5/10 |
| T | | 1150     3.70 | | 6/10 |
| S+ | 1100 | | 3.50 | 8/10 |
| S | 1050 | | 3.30 | 9/10 |

school for her. You and your students can extract the necessary statistics from any quality guidebook. Let's look up the "average" recentered SATs and GPAs for a sample of schools:

| | | |
|---|---|---|
| *Dartmouth* | *1380* | *3.90* |
| *Wm & Mary* | *1270 (out of state)* | *3.75* |
| *U. of Maryland* | *1050* | *3.0* |

| | | |
|---|---|---|
| *Vassar* | *1225* | *3.75* |
| *Lafayette* | *1210* | *3.70* |
| *Drew* | *1150* | *3.50* |

Now place them on the ladder, as shown in Figure 22-3.

FIGURE 22-3

| Code | | | GPA | Odds |
|---|---|---|---|---|
| R+ | | *Dartmouth* | | 2/10 |
| R | 1250 | *Wm & Mary* | | 3/10 |
| T+ | 1200 | *Vassar* | 3.90 | 5/10 |
| T | *Drew* | *1150* | *3.70* | 6/10 |
| S+ | 1100 | | 3.50 | 8/10 |
| S | 1050 | *U. of Maryland* | | 9/10 |

Even though admission to the so-called top 100 schools still remains a crap shoot, we nonetheless believe that Vassar will be an easier nut to crack than William & Mary for Lisa, and that Dartmouth will be a greater struggle than William & Mary. Drew University, as good a school as it is, is nonetheless a clear target with its 1150 mean SATs and 3.50 GPA. Incidentally, the kids love the odds routine; e.g., Dartmouth is a 2 out of 10 or a 20% shot.

It's probably best to play things conservatively. That way if your counselee gets admitted, it'll be all the more pleasurable an experience. She'll think that she's wonderful, and that you're a little bit wonderful.

Again, the ladder can be a fine method to demonstrate selectivity levels. Keep reminding your families that it is a *rough* analysis, and that you don't walk on water. But do keep returning to the ladder, especially when overly-anxious parents fret over their pride and joy becoming admitted, or when the negative remark, "she'll never get in anywhere" falls on your ears.

We have used this structured process repeatedly, and have found that if students do their homework correctly by distributing their selections over the ladder in a *reasonable* fashion, they will get into at least half of the schools to which they apply. Several years of tracking indicate that senior class acceptances tend to mirror the ladder odds—that is, 30% of students get into one or more of their reaches; 60% get into one or more of their targets; and 90% get into one or more of their safeties. The 9 out of 10 odds is as good as it gets. You never tell them that they'll walk through the door.

## SELECTION WORKSHEET

The worksheet shown in Figure 22-4 is a worthwhile piece that enables your counselees to record certain personal data and their tentative selections. It's an excellent device for tracking the number of reach, target, and safety schools.

## SOME PROBLEMS WITH THE SYSTEM

Arriving at reasonable reaches, or reach pluses, can be problematic. Although you don't ever want the words "never get in" to leave your lips, you nonetheless have the responsibility of alerting your counselees to their admission chances. Try, "You might want to consider not applying," or perhaps the more lofty phrase, "Do you think you have sufficient aptitude to be successful in such an intense academic environment?" If none of that works, let them apply. For, after all, it's their prerogative. Just make sure the rest of the ladder makes sense. *Whatever you do, don't take it personally.*

Uncovering a sufficient number of target schools can also be problematic for the many students who either overestimate or underestimate themselves. Some counselors consider target selection as a "realistic stretching" (nice term) maneuver: there's a 60 percent chance of acceptance, yet 40 percent chance of rejection. You'll find that most of your students will agree that 6 out of 10 is a good shot.

## YOU AS THE LEADER

Who better to do all of this than you? You're the best friend students and their parents can have in the junior and senior years. As a knowledgeable professional, you: (1) comprehend and appreciate a good many strengths and weaknesses of your students, (2) are familiar with the little subtleties of the admission process, and (3) can articulate the differences among collegiate institutions. A school counselor can use these capabilities to help the family feel even more in control of the choices they are making. Again, the more experienced the counselor, the easier and more accurate the task of constructing a six-rung selectivity ladder.

# COLLEGE SELECTION WORKSHEET

| NAME | Lisa Maier | JR. SAT: V 540 M 610 |
|---|---|---|
| ADDRESS: | 253 South Main Street Abbingdale, NJ 08520 | CLASS RANK: top 10% |
| TELEPHONE: | 609-443-1299 | GPA: 3.70 |

| RECOMMENDED SCHOOLS | SELECTIVITY CODE | PUBLIC/ PRIVATE | NOTES |
|---|---|---|---|
| Dartmouth College, New Hampshire | R+ | Private | |
| Johns Hopkins, Maryland | R+ | Private | |
| College of William and Mary, Virginia | R | Public | 2 |
| Davidson College, North Carolina | T+ | Private | |
| Fairfield University, Connecticut | T+ | Private | 2 |
| Vassar College, New York | T+ | Private | |
| Colby College, Maine | T+ | Private | |
| James Madison U., Virginia | T | Public | 1, 2 |
| Skidmore College, New York | T | Private | |
| Lafayette College, Pennsylvania | T+ | Private | |
| Kutztown University, Pennsylvania | T | Public | |
| Clark University, Massachusetts | S+ | Private | |
| Drew University, New Jersey | T | Private | |
| State U. of New York, New Paltz | S | Public | |
| U. of North Carolina, Greensboro | S+ | Public | 1, 2 |
| Hartwick College, New York | S | Private | |
| U. of Maryland | S | Public | |

| | *CODE: | ODDS: |
|---|---|---|
| | R = Reach | 3/10 |
| | T = Target | 6/10 |
| | S = Safety | 9/10 |
| | + = More difficult yet | |

**Notes:**

All schools listed have German and women's soccer.
1. Denotes Elementary Education
2. Denotes Division I women's soccer

# CHAPTER 23

# LOOKING BEYOND THE "NAMES"

Whether with their families or on a teen tour, teenagers are "on the road again" in increasing numbers; they are traveling more than ever before. Although currently the typical student in America attends college four hours from his or her home, that mean figure might well increase in the next decade, as youngsters come to realize that things aren't so bad west of the Alleghenies or east of the Mississippi. Even the 98 percent in-state figure for Texas is vulnerable.

Furthermore, as the press states and high school counselors confirm, American families are more caught up with the "name" schools than ever before. There's no disputing the fact that the so-called top 100 are on a roll. Applications to the names have been soaring. For that reason, you and your counselees will want to look at some colleges with which you may not be familiar.

The students' quest for a "name" school is reason enough for the counselor to search farther geographically for colleges and universities of quality and substance. Many interesting schools, worthwhile institutions, have not been getting the play they deserve, though. They remain buried in the pages of the standard guide books. And so we've uncovered some 100 schools outside of Barron's listing of the 40 "most" and 60 "highly competitive" institutions, and we've listed them for your examination.

Even though consideration of overall academic strength was the highest priority in our selection process, we paid considerable attention to location and setting, as well as to the attractiveness of the campus. So often students and parents exclaim, "We want a college that looks like a college." Location and setting can affect campus environment, social and cultural opportunities, and the availability of practical work experiences.

Incidentally, *don't* miss reading Loren Pope's book, *Looking Beyond the Ivy League*, published by Penguin (1990). The back cover states "A first-class education isn't always wrapped in an ivy package."

# SCHOOLS WELL WORTH CONSIDERING

*ALABAMA*

Auburn University
Birmingham Southern College
Spring Hill College

*CALIFORNIA*

Mills College
Occidental College
Pepperdine University
University of Redlands
University of the Pacific
Whittier College

*COLORADO*

University of Colorado at Boulder

*CONNECTICUT*

University of Hartford

*DISTRICT OF COLUMBIA*

American University

*FLORIDA*

Rollins College
Stetson University

*GEORGIA*

Berry College
Ogelthorpe University

*ILLINOIS*

Knox College
Lake Forest College
Wheaton College

*INDIANA*

De Pauw University
Earlham College
Hanover College
Indiana University at Bloomington
Valparaiso University

*IOWA*

Coe College
Cornell College
Luther College

*KENTUCKY*

Centre College

*MAINE*

University of Maine at Orono

*MARYLAND*

Goucher College

Washington College

Western Maryland College

*MASSACHUSETTS*

Clark University

Curry College

Simmons College

*MICHIGAN*

Albion College

Alma College

Calvin College

Hope College

Oakland University

*MINNESOTA*

St. Olaf College

*MISSISSIPPI*

Millsaps College

*NEW HAMPSHIRE*

Franklin Pierce College

Keene State College

St. Anselm College

*NEW JERSEY*

Drew University

Rowan College of New Jersey

Stockton State College

*NEW YORK*

Bard College

Hartwick College

Hobart and William Smith Colleges

Marist College

Rochester Institute of Technology

St. Bonaventure University

St. Lawrence University

Skidmore College

*NORTH CAROLINA*

Campbell University

Elon College

Guilford College

Johnson C. Smith University

St. Andrews Presbyterian College

University of North Carolina at Greensboro

*OHIO*

Baldwin-Wallace College

Denison University

Marietta College

Ohio Wesleyan University

Wittenberg University

*OREGON*

Linfield College

Willamette University

*PENNSYLVANIA*

Allegheny

Cedar Crest College

Elizabethtown College

King's College

Muhlenberg College

Susquehanna University

University of Scranton

Ursinus College

*RHODE ISLAND*

Bryant College
Providence College
University of Rhode Island

*SOUTH CAROLINA*

Clemson University
Furman University

*TENNESSEE*

Rhodes College

*TEXAS*

Baylor University
Southern Methodist University
Texas Christian University
Trinity University

*VERMONT*

St. Michael's College

*VIRGINIA*

Hollins College
James Madison University
Lynchburg College
University of Richmond

*WASHINGTON*

Evergreen State University
Pacific Lutheran University

*WISCONSIN*

Beloit College
Lawrence University
Marquette University
Ripon College

# CHAPTER 24

# COUNSELING TOWARD THE PUBLIC COLLEGES AND UNIVERSITIES

In his book, *The Public Ivys*, author Richard Moll comments on the virtues of two dozen or so public colleges and universities, and compliments the school counselor: "Who is in the best position to evaluate colleges? In my view, high school guidance counselors and college advisors are uniquely suited to do so. With a minimum of personal bias (that is compared to parents, teenagers, friends, college admission officers, alumni, and faculty), they keep up with and interpret individual institutions' offerings, strengths, and weaknesses. . . ."

There probably isn't a counselor in the nation who doesn't recognize the ever-increasing problem of keeping up with an ever-changing college admission picture. We made that statement in 1987, and we're still dealing with it. Even Moll's 1985 "public ivys" have changed. Some have withered a little, some have grown and flourished—and some are no longer the financial bargain the author touted them to be, especially for out-of-state candidates.

Public school tuition is up 70% in the past decade and is slowly catching up with the private sector. States like Michigan and Vermont are really socking it to students who cross their borders, with total annual higher education costs that exceed $20,000. And that's before personal expenses. On the other hand, some of the best financial buys continue to be the two Virginia schools, William & Mary and the University of Virginia; the University of Illinois; and certain SUNY schools.

There has been a virtual stampede toward public institutions since the early 1990s, in part because of economic conditions. Your counselee can receive a first-rate education at many of these schools. However, he or she needs to select carefully.

## 14 STATE UNIVERSITIES WITH HIGH ACADEMIC STANDARDS

California, University of, at Berkeley

California, University of, at Los Angeles

College of William & Mary

Colorado, University of

Illinois, University of

Miami University of Ohio

Michigan, University of

North Carolina, University of, at Chapel Hill

Pennsylvania State University

Rutgers the State University, New Jersey

State University of New York at Binghamton

Texas, University of

Virginia, University of

Wisconsin, University of

With some applicants, a significant consideration in the selection process is the quality of a particular department in which the student wishes to enroll. Even less selective schools can have extraordinary departments—University of Maryland, for instance, has a nationally ranked engineering department.

Another consideration that applicants should be especially concerned about for public institutions is the retention and graduation rates of the student body. The majority of secondary school students attend public colleges and universities, yet one-third or more of them are not graduating from many of these schools. Why? Undoubtedly multiple factors come into play here. Could there be a correlation between the academic reputation of an institution and retention and graduation rates of that same institution? Probably. How about between the intellectual quality of the student body and those rates? Probably.

You might want to study the freshman retention and four- and five-year graduation rates displayed in Figure 24-1 and explore them with your students. If nothing else, it should further sensitize you to this important college-selection consideration. We took Richard Moll's selections and researched them for cost, dropout, and graduation figures. Cost figures are for out-of-state students.

FIGURE 24-1

| THE PUBLIC IVYS | Total Cost | Freshman Dropout Rate | 4-year Graduation Rate | 5-year Graduation Rate |
|---|---|---|---|---|
| . . . . . . . . . . . . . . . . . . . . . . . . . . . . . . . | $ | % | % | % |
| University of California . . . . . . . . . . . . . . . . | | | | |
| at Berkeley . . . . . . . . . . . . . . . . . . . . . . . . | 17,500 | 11 | 29 | 76 |
| at Davis . . . . . . . . . . . . . . . . . . . . . . . . . | 17,000 | 7 | 27 | 67 |
| at Irvine . . . . . . . . . . . . . . . . . . . . . . . . . | 17,000 | — | — | — |
| at Los Angeles . . . . . . . . . . . . . . . . . . . . | 18,000 | 6 | — | 69 |
| at Riverside. . . . . . . . . . . . . . . . . . . . . . . | 18,000 | 10 | 42 | 58 |
| at San Diego. . . . . . . . . . . . . . . . . . . . . . . | 18,500 | 9 | — | — |
| at Santa Barbara . . . . . . . . . . . . . . . . . . . | 18,000 | 12 | 36 | 63 |
| at Santa Cruz . . . . . . . . . . . . . . . . . . . . . . | 17,500 | 12 | 25 | 68 |
| Miami University of Ohio. . . . . . . . . . . . . . . . | 17,000 | 5 | 70 | 81 |
| University of Michigan at Ann Arbor . . . . . . . . | 25,000 | 4 | 63 | 82 |
| University of North Carolina at Chapel Hill . . . . | 17,500 | 5 | 55 | 68 |
| University of Texas at Austin . . . . . . . . . . . . . | 12,000 | 15 | 35 | 56 |
| University of Vermont at Burlington . . . . . . . . . | 24,000 | 16 | 59 | 74 |
| University of Virginia at Charlottesville. . . . . . . | 20,000 | 4 | 77 | 90 |
| William and Mary College of Virginia . . . . . . . . | 20,000 | 7 | 77 | 89 |

| THE BEST OF THE REST | | | | |
|---|---|---|---|---|
| University of Colorado at Boulder. . . . . . . . . . . | 18,500 | — | 36 | 58 |
| Georgia Institute of Technology at Atlanta . . . . . | 15,000 | 14 | 16 | 67 |
| University of Illinois at Urbana/Champaign. . . . . | 15,500 | 5 | 52 | 78 |
| New College of the University of South Florida. . | 15,000 | 20 | — | — |
| Pennsylvania State University at University Park . | 18,000 | 16 | 34 | 59 |
| University of Pittsburgh . . . . . . . . . . . . . . . . . | 18,000 | 14 | 36 | 57 |
| State University of New York at Binghamton. . . . | 17,000 | 10 | 70 | — |
| University of Washington at Seattle. . . . . . . . . . | 16,000 | 10 | — | — |
| University of Wisconsin at Madison. . . . . . . . . . | 15,500 | 9 | 33 | 77 |

Sources:   *The Public Ivys*, Richard Moll, Viking Penguin Inc., New York, 1985
*Lovejoy's College Guide* (22nd edition), Prentice Hall, New York
National Collegiate Athletic Association (NCAA) 1994 Graduation-Rates
Report
Note:   — indicates that the school did not report statistics

## *Enrollment Size as a Factor*

Size of enrollment is, of course, a characteristic of a college or university. Most of the public colleges and universities range from medium (6,000 to 15,000) to large (16,000 to 25,000), to extra large (26,000 to 45,000). Students need to understand that the size of any student body can be a critical factor in the success of one's personal adjustment. There *is* a considerable difference in being in a school of 2,000 students and being in one of 40,000.

Your counselee should not believe all the clichés he or she hears about the size of a school. Contrary to public opinion, close faculty relationships and small classes can be enjoyed at large universities, especially as students move into their major field of study. In addition, public universities do have many redeeming characteristics:

- A public university can be alive, vibrant, and always surprising. There are endless new social contact possibilities.

- The curriculum is one big smorgasbord of course offerings.

- There is usually an extensive cultural affairs program, and every intercollegiate sport imaginable can be found. If you can't make a team, a club or intramural sports program is there waiting for you.

- In some public universities, e.g., the University of Virginia, you can witness a great cross section of students arriving on campus each year from all parts of the country—from all parts of the world. Clemson pulls them in from all over the nation as well.

- Some of these schools pride themselves on the attention they pay to freshmen and to the teaching quality the newcomers receive.

In assessing the suitability of public institutions for your counselees, there are, however, some questions to ponder:

1. The world is shrinking. Some public schools accept very few out-of-state students; states such as North Carolina and Pennsylvania even have established quotas. Other schools have their doors wide open. Are students at an increasing disadvantage in this shrinking world of ours, when they attend schools where most of the students come from the same geographic region?

2. How much consideration should students give to the financial condition of a public university that can be sometimes battered by a slumping economy?

3. Keep 'em in state! But if the state is so broke that it can't offer adequate educational services, won't the kids leave anyway?

4. Is it not cheaper to attend certain private schools? Some public institutions are more costly than some top-flight private schools like Washington & Lee University, Rice, and Davidson College.

5. If some of the public schools spent more time and money shoring up undergraduate programs and improving their support services, would their retention and graduation rates rise?

6. Is there an existing problem with some professors and teaching assistants not being able to speak the English language at more than a few universities?

7. Should the schools with enrollments exceeding 30,000 be "shrinking to excellence," rather than maintaining a "land grant" mentality whereby the door opens to everyone, then quickly closes again on a host of freshmen who can't make it?

8. With the exception of a handful of prestigious schools, including Berkeley, Michigan, and the two Virginia schools, is one public university really better than another? In other words, maybe the deciding factor might be the youngster's desire to see another part of the country or to pursue an unusual major.

# CHAPTER 25

# ADVISING THE STUDENT-ATHLETE

The American ideal: an outstanding athlete with charm, good looks, savoir faire, and intelligence, who is articulate and humble as he or she speaks with eloquence. Or is it an unusually talented student who performs athletically with taste and exceptional skill? Perhaps it's the young man or woman who is not an excellent student or a great orator, but is so good in a particular sport that he or she will be a "pro" someday, rich and famous? Or is it the young person who does not expect to be the "best" athlete or the "best" student, but who wants to pursue both avenues, because he or she loves doing both?

Actually, it's all of the above, and this "ideal" generates yet another goal that has enormous influence on the college- and career-planning process—which is your entrance cue as a school counselor.

Of course, the picture contains some shadows as well. One has only to pick up a magazine or newspaper to understand that there is trouble in the River City of student athletics. College athletes, confused and disillusioned, continue to transfer schools or dropout altogether in substantial numbers. Some who do stay to graduate read only at the grammar school level.

The impact of athletic participation on the personal growth and development of adolescent youth is undoubtedly the most serious, albeit often neglected, challenge for the school counselor. Student-athletes are under enormous pressure, both from within—they want to *be* good and *be seen* to be good—and from without: the colleges, the coaches, parents, peers, alumni. Athletes must do an exceptional balancing act; the sport they love needs time and concentration, but it cannot be pursued at the collegiate level unless sufficient time and concentration are spent on the academic life. Athletes *must* bring the same amount of discipline and energy to the classroom that they bring to their athletic endeavors. Even the "stars" need to fully develop their intellect and ready themselves for life beyond the world of sports.

Athletes receive mixed messages from their dual, often conflicting roles as student and athlete. In his 1984 work, *The Athlete's Game Plan for College and Career*, author Howard Figler refers to it as a double bind. Friends value athletic achievement more than educational achievement; and parents and community praise and cheer on their sons and daughters for whom a team's record becomes a reflection of their parental selves, the school, and the community. In the same breath with which student-athletes are lauded, they're maligned as pampered problem children—a privileged minority.

Athletic involvement has important ramifications that must be understood by counselors who in turn will explore them with their counselees. Counselors need to be knowledgeable about (1) how such involvement can impact on the various stages of identity-formation in a person; (2) personal and societal factors that might foster or retard the student-athlete's psychosocial development; and (3) life after high school for this special population, specifically college *and* world-of-work experiences. These issues can be a great vehicle for the development of identity exploration activities with this targeted group.

For the student-athlete, the glamour and short-term rewards of competition can obviate one's developing an identity *outside* of athletics. This can be serious business, especially when an athlete's star begins to descend, i.e., he or she is no longer a starter, or is simply losing playing time. Serious depression can take hold. At the collegiate level, such depression can translate into dropping out. Any loss of primary role, whether it be scholarship, job, or athletics, can cause a void that must be filled. Unfortunately, all too many athletes have not acquired the background experiences and internal resources to fill the void.

## COUNSELOR INTERVENTION

Even though your intervening on behalf of an athlete can be a complicated endeavor, the situation will become more manageable if you realize that the best path is one of *prevention*, not therapy. In short, your primary role should be that of a preventative mental health specialist. Here you become educator and consultant: you become an educator to students, coaches, and parents as you identify relevant issues, and then create and conduct seminars that address these issues. You are a consultant to students, coaches, and parents through emphasizing the positive role athletics *can* play in the lives of young people, and by working with everyone concerned to develop a healthy system of values that is applicable *while* the youngster is engaged in sports activities, and *after*, in life beyond the playing field.

Because of your teaching skills, knowledge of human development, and expertise in consultation, you're in the perfect position to help students, coaches, and parents. Never forget that coaches play a significant role in the personal and social development of high school athletes. Similarly, in some districts, coaches are no longer teachers who have regular contact with their players during the school day. These coaches, from outside and for hire, often have little or no contact with, or understanding of, their players in any arena other than that of athletics. As models for students, coaches' handling of their own emotions and the manner in which they communicate with their players have a direct bearing on the parallel processes of athletes. Counselors and coaches can work together to intervene and *teach* such things as coping with stress, self-control skills, decision making, responding to failure, assertiveness versus aggressiveness, goal setting, and the resistance of drugs and alcohol. All of these factors are mentioned in an attempt to teach athletes a wide range of social skills, and at the same time, improve individual self-image.

Finally, thought should be given to dropping the hyphen in the name "student-athlete"; the non-hyphenated "student-athlete" might more strongly represent the "student who engages in athletics." While we're sensitive to the amount of time and energy that athletics requires, we feel educators need to redirect their priorities; one method would be to redirect the language.

## ISSUES WORTH EXPLORING

With the athlete, then, you will try to compensate for any lag in the development of other aspects of his or her personality. Here are some provocative issues around which you can construct seminars to properly prepare student athletes for the numerous problems that might confront them at the secondary school and collegiate levels. During their high school career you could work toward:

- Counseling the athlete to keep his or her special talent in perspective. (Athletics should be secondary to academic work.)
- An in-depth exploration of life after the locker room.
- Awareness exercises that relate to the penalties of academic neglect.
- Long-range academic planning of appropriate coursework, and then the fine-tuning that must follow each spring for the ensuing school year.
- Encouraging reluctant counselees toward athletic participation.
- Operating in concert with a coach and parents on college selection so that you, coach, and parents aren't working at cross purposes.

Questions can arise that are directly related to a particular college:

- Even the tough get homesick at times. The transition to college can generate normal feelings of homesickness, but the athlete can be readily caught off-guard. Feelings that might be acceptable to the general student population are not necessarily acceptable to the athlete who has been socialized to "hang tough."
- What does collegiate housing look like for the athlete? Are athletes housed separately? Do they take their meals together? Attend classes and study together? In other words, how far removed from the mainstream will they be? What effect, if any, will all of this have on the athlete's development of self-identity outside the circle of athletics?
- What are the prevailing campus attitudes toward various minorities, ethnic groups, and religious faiths?
- What is the academic reputation of the particular college or university? What are the course requirements of the academic department in which the athlete is interested? What time demands will be placed on the athlete?

# WHAT'S IN IT FOR THE ATHLETE?

- "High school athletes have higher grades and lower dropout rates, and are more likely to attend college than non-athletes."—Women's Sports Foundation Survey

- "Students who do not participate in sports average 2.39 GPA, while those who participate in one sport average 2.61; those active in two sports average 2.82."—Iowa High School Athletic Association

- "Grade point averages of athletes improve the overall GPA picture of the general student population (in-season and out-of-season)."—South Bend (Indiana) Community Schools

- "Ninety-five percent of school principals believe that extra-curricular activity programs contribute to the development of 'school spirit' among the student body."— Indiana University study

- "Eleven percent of the athletes had discipline referrals compared to 25% of the general population. No athletes dropped out of school, while 3.7% of the general population were dropouts."—Randolph County (North Carolina Schools)

- University of Chicago research suggests:

  a. By a 2 to 1 margin for males and a 3 to 1 margin for females, student athletes do better in school, do not drop out, and have a better shot at getting through college.

  b. Student athletes tend to pursue more challenging coursework.

  c. Student athletes' parents are more involved in the educative process.

  d. Student athletes tend to focus more on long-term life accomplishments than short-term goals.

  e. Ninety-two percent of athletes do not use drugs.

  f. Student athletes are more self-assured. Aggression intertwined with teamwork can be extremely beneficial for the future, especially on a woman's corporate career path.

- "Ninety-five percent of *Fortune* 500 executives participated in some form of athletics. Only 47% were National Honor Society members."—Fortune Magazine

# THE RECRUITMENT HEADACHE

Each year millions of secondary school students participate in some sort of organized sports activity. Thousands anticipate competing at the collegiate level. Similarly, more than 2,000 collegiate institutions field teams in an unbelievable number of sports. Since college athletes are engaged in play for a brief period of time, coaches are themselves engaged in a never-ending, year-in-year-out search for promising replacements.

Sounds relatively simple and straightforward, doesn't it? Loads of high schoolers who want to keep "doing their thing," and loads of colleges determined to see to it that they do so—often by offering hefty financial aid packages.

But athletic recruiting is anything but simple! The big problem is the lack of structure that would enable high school athletes and college coaches to mesh their respective needs and interests. More to the point, there is no real mechanism for student athletes to search for openings on college teams, other than the various for-profit exposure services (explained later in this chapter). There's no classified ad program whereby colleges can advertise for quarterbacks or goalies. Rather, it's a hit-or-miss proposition of telephone calls, direct-mail contact, and, occasionally, face-to-face interviews.

All parties, then, scurry around as they carefully pick their way through a complicated minefield of rules and regulations that govern the conduct of coaches, prospective athletes, and parents—yes, even parents. Imagine, if you will, America's *Fortune* 500 companies each year trying to locate prospective employees through word-of-mouth references and little else, and you'll get some idea of athletic recruiting as such an arduous and perplexing process.

# PLAY, DON'T PAY

For a few students, athletic prowess can be turned into a ticket to college—maybe even, in time, to the pros. Such prowess can also be a passport to financial assistance. For the aspirant, proper and long-range planning is the key, and ninth grade is none too early to begin the search.

There is a vast difference between the top level of high school athletics and the bottom level of college sports. Unless your counselee is a star or, at the very least, a starter, his or her chances of making varsity in college are slim. Consider the following:

- Of 400,000 high school seniors playing football or basketball, only about 20,000 will be signed by the 800 NCAA (National Collegiate Athletic Association) member schools.
- An additional 5000 students will play for the 400 colleges affiliated with the NAIA (National Association of Intercollegiate Athletics).
- 3000 will take the field for the 500 members of NJCAS (National Junior College Athletic Association).
- Only 300-some colleges and universities award full athletic scholarships.

Early planning can provide your counselee the needed time to select the *appropriate* college or university. Where there is a choice, the student's first priority should be the institution's academic reputation—not its athletic record, facilities, or even the coach's personality. In short, go where brains are important. One avenue to selecting the appropriate school is to check out graduation rates of both athletes and total student body. Usually the higher the graduation rate for the total student body, the higher the rate for the athletes. (See Figure 25-1 later in this section.)

## *The Knight Commission*

In 1992, the Knight Foundation Commission on Intercollegiate Athletics issued a report entitled *Keeping Faith with the Student-Athlete: A New Model for Intercollegiate Athletics*, in which the commission explored the role of athletics on the college campus, including the need to place the well-being of student athletes at the forefront of concern. Athletes should not be considered for enrollment, the report maintains, unless "they give reasonable promise of being successful" at a given institution.

Of course, what is "reasonable promise"? It certainly varies from college to college, with the overall academic quality of the student body as one important consideration. The effort by NCAA during the past decade to improve eligibility requirements (strengthen academic preparation of high school athletes), while well-intentioned, might tempt high school counselors and coaches to focus exclusively on problems of eligibility and the monitoring of student progress.

In its Statement of Principles, the commission urged college presidents to admit athletes solely through their admission offices: "The admission of student athletes—including junior college transfers—will be based on their showing reasonable promise of being successful in a course of study leading to an academic degree. That judgment will be made by admission officials. Student athletes should undertake the same courses of study offered to other students and *graduate in the same proportions* as those who spend comparable time as full-time students."

Some of that graduation problem is evident in the data shown in Figure 25-1 gathered by the Associated Press on football players and student bodies as a whole. The AP Rank was for a given week in the 1994-95 season.

**FIGURE 25-1**

| ASSOCIATED PRESS PROJECTED TOP 10 FOOTBALL TEAMS, 1994 | | | |
|---|---|---|---|
| SCHOOL | FOOTBALL TEAM GRADUATION RATE | STUDENT BODY GRADUATION RATE | AP RANK |
| Penn State U. | 92% | 77% | 9 |
| U. of Michigan | 81% | 85% | 5 |
| Notre Dame U. | 73% | 95% | 3 |
| U. of Wisconsin | 61% | 72% | 10 |
| U. of Miami | 56% | 60% | 6 |
| Florida State U. | 53% | 61% | 4 |
| U. of Colorado | 46% | 64% | 8 |
| U. of Nebraska | 46% | 53% | 2 |
| U. of Arizona | 40% | 49% | 7 |
| U. of Florida | 37% | 63% | 1 |

*Source: National Collegiate Athletic Association 1993 Retention Rate Report*

## YOU, THE COLLEGE, THE TEAM, AND THE COACH

If your students are planning a campus visitation, they might be encouraged to tie the visitation to their favorite sport—that is, take in a game, and watch their future team play. Figure 25-2 is a handy handout that suggests what they might look for from the athletic perspective.

FIGURE 25-2

## What to Look for During the Campus Visitation

- When you visit a particular campus, one of the important things you can do is watch your future team practice or play. Such observation can tell you much about the school and the sports team.

- When observing the team, watch its style of play. For example, if it's soccer, is the team playing a lot of balls into space? Or does the team play the ball to feet? Or is it a combination of both factors?

- How do the players interact with each other?

- Are they extremely defense-minded?

- How aggressive is the team? How much contact? What is the size and speed of the players?

- Is this the way in which you presently play or would like to play?

- While watching the team, watch the coach. Is the coach constantly directing the game? Is he always screaming at the players? Could you deal with that kind of an approach?

- Or is the coach just sitting there, fixed in stone, showing little or no emotion?

- What is the coach like when players make mistakes? Does he scream at them from the sidelines? Or does he calmly pull them from the field, correct them, and then send them back into the game?

- Watch the players in your position. What year are they? What are their strengths and weaknesses? How do you stack up?

- Observe players in other positions. Even though you play a particular position, could you play another one?

- Be honest with yourself! Do you think you could compete at that level?

# EXPOSURE SERVICES

Of course, there are the so-called exposure services where, for a fee, student athletes will be brought to the attention of college coaches. For about $500, your counselee will be counseled on NCAA or NAIA rules and regulations, be evaluated as to his or her athletic skills, and have a personal résumé developed that will include admission test scores and grade point average. The resulting information will then be forwarded to coaches at colleges where athletes with profiles like your counselee's might expect a reasonable welcome. Sounds good, doesn't it, considering that test preparation firms charge similar or even larger fees? But buyer beware! There are exposure services *and* exposure services. Talk is cheap and not all deliver.

Two services that do deliver appear to be "College Prospects of America," the industry giant based in Ohio, and "College Bound Student Athletes," based in Wisconsin. Both have regional offices and use regional representatives. Because of the credibility factor, the services say they routinely reject applicants who exhibit little or no chance of engaging in college sports.

Figures 25-3 and 25-4 are handouts for the athlete who wants to bypass the exposure services, and submit his or her own query letter and résumé.

## *A Note About the NCAA Clearinghouse*

The Clearinghouse's decision as to what courses are or are not acceptable, doesn't call into question the relative worth of a given course, only its use as one of thirteen core courses according to NCAA standards. In all actuality, this uncommon gatekeeper organization merely applies the Bylaws of the NCAA member institutions, but the Clearinghouse doesn't mind citing chapter and verse. In the unacceptable category: courses chiefly oriented toward personal service rather than the teaching of material as defined by one of the five academic areas (14.31.3); courses that are vocational in nature (14.31.3); courses that are primarily a review of previously covered material (14.31.3); dual sequence courses such as Algebra I taught over a two-year period (14.31.3); changed definition courses such as Pre-Algebra (14.31.3).

It seems the House doesn't like pre-anything. They refer to such courses as "preparatory"—courses pursued prior to the first course usually taken to fulfill the progression of a core-curriculum sequence. They also have difficulty with course levels, e.g., a slower moving/less depth version of French III. Don't call it French III B or you're dead in the water. Is the Clearinghouse yet another champion of heterogeneity—everybody enrolled in the same level, except, that is, for honors? (See commentary in Chapter 2.) For a while, the House was even having problems with Discrete Math. Maybe they thought the course content was too "finite."

On a more serious note, the Clearinghouse requires the submission of but *two* transcripts: one at the *end* of the junior year that reflects final grades for purposes of preliminary review, and a second one at the end of the senior year for final certification. Sending senior mid-year grades is a waste of time.

FIGURE 25-3

## Tips on Writing a Good Résumé & Cover Letter

1. *Don't* open with "Dear Coach." It makes it look like a form letter that you're sending to a list of schools. Take the time to find out the coach's name, and personalize your piece.

2. Make sure your letter explains *why* you want to attend a particular college or university. Is it because the school has a topflight chemistry department? Maybe it's the location of the campus that attracts you to it. College coaches continue to receive hundreds of generic letters that simply say, "Dear Coach, I want to play soccer in college. Could you send me information about your school and about scholarship opportunities?" Remember that your academic standing is usually the first thing coaches examine.

3. Make certain your name, address, and telephone number appear on the cover letter. Coaches work in offices that are crowded with papers, books, and equipment.

4. If you are going to be in a big tournament, mention it in your letter. Tell him your club name, jersey color, and number. If the coach himself can't attend the particular tournament, he might send someone else.

5. Include a brief résumé in your letter. Don't say, "I think I can play for you because . . ." Be more objective. Say something like, "During the past two years I have been on a state traveling team . . . ," or "My team recently won two tournaments and. . . ."

6. At the top of your résumé you should list academic information such as grade point average, class rank, and ACT or SAT scores. If your school computes GPA on other than a 4.0 scale, *briefly* explain the procedure.

7. If you are good at other sports, mention them. If you've set the school record in the 200 meter, state the fact and put down the time.

8. Experience in any sport carries a lot of weight. Club play can be very important. The problem with high school athletics is that the quality of play throughout a particular conference can be very uneven.

9. Don't stack the deck. It's not necessary to list everything. Club and high school participation will do.

10. Include the names of present and former coaches on your résumé. Be sure to ask these coaches for permission to use their names as references. Don't assume that a college coach knows your high school coach. There are 25,000 high schools in America.

FIGURE 25-4

## Frequently Employed Terms

**Prospective Student Athlete**   A student who, because of special athletic ability, can contribute quickly and substantially to a collegiate program. These candidates are also referred to as "highly recruited" due to extensive media coverage, and the attention paid to them by many schools.

**Red Shirt**   Someone who is held out of competition for a season, so that he remains eligible for a fifth year. This happens when athletes are injured ("injury" or "hardship" red shirts), need to develop more physically, or when there is a "crowd" at a given position.

**Core Courses**   NCAA dictates that student-athletes must present within the four-year period of high school 13 recognized academic courses. They must achieve within the core a minimum grade point average of 2.00 based on a maximum of 4.00.

**Proposition 48**   That portion of NCAA rules that requires a student athlete to attain the above-mentioned minimums, both GPA and admission test scores. Anyone entering an NCAA Division I college without attaining these minimums must sit out one full year of competition to improve his or her academic standing, and cannot receive a scholarship at that time.

**Qualifier**   A prospective student-athlete who has met (prior to senior year) grade requirements in core academic courses and attained the minimum qualifying score on the SAT or ACT.

**Contact**   Any "face-to-face encounter" that takes place between a prospect or his/her parent or guardian and "an institutional staff member or athletics representative," during which dialogue occurs in excess of a greeting. Telephone calls are also subject to strict recruiting rules that limit time and frequency of phone contact.

**Early Signing Period**   A one-week period in November during which athletes engaged in sports other than football can sign a national letter of intent that commits them to a specific school.

**Signing Day**   The exact day NCAA designates as the beginning of the time period when student athletes can sign letters of intent. The first Wednesday in February is usually set aside for football. All other sports have a different signing day in April.

**On the Bubble**   Athletes who can't make up their minds as to which offer to accept. Or, athletes who deserve scholarship money but have yet to receive an actual offer of same.

**NCAA**   The National Collegiate Athletic Association, an organization that establishes rules and regulations governing athletic eligibility, recruitment, and competition for some 800 member colleges and universities.

**NCAA Clearinghouse**   A division of NCAA that collects prospects' admission test scores and academic records, and then submits the information to those collegiate institutions that request it. Student athletes who wish to be recruited by NCAA Division I or II schools must furnish the Clearinghouse with such data, as opposed to sending it directly to the interested college or university.

**NAIA**   The National Association of Intercollegiate Athletics, a federation of some 400 schools, about 75 percent of which are Christian colleges. NAIA has two divisional levels within which some 60,000 athletes participate.

**JUCO**   An abbreviation that stands for private junior and community college. Players who are recruited from this type of school are often referred to as JUCOs.

For the sports of football, field hockey, water polo, women's volleyball, and men's and women's soccer, a student *does not* have to be registered with the Clearinghouse to do any *official* visiting of campuses. Some over-zealous coaches, e.g. in football, have been urging their players to register with the House in the spring of the junior year *prior* to final grades being issued. The danger here is in forgetting to send an updated transcript during the summer or once school opens in the Fall. Again, the Clearinghouse would prefer that students wait to register until the *end* of the junior year when final grades are available. Any transcript submitted to the Clearinghouse for preliminary review, then, should also reflect senior courses proposed or in progress.

## SUGGESTED CONTACTS AND READINGS

National Association for Intercollegiate Athletics (NAIA) 1221 Baltimore Avenue, Kansas City, Missouri 64105.

National Collegiate Athletic Association (NCAA), College Boulevard, Overland Park, Kansas, 66211.

College Bound Student-Athletes, W62 N179 Washington Avenue, Cedarburg, Wisconsin 53012.

College Prospects of America, 12682 College Prospects Drive, Logan, Ohio 43138.

Figler, Howard (1984), *The Athlete's Game Plan for College & Career*, Princeton, NJ: Peterson's Guides, Inc.

Reischl, Dennis K. (1994), *Winning an Athletic Scholarship*, Huntsville, AL: FPMI Communications, Inc.

# CHAPTER 26

# DISABILITY AND COLLEGE ADMISSION

When today's college-bound students began kindergarten, we could count on our fingers, and maybe our toes, the number of colleges and universities in the nation that accepted and served students with learning disabilities (LD). The publication of guides such as *Peterson's Colleges with Programs for Students with Learning Disabilities*, which presently contains almost 1,000 collegiate LD programs, is tangible evidence to the changes that have transpired since the early 1980s.

The Heath Resource Center, an arm of the American Council on Education in Washington, D.C., led the way with a published paper on the topic in 1981. Heath cited nine collegiate institutions with LD programs. It was this core of programs that many colleges and universities emulated as they moved to provide for students with learning disabilities

Since then, there has been a significant increase in the number of students attending college with both physical and learning disabilities. In 1978, the first year disability-related data on college students was published in *American Freshman: National Norms*, 3% of full-time freshmen claimed a disability. In 1991, some 9% of college freshmen reported some sort of disability. Of the 1991 reporting freshmen, one quarter or 35,000 of them stated they had a learning disability.

In the mid-1970s, two significant pieces of legislation became law: the Education of the Handicapped Act (now titled the Individuals with Disabilities Education Act) and the

Rehabilitation Act of 1973, followed by the 1977 regulations implementing Section 504 of the 1973 Act. The drafting of these pieces of legislation reflected the country's desire to include people with disabilities in regular education, and led to the changes necessary in those programs so that people, including those with LDs, could participate. These desires were further validated with the enactment of the Americans with Disabilities Act of 1990.

However, we can go back further to Dr. Gertrude Webb, who, in 1970, began the first college program for LD students at Curry College in Milton, Massachusetts. Dr. Webb recognized that a good number of these students had both the capability and the desire to attend college. Webb felt they deserved a shot at a college education and could, in fact, earn a college degree if they were provided with special personal assistance to meet the demands of collegiate study.

In the past fifteen years, all secondary school students have become better prepared for college. As students with disabilities have had their aspirations raised by supportive parents, teachers, and counselors, and as collegiate institutions have come to understand the strengths and potential that such students can add to the quality of campus living, the number of college and university programs in the country has swelled.

## CHARACTERISTICS OF COLLEGE STUDENTS WITH LEARNING DISABILITIES

A learning disability is often referred to as "the hidden handicap." Many lay persons have trouble understanding what is meant by "LD." The public needs to understand that a learning disability is a *permanent* disorder that affects the way in which a student with average or better-than-average academic ability internalizes, retains, or communicates information.

The characteristics associated with LD students can be grouped into seven major categories: cognition, language, perceptual and motor skills, academic matters, work and study habits, social skills, and emotional development. There can be an overlapping of categories, and virtually no one will present all of the characteristics. Cognition has to do with the manner in which students think and reason, for instance; LD students in college can have difficulty in both spoken and written language; perceptual-motor deficits are quite common. As youngsters mature they learn to compensate for these deficits, though traces of any problem(s) can remain into adulthood. Often a learning disability is accompanied by significant underachievement in one or more of the five normal academic areas: mathematics, science, English, foreign language, and social studies. College students can have continuing difficulty in any one or more of these areas.

LD students often drop out of college because of their inability to handle the social demands placed upon them, as opposed to their inability to handle academic matters. LD students frequently encounter difficulty in interacting with peers, professors, and advisors. LD students can also have trouble in handling their emotions and feelings. Their behavior might continue to be childlike as they fail to demonstrate a mature set of responses typical of adult behavior.

To succeed in college, LD students need to present at least average intellectual ability, but they also need to possess a rather sophisticated set of work and study skills. Collegiate programs can be in place to enhance such skills.

# TRANSITION TIPS FOR THE LEARNING DISABLED

The transition from high school to college can be difficult for anyone; for the learning disabled, it can be especially troublesome. To prepare for such transition, students with learning disabilities are urged to carefully weigh the following issues.

## *Preparing for the Transition*

1. Get a grip on your strengths and weaknesses, and how they might apply to your personal learning style. In short, be able to explain in simple language just how your strengths and weaknesses affect your learning.
2. Be assertive, but not aggressive. Learn to self-advocate (look after your needs) in order to make your present support services work for you. You'll be doing a lot of self-advocating in college, so learn how to do it in high school.
3. Be sure to attend all IEP meetings. Senior-year meetings often focus on the transition to post-secondary education. Ask questions at IEP meetings and become involved in planning your future. By the time you are a senior, you should be running the meetings.
4. Find out about financial aid. You may qualify for more financial assistance than you realize. The Heath Resource Center has compiled a list of financial aid resources. For a free copy, write to the Heath Resource Center.
5. Visit as many colleges and universities as possible. Set up an appointment with a learning disabilities support services staff member. Be prepared to ask specific questions. Remember that the quantity and quality of programs vary greatly from college to college.
6. Prepare a personal folder that you can take with you when visiting. The folder might include an unofficial transcript, applicable test scores, letters of evaluation, documentation of disability—any information that might assist in determining *your* special support service needs.

## *Guidelines for Interviewing: Issues to Raise*

1. Learn what the admission requirements are for LD students. (Admission requirements vary from college to college.)
2. Is it possible to get an updated LD assessment once on the campus? If so, is there a fee?
3. Are there any additional charges for support services? If so, what are they?
4. Most guide books now outline and rate support services as to their expense. How does the particular college view its services: light, moderate, or heavy?
5. Who is the director of the program?
6. Who will help me obtain housing and counsel me as to my legal rights and responsibilities?
7. Are learning disabled students permitted to take a reduced course load?

8. How barrier-free is the campus for me if I am physically disabled? Most students seek 90% access to facilities. Beware of anything under 75%, and then determine what the remaining 25% represents.

## *Now That You're There*

1. Once on the campus, identify yourself again to support services personnel as a student with a learning disability.

2. Work with the personnel to fine-tune your academic program, including any personal adjustments that might be warranted.

3. Remember that assistance should be sought early in the semester, not just before midterms or finals.

4. Don't leave anything to chance! Make sure there has been some communication between the support services office and your professors by personally speaking to them about your disability.

5. Time-management skills are of critical importance at the collegiate level. Design and then adhere to a schedule that includes study, part-time work, campus activities, and social life.

6. If you are assigned to a regular academic advisor, use him or her well. Don't panic. A major field of study need not be declared until the sophomore year or later. But do sit down with your advisor and plan as early and carefully as possible. Most colleges have career planning specialists who are housed in placement offices. Use these people to good advantage.

# NEW SAT SERVICES FOR THE DISABLED

The College Board has instituted a number of changes in the special SAT services offered to disabled students, beginning with the 1995-96 testing year.

- An expanded testing program of seven testing periods that correspond to each national test date. More precisely, each period will have an eleven-day untimed testing window.

- A single eligibility form for Plan A and Plan B. Plan A continues to be available to SAT I and II takers who have documented hearing, learning, visual, and physical disabilities. The plan provides such accommodations as special test editions in Braille, cassette, large type, regular type, or script. Also, the test taker can order machine-scannable or large block answer sheets. Untimed is defined as approximately 6.5 hours of testing time. Plan B is available to students taking SAT I who can document disabilities, and who can test at national test centers using a regular test and a machine-scannable answer sheet. Plan B students receive an extra 90 minutes or 4.5 hours of testing time. The Board is *not* increasing the number of Plan B testing opportunities. The extended time option will continue to be offered on the national test dates of November and May only.

- Section 504 plans on file at a given school will now be considered an element in the need for special accommodations.

- An admission ticket/correction form will now be mailed to each disabled student.

- Extended and untimed testing can take place at a single site within a school district, or at a special site developed by a group of secondary schools.

- Nonstandard scores will be released on the same schedule as score reports from standard administrations.

# QUALITY RESOURCE GUIDES

College guides for the learning disabled are a relatively new category of reference material. What's even newer is *Hunter's Guide to the College Guides, 1995*—the first book to review the hundreds of comprehensive and self-help guides currently on the market. Author Bruce Hunter devotes a section of his work to the learning disabled student. He does an excellent job of critiquing the worthwhile publications in the readings below. Hunter's book can be obtained by writing to Hunter's Guide to the College Guides, P.O. Box 9647, Naples, Florida, 33941.

# SUGGESTED READINGS

*The College Guide for Students with Learning Disabilities*, Laurel Publications, Miller Place, NY 11764. Telephone: (516) 474-1023.

*Guiding the Learning Disabled Student: A Directory of Programs and Services at NACAC Member Institutions*, National Association for College Admission Counseling, 1631 Prince Street, Alexandria, VA 22314. Telephone: (703) 836-2222.

*Heath Resource Directory*, Heath Resource Center, Suite 800, One Dupont Circle NW, Washington, D.C. 20036. Telephone: (800) 544-3284.

*The K&W Guide for the Learning Disabled*, HarperCollins Publishers, 10 East 53rd Street, NY 10022. Telephone: (800) 331-3761.

*Lovejoy's College Guide for the Learning Disabled*, Monarch Press, 15 Columbus Circle, New York, NY 10023.

*Peterson's Colleges with Programs for the Learning Disabled*, Peterson's Guides, Princeton, NJ 08540. Telephone: (800) 338-3282.

# CHAPTER 27

# THE COLLEGE APPLICATION

Many issues must be addressed and then resolved before the student takes pen to paper; just as there are many nuances of application completion, including whether or not the student uses a pen, typewriter, diskette, or electronic data interchange to produce the final copy. We have divided the material in this chapter into two major categories: (1) factors that affect the application process, and (2) the completion of the application itself.

## FACTORS THAT AFFECT THE APPLICATION PROCESS

Each year, thousands of high school seniors make a decision to apply to their very favorite college or university under one of two "early" programs, Early Decision or Early Action. This does impact on how an application is completed, including the quality and thoroughness of the presentation.

Time was when it was just Early Decision, but then along came Early Action in the 1980s—a best-of-both-worlds plan with the attraction of "take me, but I might not take you." Maybe Early Action is not long for this world. Both Yale and Princeton dropped the program in 1995 and returned to Early Decision.

## Early Decision

Under Early Decision, the student applies to *one* participating college or university, usually by mid-November. (The institution will generally render a decision by mid or late December.) There are, or perhaps more accurately were, two forms of this plan: (1) the student is *not* permitted to apply to other colleges while a decision is pending, and (2) the student *is* permitted to apply to additional schools, but once admitted by the early decision institution, he or she *must* accept the offer, and withdraw all previously submitted applications. Hardly anybody seems to be doing plan #1 these days; consequently, nervous students can be seen spending literally hundreds of dollars on application fees in October and November as they bide their time waiting for that "early decision" decision. Not-so-nervous students ready all or most of their applications, don't write any checks, and then if accepted to that "dream" school, take their counselor out to lunch with some of their application fee savings. Does all of the foregoing affect the application process? You bet!

If an applicant indicates a *strong* desire to attend a given institution, by applying early most colleges will give him or her special consideration in the evaluation process. Indeed, at many of these schools, the acceptance rate of early-decision candidates is a bit higher than that of applicants who choose the regular route. This phenomenon is largely due to the weight assigned early-decision applications (colleges love to be loved), as well as to the strong credentials of the applicants. (Most school counselors believe a student should be at least "target" qualified to have a running shot.) Nonaccepted applicants are almost always deferred to regular decision; but, *the applicant should read the fine print.*

## Early Action

Then we have Early Action with its luxury of applying early, but once accepted not having to go. Fortunately, only a handful of collegiate institutions still subscribe to this program, which some counselors believe undermines the development of student decision-making skills that include a most serious approach to the college-planning process. Warning! Unlike Early Decision, your student could be rejected outright and not deferred. Again, the applicant should read the fine print.

## The Counselor's Role

The Early Decision program has been around for some thirty years, but because of a perception by the colleges of an abuse of the system, high school counselors have become major cooperating players. This is as it should be. In fact, counselors should be playing an even larger role, since the program continues to be administered very unevenly; e.g., some colleges require school counselors to sign off and some do not.

The original intent of those colleges that created the Early Decision program was to develop a "first choice" plan. For those of us in the counseling profession for longer than we care to admit, we remember that thrust well. It *was* a "first choice" plan! But there are still counselors today who endorse the idea of submitting more than one early-decision application, arguing that if you ask students to withdraw other applications once accepted, that implies that students can apply to other programs, including early-decision ones. That's quite a stretch.

NACAC guidelines stipulate that Early Decision programs are a *recognized exception* to general admission policies and practices, and that a student "may have only one early decision application pending at one time." That seems to make sense. Besides, how can you say that two somethings are your first choice? Of course, it is possible for a student to apply to two different Early Decision programs, but only in succession, not concurrently.

As school counselors, we must remember that a violation of an early-decision agreement not only damages a student's chances of college matriculation, but the high school's credibility as well. More and more colleges expect us to both counsel on the early option and supervise the execution of it.

### SUGGESTED POINTS TO COVER WITH EARLY-DECISION CANDIDATES

1. Students should have visited the campus *at least* once—the longer the stay, the better.

2. Early decision should come from "best possible fit." Students should not use the option unless they are totally convinced that the particular college or university is the most appropriate one for them.

3. Students need to know why applicant pools of highly selective colleges and universities are purposely kept high for early-decision candidates. Answer: What *will* the applicant pools of these "highly selectives" look like in the spring? Who can tell. Certainly not the collegiate institutions.

4. If a student plans to apply to an early-decision school that does not defer a portion of its pool, and if the student's credentials are marginal, the student might want to wait to be considered with the total applicant pool when his or her credentials could appear stronger in comparison to others. In short, will the record look more impressive in January than it does in November? Will test scores be higher? Will grades be better? Will there be other additional achievements?

5. Students need to understand that how they "package" themselves is crucial. Some educators believe that the polished application, with an accompanying essay, should be the best writing effort to date.

6. Once admitted to an early-decision school, the student is going! He signed a statement that if admitted, he would definitely attend, and he is therefore obligated to enroll at that college or university and must withdraw all applications to other schools. If the student refuses the school that has accepted him, there is an ethical question of his filing additional applications elsewhere during that school year. The only exceptions would be real hardship: changes in family structure, insufficient financial assistance, etc.

## Rank-In-Class

RIC. Is it one big impediment to the love of learning? It certainly has an impact on the college application process. Even the students are growing weary of the cut-throat competition it engenders. In the 1994 findings of a survey commissioned by National Association of Secondary School Principals (NASSP), class rank was found to be valued more highly by colleges than by secondary schools in terms of its use in making admission decisions: class rank has more pull in the college admission decision than high school counselors or secondary school students would like to see.

(Incidentally, the 38-page study is well worth purchasing from NASSP, 1904 Association Drive, Reston, Virginia 22091. Remember that NASSP is now working closely with NACAC. Nice to see!)

NASSP commissioned George Mason University in Virginia to survey 1,109 four-year colleges and universities and 2,175 high schools. Result: 61.9 percent of the colleges named class rank as one of the top five factors for admission, while only 28 percent of the high schools indicated that rank was among what *should* be the top five admission factors. (See Figure 27-1.)

## FIGURE 27-1

### FACTORS COLLEGES & SCHOOLS RATE MOST IMPORTANT IN COLLEGE ADMISSIONS

Following are the rankings colleges and high schools gave to various admissions factors, taken from a survey of 2,175 high school principals and 1,109 college admission deans.

#### Colleges

1. High school grade-point average (GPA)
2. High school courses completed
3. Standardized test scores
4. Rank in class
5. Difficulty of curriculum

#### High Schools

1. Courses completed
2. Difficulty of curriculum
3. High school GPA
4. Standardized test scores
5. Portfolio
6. Recommendations
7. Extracurricular activities
8. Competitiveness of high school
9. Achievement scores
10. Rank in class

Source: National Association of Secondary School Principals, "Rank-in-Class, Grade Point Average, and College Admissions," February, 1994

Student participants in the study indicated overwhelmingly that they would favor discontinuation of class rank as an admission factor. The students were of the opinion that rank is not a standardized comparison among schools, and that class rank discourages students from taking more challenging coursework.

It seems that students from top-flight high schools who are in the mid-range of their class are those being hurt the most. Some of these students have grade point averages of 3.1, yet are just below the middle of the class. Others with 4.0 averages don't even cut the top ten percent of their classes—and in some rather rare instances, not even the top fifth. An example of this can be found at East Brunswick High School in New Jersey, a nationally ranked school of excellence: in the class of 1996, 46 students out of 456 had GPAs of 4.0 or better—that's more than 10%; the top weighted GPA was 4.6.

Past national president Cleve Latham, in commenting on the findings in the March 1994 *NACAC Bulletin*, states: "It is misleading to assign students a class rank because of the inherent limitations of a whole number system. A student could miss being in the top ten or twenty percent of a given class by a hundredth of a point, and the admission process would have been poorly served by the attempt to quantify an academic record that is not always easy to quantify."

The results of the NASSP survey vividly demonstrate just how far apart the secondary schools and colleges are with regard to RIC. "Save us all from the artificial and superficial," cry the students! "Rank-in-class is meaningless, unfair, and subjective." But who's listening? More than a few secondary schools, it seems—they've abolished rank-in-class. Others are contemplating doing so, but far too many high schools continue to run scared. Some of the high schools that have eliminated rank are undoubtedly the very ones that have had the courage to develop their own Secondary School Report form.

As a school counselor, you can help foster a greater love of learning in your students. One way is to face down the 125 "most" or "highly" selective colleges and universities of the nation, who might be holding on for dear life to rank-in-class, chiefly for their own reasons: it's easier to use cutoffs; they can boast about their "statistics"; and they've always done it.

The proponents of ranking maintain that the way to make ranking more accurate lies in changing the system of weighted grades and being less generous with high marks. That is true, and whether or not you plan to drop class rank, you'll want to look carefully at weighting and high grades. Some high schools have gotten themselves into a bind with the adoption years ago of sophisticated weighting systems. Our advice is that if you are going to continue to weight, the system should only encompass honors and advanced placement work, and that the difference between standard college preparatory and honors/AP should be a modest one.

Schools can be less generous with high marks in two ways: caution the teacher who gives an "easy A," or spreads the grading scales so that an "A" is between 93 and 100, instead of 90 and 100. Note in Figure 27-2 that some of this generosity can also be tempered by using the plus (+) and minus (-) system; the teacher keeps the numbers in his or her grade book, and then presents the letter grade.

FIGURE 27-2

### Recommended Table of Weights

Level of Courses Weighted: Honors and Advanced Placement Only

Grading Scale: 4.0 with highest assigned value being 4.95

| Grade | Numeric Equivalent | Standard Scale Grade Value | Honors/AP Grade Value |
|-------|--------------------|-----------------------------|------------------------|
| A+ | 98-100% | 4.3 | 4.95 |
| A | 92-97% | 4.0 | 4.60 |
| A- | 90-91% | 3.7 | 4.25 |
| B+ | 86-89% | 3.3 | 3.80 |
| B | 82-85% | 3.0 | 3.45 |
| B- | 80-81% | 2.7 | 3.11 |
| . . . . | | | |
| D- | 60-61% | .7 | .81 |
| F | below 60%—failing | 0 | 0 |

Then there are those who argue that, among other benefits, weighting encourages students to go for the challenge—and that students who pursue honors or AP programs deserve a *little* extra credit. There is some merit to that thinking. But you couldn't convince Scarsdale High School in Westchester County, New York of that idea.

### *The Scarsdale Plan*

We don't mean the Scarsdale Diet. The closest thing to "diet" might be that Scarsdale High School's reporting of student performance is, to say the least, on the lean side. The venerable and high-powered school, where 97% of the students attend senior colleges and universities, hasn't ranked students since 1981; it was one of the first in the nation to abandon RIC. They don't even weight courses: Scarsdale believes that students who have the "smarts" to carry honors and advanced placement courses are already advantaged. Enough is enough. No valedictorian or salutatorian, either. The presidents of the senior class and student government deliver the commencement addresses. What the professional staff and community-at-large have discovered through the years is that college admission officials more carefully eyeball every course and accompanying grade on the transcript before rendering a decision.

Many teachers, counselors, and students support dropping rank because it would encourage students to take a broader array of courses and cut down on cheating and plagiarism, a phenomenon that to some extent can be attributed to rivalry over rank-in-class. In addition, more than a few students shy away from the arts and other courses that carry less weight in favor of more heavily weighted ones.

### *If Rank Is Eliminated, You Could:*

- Calculate rank-in-class but not release any individual rankings to students or parents.
- Provide families and collegiate institutions with information on grade point average *ranges* to determine approximate rankings.
- Release a student's specific rank directly to an institution if the student needed the information for a scholarship, military academy, or other competitions.
- Have none of that, and insist that all competitions and military academies work exclusively with grade point average and quality of coursework pursued.

## COMPLETING THE ACTUAL APPLICATION

All the months—even years—of preparation (the analysis of self, the national college fairs attended, the campuses visited and interviews taken) come together with the completion of the application. Some seniors find the selection process and the completion of a half dozen or so applications akin to having an additional course in their schedules. You, the counselor, might want to be sensitive to the pressure that "course" puts on certain of your counselees.

As you know, the more selective the college is, the more it considers *nonacademic* qualities. If your counselee is up against someone else whose academic record is equal to hers, the college will be searching to find which of the two can bring the more worthwhile "something" to the mix.

That "something" can be discovered on an application. And with the word "application," we take the broadest possible definition—one that encompasses the personal essay, supplementary materials, teacher recommendations, counselor evaluation, and any other supporting materials. In short, the application *packet.*

It is most important that students' submitted materials are prepared as thoroughly, thoughtfully, and creatively as possible. Is this kind of packaging dehumanizing? No more than a résumé is for a job.

Perhaps we should become more involved in advising on application completion, thereby enabling our clients to do a better job with these two- to six-page documents. But, alas, *comprehensive* advising is not always easy, particularly for some heavily case-loaded public school counselors. Nevertheless, as a counselor, you've worked to get a young woman/man to internalize the concept that she or he is one of a kind. If that person wants to be accepted somewhere, especially at one of the 100 or so highly selective institutions in the nation, then that person has to figure out what she or he has *really* got and who she or he really is, and let it come through, quirks and all.

### *Thinking Less of the Handwritten Essay? Think Again*

It can be both unsettling and a pleasant surprise when the results of one's study reflect what you had *not* expected to find. Such was the case with researchers at Educational Testing Service in Princeton, New Jersey, who discovered that typed essays and those written on a word processor scored lower than the handwritten. The researchers had asked selected students to submit two identical essays for a teacher's licensing examination. The findings were published in the Fall 1994 issue of the *Journal of Educational Measurement.*

It appears that the handwritten personal essay could be quite advantageous to applicants to college. Graders might feel empathetic to the student, identify more with the author because handwriting is more personal. That is, if it can be read. Word-processed copy need not look reworked, whereas edits to a handwritten piece are more apparent and available to the reader. Counselors are seeing some of this in the increased number of colleges and universities that are requesting graded papers as yet another means of examining student writing capability and authenticity.

You and your department might want to carefully examine this issue with the thought of advising certain of your counselees to consider penning their essays. Again, legibility is the key here, and many students possess excellent penmanship skills: they might not have come through the old Gregg or Pitman programs, but they can really form those letters. One English teacher was bemoaning the fact that with the advent of the word processor, handwriting was fast becoming a lost art. Fortunately, we are now seeing both elementary and secondary teachers mandating that a portion of their students' out-of-class essays be handwritten. There is much to be said for the more personalized handwritten essay—even if it does mean writing the work seven times for seven different colleges.

### *Procuring Those Teacher Recommendations*

When we speak about any type of recommendation writing, we are usually referring to support systems. We are making an effort to demonstrate that other people—besides the applicant—think this person is worthy of acceptance. Much of this is done by weaving together academic and personal information from various perspectives. Most colleges and universities request supporting materials. Others simply suggest that they are open to the receipt of such information. Few if any state that such material is not welcome.

A teacher recommendation is considered by some colleges and universities as a powerful piece of supporting information. It can be especially helpful to those candidates who are marginally admissible. Figure 27-3 is a nifty handout for your students—guidelines that should help him or her procure more meaningful and substantive recommendations.

FIGURE 27-3

**How to Handle Teacher Recommendations**

Dear Student:

Here are some guidelines that should help you obtain more meaningful and substantive recommendations.

1. Learn about your school policy and procedures for the handling of teacher recommendations; they do differ from school district to school district. For example, in some districts, the procurement and eventual processing is the sole responsibility of the students, with the students viewing most or all of what had been written prior to submission. In other districts, all recommendations are channeled through the counseling department and students may or may not get to see them. In this situation, the counseling department does all of the collating and submitting.

2. Give your recommenders plenty of lead time, i.e., thirty days. Some teachers, especially in English and social studies, are swamped with requests. Some teachers even like to work on junior requests over the summertime.

3. Supply your recommenders with all necessary materials, such as stamped addressed envelopes, unofficial transcripts, and possibly college literature.

4. Some teachers might ask for written input from you, such as what short story, novel, or portion of the course you enjoyed the most and/or in what area you experienced your greatest success. If they don't request such information, you might offer it to them.

5. Waive your confidentiality rights. Not waiving your rights can, in some respects, tie the hands of your recommender and lead to less honest and purposeful writing. Remember that colleges are not looking for "walk-on-water" candidates. They're seeking real human beings with some or all of their frailties.

6. Select your recommenders wisely. Don't select a teacher simply because you got an A grade in the course. It is important that the teacher knows you on a personal level. If you can select teachers who write well, so much the better.

7. Where permissible, don't hesitate to use community folk as recommenders: pastors, camp directors, employers, etc. They can bring another perspective to bear. The important point here is that the recommenders know you and your contributions well. From a familiarity standpoint, the worst people to select can be school superintendents, mayors, and congressional people. Families sometimes select these people because they see them as "heavyweights." But colleges and universities are usually not impressed, especially when they detect that these prestige people don't really know their recommendees well. Heavyweights can be found writing lightweight stuff. Gently remind your "outside" recommenders that substance and specifics are what colleges and universities seek in a written evaluation.

8. Send thank-you notes! Eventually inform your recommenders where you will be matriculating.

### *The Common Application: It's Growing*

Indeed it is, and taking on more respectability, as well. Dartmouth joined the group in 1995 and the Hanover, New Hampshire school makes things quite clear in its October 1995 report to secondary schools: "Applicants may use either the Dartmouth form or the Common Application—both forms will carry *equal weight* in our deliberation process." Of course they will, especially since institutions continue to gravitate toward the common application program. One reason is pressure from secondary schools for more standardization.

The common application group has always tried to reassure families with their front-cover statement:

> *The colleges and universities listed above have worked together to develop and distribute the Common Application. . . . All encourage its use and no distinction will be made between it and the college's own form . . . Students are urged to use this form, rather than writing to participating colleges for application materials.*

In spite of these rather strong words of advice, some counselors still believe students will receive more favorable treatment if they submit a participating school's regular application. The fact that counselors even instruct their counselees not to use the common material is mystifying, in that certain member institutions such as Harvard, Bucknell, and Franklin and Marshall use only the common application. Oh well, attitudes are changing. Students are now using such computer-based programs as *College Link*—even applying on-line through Electronic Data Interchange (EDI). For better or worse, speed, efficiency, and standardization are here to stay.

### *Tackling Optional Questions*

"Feel free to tell us anything else you think we'd like to know about you." Such a statement might be construed to be an optional one on the application. Counsel your students not to believe it. In fact, your students should not ignore any of the so-called "feel free" or noncompulsory sections of the application. The tackling of optional questions can demonstrate a sense of thoroughness, industry, and seriousness of purpose in a candidate. With applications that do not require an essay, bypassing these noncompulsory items is an even greater risk.

### *The "Improved" Student*

The number of academically capable students who produce mediocre or poor work prior to the senior year is staggering. If your counselee falls into this category, he or she should take heart—it's not too late: colleges love to see an "improved" student. Obviously, the sooner the student comes alive the better, but even if the student has bombed in his or her first three years, there's still hope. The student might not think so, but you know better. Usually the greater the academic potential (as measured by standardized testing), the greater the attraction. Your counselee is going to need some very good mid-year senior grades, however.

The applicant needs to find a spot somewhere on the application, or use a separate piece of paper, to *briefly* explain just why he or she had not been working toward his or her ability. Here are some do's and don'ts:

Don't waste the essay section with such an explanation.

Do be thoughtful, objective, and honest in your writing.

Do shoot for understanding, not pity.

Don't lay the blame for your underachievement at the school's or someone else's feet.

Do conclude your statement with a few words about how your handling of the mess has made you a better person.

## *Supplementary Materials*

The process of submitting supplementary materials continues to be abused. You can do much to remind your counselees of the old adage, "The thicker the folder, the thicker the student." For example, submitting an entire term paper is not the way to go with it. Neither is a book of poetry. Colleges take pride in developing application materials where the amount and depth of information requested reflects specific institutional needs. Going beyond that point can find the candidate in dangerous waters.

The issue seems to be especially pronounced with the "most" and "highly" selective colleges and universities that are often "reach" schools for a candidate. Granted that these schools are interested in an applicant documenting a portion of his or her life that cannot be fully presented on the actual application. On the other hand, the same schools can be a bit wary about a packet that takes up too much space in a file drawer; with some admission officials, it's called "stacking the deck." Your counselees need to proceed with caution; students should be judicious, both in their selection of materials to be submitted and in the number of submissions.

**What *not* to send:**

- More than the number of letters of recommendations requested. If a college or university does not require such letters, and the candidate wants to submit them, then no more than two should be submitted.

- Term papers, long essays, or original short stories.

- Special documentation of scholastic or co-curricular achievement. It is not necessary for an athlete to rip the letter off her varsity jacket and send it in as evidence of her prowess on the soccer field. Most colleges will take the word of the applicant as to awards and honors received. A relatively new phenomenon is that colleges might ask for length of commitment as expressed in number of hours devoted per week.

**What to send:**

- A *piece* of original poetry, a small sample of artwork or a photograph of a larger piece, a newspaper article about or by the applicant, a video or audio *clip* of an instrumental or dance performance, and a photograph that illustrates a particular project.

### X-ing the Box Marked "Race"

We have gone through stages in the identification of race: once-upon-a-time it was required, including the submission of a photograph; then we said we didn't *have* to know, so we made identification optional. Now what? It's still optional. But young people have been shifting their perspective on revealing their ethnicity, some for the better, some for the worse.

Essentially, it is a question of what the youngster wants to project to the admissions office. Some tend to hold back on their belonging to a "group," whether that be religion, or race, or socio-economics, or sex; they have a strong desire to be seen as an individual. Some are strongly invested in their "group"; being Jewish or Christian or Black or Oriental or male or female is part of what they want to project. Some are "different" from the majority and want to be accepted apart from that difference; some are different and want to be accepted *because* of that difference.

Your job as counselor is to help your counselee reflect on these matters. (We treat them more thoroughly in Chapter 12 on self-concept.) When this has been accomplished, the student will know whether or not to "X" the box.

You can be an encouraging force on "disclosure" (properly identifying oneself on an application) if you highlight a few things:

1.  Your heritage can be an acceptable "edge" as many collegiate institutions avidly search to build cross-cultural campuses.

2.  If your race or ethnicity is an issue and you're accepted, then you will know that the school *wants you*—it's not just luck of the draw.

3.  Disclosure could mean certain financial benefits.

4.  And most important: you are what you are—*and you should be proud of it!* This is a land of differences and opportunities. Colleges don't like candidates who try to *use* their ethnic status—but they don't like students who try to hide it, either.

A cautionary note. We said at the beginning of this section "some for the worse." In the identification of ethnicity, as in other areas, some people stretch the truth. Luke's great-grandfather was Cherokee, but all other members of his family were of European descent; does he classify as Native American? It's up to the college or university. The rule of thumb seems to be fifty percent, or one parent, but even that's becoming meaningless: "mixed marriages" are increasingly common.

Which box does the student check? It seems reasonable that he or she should go with the greatest share, or check two boxes, or maybe three. Or proudly note that the ancestry is mixed.

But what is the counselor's ethical responsibility? If Luke applies for a scholarship, basing his claim on a small part of his heritage, should the counselor intervene? Or should it be the institution's responsibility? Are you going to handle it or are you going to punt? It's up to you; ethical lines are rather fuzzy. Perhaps if there is a gross misalignment, you'd want to withhold your approval. Honesty still seems to be the best policy—if not for the moment, surely later, when you can sleep at night.

# A FINAL WORD

The process of a family getting a son or daughter into college today has taken on the aura of any other marketing campaign. We hesitate to use the term "package," but for certain collegiate institutions and for purposes of acceptance, that's what it has come down to: how well the candidate has *packaged* him- or herself. The quality of completion of the application has become a major instrument in such packaging.

# SUGGESTED READING

American Educational Research Association, 1995, *Will They Think Less of My Handwritten Essay If Others Process Theirs?*, 1230 17th Street NW, Washington, D.C. 20036-3078.

# CHAPTER 28

# ADMISSION TESTING

For admission testing and college entrance, it would be nice to have a level playing field, but such is not the case. Some college officials have snidely remarked that without the monied crowd, there'd be no playing field at all. Perhaps. But it continues to be obvious that the more affluent families are at a decided advantage when it comes to "getting in." And scores on tests such as SAT I *are* closely correlated with family income; with some exception, the highest scores can be found with youngsters from the most affluent families.

Another term heard frequently at state and national conferences is "unfair." Admission officers concede that their actions are often unfair. Interesting. As a school counselor you can help temper the impact of some of this unfairness, e.g., admission test results, to certain of your less fortunate counselees. Such help can come through good counsel related to academic achievement (dropping class rank if you are working in a high-powered school system) or even through more substantive and purposeful evaluation writing. There are lots of ways you can help, because admission testing is going to be with us for some time to come.

Although the product has been improved, its adverse impact will continue to be felt on a sizable portion of the student population. Whether or not SAT/ACT scores are biased or whether they mean anything at all will be debated for years to come with little or no resolve. The larger issue is that the most prestigious colleges and universities seek high test scores, and that translates into an advantage for the more well-to-do.

In the exhibit halls in America, Stanley Kaplan, the *Princeton Review*, and others offer their wares to school counselors who attend particular conventions. Through personal contact and the media, test preparation firm representatives boast about the increases their clients have enjoyed. Prep courses don't come cheap: the $500 to $1,000 price tag can put them out of reach for many lower- or middle-class families.

Does any of this matter? To some extent, yes. We know that in times of recession, corporations do not stop sending their personnel recruiters to places like Harvard, Yale, and Princeton. Class bias in higher education has its exceptions, but they are, after all, exceptions. Henry Ford and Thomas Edison scoffed at the importance of higher education. But they, too, were exceptions.

# IS TWICE BETTER?

Some people believe that scores always rise when students take the SAT I more than once. A study by the College Board, however, shows that this is not the case. The Board based its findings on some 400,000 students who took the SAT I in the spring of 1994 as juniors, then again in the fall of 1994 as seniors. Fifty-five percent of 1994 juniors who took the test for a second time as seniors improved their scores; 35 percent had score decreases; and 10 percent had no change at all.

School counselors *and* college admission officials must become knowledgeable about such data. Regrettably, some colleges continue to encourage students to "take it as often as you like." The same colleges tout the fact that they will always take the highest score. Most counseling departments now strongly advise families that twice is nice, and let's not overdo it. As you know, virtually all colleges and universities will take the highest verbal and the highest math, even splitting the scores where necessary, *if* the test is taken but twice. How about taking it just once?

According to the same College Board report, the higher a student's scores as a junior, the more likely that subsequent scores will be lower. The lower the initial scores, the more likely subsequent scores will be higher. So, when is high enough? When is it appropriate to take the SAT only once? When the combined score hits 1350 or 1375? Probably. It really becomes a matter of personal preference, yet when John or Jennifer come seeking your advice, we believe you're on safe ground with 1375. One problem is that the 1375 youngsters often want to see if they can "break" 1400. Sound familiar? Others get nervous about the Ivy League and want to see how high they can go.

The Board further discovered that on *average*, juniors repeating the SAT I as seniors improved their verbal scores by about 13 points, and their mathematics scores by about 12 points. Also, among students who repeat SAT I, about 1 in 30 gains 100 or more points on verbal or math, and about 1 in 30 loses 100 or more points. The College Board keeps reminding the public (many are not listening, including test preparation firms) that a verbal or math score must vary by some 70 points before it can be viewed as reflecting a genuine difference in ability.

# INCREASED STUDY MEANS HIGHER SCORES

It appears that SAT/ACT scores are directly related to the number and level of academic courses reported by students. The more academic courses pursued, the higher the SAT scores. The higher the level of coursework pursued, the higher the SAT scores. So, the *number and quality* of academic courses selected seems to dictate how well students will do on college admission tests (SAT or ACT). According to a September 1995 College Board bulletin, students who had 20 or more academic units had SAT averages of 474 verbal and 531 math, while those with fewer than 15 units had average scores of 354 verbal and 406 math. (The Board reported out the 1995 scores on the original, not the recentered scale.)

In reporting out, the College Board also mentioned that 1995 scores were the highest in years, most of the increase attributed to the better-prepared students—those in the top fifth of their class. The class of 1995 had also pursued a record number of honors courses, especially in the areas of English, mathematics, and science.

Undoubtedly you've been witnessing more students opting to take more challenging work. You can be a major factor in seeing to it that your counselees "stretch" themselves academically, of course doing so in a realistic manner. The term realistic can be translated into a course grade. For example, is there anything wrong with a student earning a final grade of C+ in an honors course? We believe not. You and your department *can* agree on a certain bottomline performance, and then communicate that to your many publics. A "C+" is an excellent bottomline grade.

For the most part, the sun is setting on those parents who believe their sons and daughters *must* pull an "A" or even a "B+" grade in an honors course. The message has been delivered! As a counselor, you know better than anyone else that all honors courses are not of equal intensity, just as all honors teachers are not equally demanding. You are also aware that there must be a bottom line—that several of the so-called top fifty colleges and universities want it all: honors and advanced placement pursuit *and* good grades.

And so, as an advocate, you walk a fine line between reality and idealism. Nonetheless, you need to encourage your students to challenge themselves academically. If you do just that, you will end up helping far more students than you will be hurting. A youngster can always back down to the next level, even once school has opened. Remember the old adage that should be pinned to every counselor's bulletin board: "Nothing ventured, nothing gained." Or, the slogan we saw posted in one counselor's office: "It's putting yourself on the line that counts—not whether you win or lose."

# SAT II SCORE CHOICE

When the College Board introduced SAT II Score Choice several years ago, the intent was to further empower students, to help them control their own test scores. The thought was to enable students to construct profiles that would reflect their greatest strengths. Also, it was hoped that Score Choice would encourage greater risk-taking in that Sat I and Sat II scores had been previously reported out on a cumulative basis and on the *same* reporting tape. For the most part, Score Choice has worked well.

Having the option to hold SAT II scores has proven to be a very popular feature with youngsters, but high schools and colleges are concerned that students are not using the option appropriately. As a school counselor, you might be concerned that students do not fully understand how the program works; if you're a college admission official, you might be concerned that your school is not receiving score reports as early as it would like. Here are some points worth exploring with your counselees:

- Score Choice does not work well with seniors, especially those who are applying Early Decision. Perhaps you need to alert your senior counselees to certain pitfalls of the program, e.g., score delay.

- If students select Score Choice, the scores from *all* of the SAT II examinations they have taken at a single administration will be placed on hold. After reviewing their scores, your counselees can then pick and choose; that is, release *individual* scores and have them sent to colleges. Students need to understand, however, that this can be a time-consuming process.

- Score Choice works well with juniors, provided they learn to release their scores on time. More than half of the Spring 1995 test takers, mostly juniors, participated in Score Choice.

- When students are ready to take their scores off hold, they need to complete an authorization form, which the Board has designed around a series of numbered steps that supposedly clears up misconceptions and reporting procedures. Students should realize that "release" is not the same as "send." They are two very different operations. Fortunately, the two-sided authorization form can be used for *both* maneuvers.

Dartmouth has addressed the suppression and delay problem quite well. The college only uses the three highest SAT II subject tests in making its decisions. Dartmouth urges students to send *all* scores and avoid any confusion or delay that might arise by suppressing scores.

# CHAPTER 29

# FINANCIAL AID

There have been two major occurrences in the college admission financial picture since the late 1980s. First, there has been a shrinking pool of academically talented applicants; and, due to soaring tuition costs, especially at the private schools, such shrinkage has provided an impetus for families to do more shopping around for the best financial deal possible. The crucial number underlying today's search for affordable quality education is actually the nation's shrunken college-age population, which has declined nearly 14% since 1975. As a result, savvy families can now negotiate financial aid packages that eliminate 50% or more of a college's total sticker price. Second, the very colleges and universities that are competing for the best and the brightest are hiking tuition rates at the same time in order to pay for "diversification" *and* to compensate for dwindling federal and state financial support. The two happenings are related, even though they tend to work against each other.

It is well known that college costs have continued to far out-pace real family income. For instance, tuition costs went up another 6.5% for the 1995–96 academic year, to an average of $10,333 at private schools and $2,780 at publics. At the same time, an increasing number of youngsters from disadvantaged backgrounds are seeking a college education. Because of this and other factors, more candidates than ever are holding out their hands for what is rapidly becoming a limited number of dollars.

Are the Ivy Leagues and other leading colleges using a record amount of revenue from tuition, which for these schools, averaged $19,110 in 1995, to subsidize grants for the less affluent students? A number of people would say "yes." Again, the colleges argue that the increase is warranted because of waning state and federal subsidies, and by the thrust of the institutions to diversify their student bodies. It's kind of like the Robin Hood principle—colleges and universities charge more to those who can pay in order to provide financial aid to the more needy applicants, rather than have empty seats or a monocultural student body. It is not a new phenomenon; it's just gotten worse in the past ten or so years. And usually the more diverse the entering class, the more tuition revenue is required to meet the need.

Nearly everyone in higher education believes that campus diversity and the educational opportunity made possible by scholarships are necessary; nevertheless, there are mounting questions about just how much more of the costs of financial aid can be shifted to the shoulders of the more affluent candidates.

According to a *New York Times* article of March 22, 1995, there is a "direct relationship between the amount of tuition devoted to scholarships and the number of students receiving them." Mount Holyoke College and the University of Rochester not only use the most tuition to provide scholarships, they also provide scholarships to the most students—2 out of 3.

Rochester decided to streamline its aid situation somewhat when it announced in the Fall of 1995 that New York State residents and children of alumni would automatically receive a $5,000 grant. Evidently, the approach has worked for Rochester—applications from state residents are up 20 percent.

At the bottom of the list of expenditure of tuition monies for scholarship assistance is Princeton University. The venerable Ivy has the luxury of spending just 1 percent of tuition revenue to meet students' financial needs because it has a 450-million-dollar endowment earmarked for that purpose only.

Some families are becoming rather rebellious about the situation; and, since the college admission scene continues to be a buyer's market, we are seeing a virtual bidding war on the part of collegiate institutions for the academically talented. Unlike voluntary charitable contributions, that portion of tuition used to provide scholarships is *not* tax deductible.

As a school counselor, and in an effort to help your families, you need to be aware of the methods that some collegiate institutions currently employ to adjust to this phenomenon. Financially strapped institutions can be seen pursuing one or more of the following paths:

1. Admit a top applicant, but offer only partial financial aid with the hope that the family can make up the difference.

2. Wait-list the applicant and see if aid dollars committed to other students will free up by late May or early June.

3. Be totally candid with the applicant. Admit the person, but announce to him or her that you can't award any aid because you've run out of funds.

4. Reject the applicant outright, claiming that too many highly qualified youngsters applied that particular year.

# LIFTING THE MASK ON NEED-BLIND ADMISSIONS

Remember when "blind" really meant blind, and not even a speck of daylight crept under the college's admission mask? There was a time when many colleges had funds to meet the needs of *all* students who qualified for admission, and consequently no one was turned down for financial reasons. Remember?

Well, now the mask has been lifted by a number of schools. In some cases, ever so discretely—some would argue secretively; in others, violently. Things *are* getting tight. Even the colleges are bickering among themselves, as they accuse each other of not being honest in their literature and in their presentations to school counselors and prospective students.

A growing number of colleges and universities are owning up to the fact that their pots are no longer full. Indeed, schools such as Carleton College, Wheaton College, and Brown University have openly dropped need-blind admissions guarantees. Of course, there are some colleges and universities with huge endowments that will continue to meet the full need of all of their applicants.

## *Tips on Handling the Problem*

There are ways in which students and their families can shield themselves from this growing problem if they believe they are deserving of financial assistance.

1. Start early (late sophomore year) to research colleges that are a good match for the student's academic interests.

2. Don't hesitate to contact certain admission offices either by telephone, letter, or in person to discuss their financial aid policies. Asking pertinent questions—the average amount of financial aid awarded each year, for instance—is the way to go. It is probably best to make your initial contact with admission people, rather than with financial aid people. Save them for later.

3. If financial aid is a major factor, it is probably a good idea to apply to a few more schools than normal, e.g., eight rather six. Because dollars are tight and application fees heavy, at times a family must pull back and apply to only a few schools; but if it is at all possible, the family should attempt to make an investment in potential grant awards by submitting several applications.

4. Just as a family should spread its applications up and down the ladder of academic selectivity, so too should they spread their selections across a range of schools based on cost.

5. The private junior college or community college can be a great beginning for the marginal student who is looking to save money. Four-year colleges often view the academically successful transfer applicant as a low-risk candidate to whom they will only have to commit two years of financial aid.

6. Once a student is admitted to a particular college, but no aid is offered or the amount offered is considerably below the expectations of the family, the family can sometimes negotiate with financial aid officers. An interview to review the offer should be requested. Maybe the picture was not sufficiently clear on the aid application, or the college or university really wants the student, or dollars have subsequently been freed up at the given institution. Admissions history is replete with cases where financial aid packages have been improved after the initial offer.

As you can see, the potential could hardly be greater for school counselors to render support to families in their quest to make that "best match" a reality. Simply doing an effective job of counseling on the basics of financial aid has taken on added importance for counselors. For example, today it is critical that families distinguish between the *price* of an institution and the actual *cost*. Sometimes, if the initial price looks too high, families won't explore further. Parents need to know that numerous colleges and universities have some very innovative financial aid programs in place. The University of Rochester, discussed earlier, is but one example. Many of these same schools openly advertise that they *can* and *will* meet full need.

### *Price Versus Cost*

What *is* the difference between price and cost? *Price* is the amount charged by an institution for tuition, fees, room, board, and personal or miscellaneous expenses. Cost is the determined amount that a family must pay out-of-pocket toward these educational expenses. *Aid* is the difference between price and cost, which is determined by *need*. As you know, price can vary greatly from institution to institution. But what a family can afford to pay doesn't often change. In other words, the amount the family is expected to contribute remains basically fixed, whether the college or university is priced at $10,500 or $20,500.

## FINANCIAL AID IS NOT FINANCIAL PLANNING

The two terms, which are "poles apart," should not be confused. Financial aid might be thought of as getting your hands on someone else's money, whereas financial planning is making the most of your own resources. There are many individuals wandering around the country calling themselves financial planners in order to sell a product. Financial planning is not a product: it is a process—a lifelong one, at that.

Since the mid 1980s there has been much advancement in bringing the "planning" message to families with respect to the significance of early financial preparation for post-secondary education. An ever-increasing number of secondary schools are conducting evening programs for parents, as early as the sixth grade. Information-starved parents can be seen flocking to these sessions. Considering the times, why shouldn't these programs be well-attended? If parents know they won't be getting financial assistance from outside sources, they can then shape their investment programs differently.

An organization that is ready and willing to offer such advice is the International Association for Financial Planning. For a complimentary membership directory that includes the names of planners in your immediate area, telephone (800) 945-4237. In addition to the usual certification, candidates for membership must also have three years of field experience, produce peer and client recommendations, submit a sample plan, and perform satisfactorily on a special five-hour examination. For other information, write IAFP at Suite B-300, 5775 Glenridge Drive NE, Atlanta, Georgia 30328; or telephone: (404) 845-0011.

Of course, to qualify for financial assistance, a student must demonstrate the financial necessity: a family does not have to be poor to qualify for aid, but there must be a genuine need for such aid.

### *"Package" Defined*

When financial assistance is offered, most families receive an aid "package," a combination of four types of financial assistance:

1. *Grant or scholarship:* Money that does not have to be repaid.
2. *Student loan:* Borrowed funds that usually carry a low interest rate and do not have to be repaid until after the student graduates, and then over an extended period of time.
3. *Parent loan:* Same as above, except that repayment begins almost immediately.
4. *Work study:* 10 to 15 hours per week of on- or off-campus employment through which one can earn money to help pay his or her way. (Freshmen hours are kept purposely light.)

To receive financial assistance, there are, of course, forms to be completed.

## TWO BASIC FINANCIAL AID FORMS

### *PROFILE*

Remember the FAF? Well, now its PROFILE. The College Scholarship Service (CSS) has created Financial Aid PROFILE to consolidate the institutional form and the CSS form. Several hundred member colleges and universities have agreed to use PROFILE, the intent being that of streamlining the process whereby families apply for financial assistance. PROFILE allows families to fill out a standard form with additional questions tailored to each college's individual requirements. All aid applicants *must* still complete the free form, FAFSA, which determines, among other things, eligibility for federal monies. Information disclosed on PROFILE will not affect a student's federal aid package.

Most collegiate institutions—especially state schools—do not use PROFILE, however. Frankly, the pricier the college, the greater the likelihood it will require PROFILE; but, since the program is new and colleges have to pay a fee to CSS for customization, some schools continue to opt for their own institutional piece.

It's easy to uncover those colleges that use PROFILE by examining the list of member schools in the registration booklet. It costs $5 to register and $14.50 for each report up to ten. If money is an issue, CSS offers a waiver program administered through designated high schools. (High schools are eligible based on the economic makeup of the community they serve *and* by the number of students who typically apply to colleges and universities participating in the PROFILE program.)

Colleges can purchase fee waiver cards on their own from CSS. Colleges can then distribute them to applicants exhibiting financial need. If a student has already had an application fee waived, there's a good chance he or she will also receive a waiver card to cover the cost of PROFILE.

Families can return the completed five-dollar PROFILE registration form to CSS by mail, fax, or electronic data submission, using the College Board's ExPan network. At that point in time CSS will send the applicant a packet containing:

- A letter explaining packet contents.
- A four-page core PROFILE form.
- Any institutional questions (Section Q of PROFILE) if required by one or more of the member schools.
- CSS supplements if required, e.g. divorced/separated parent's statement.

## *FAFSA*

It began with the 1995-96 school year, and it will probably never end: parents can now apply for financial aid to most colleges and universities without having to spend a dime on reporting fees. All students applying for any federal assistance *must* file the Free Application For Federal Student Aid form. It is the only application form families have to complete to be considered for federal Pell Grants, Supplemental Educational Opportunity Grants (SEOG), Stafford Loans (including the new unsubsidized Stafford Loan), Perkins Loans, Work Study, and other federal financial aid programs. The application process is free!

When completing the FAFSA, students can send data to six colleges or universities. If they wish to send more reports, students can follow instructions on the SAR (Student Aid Report), which applicants usually receive within four weeks of application submittal.

Most states are now able to award their grants solely on the basis of information derived from the FAFSA.

The FAFSA, distributed initially by the College Scholarship Service, is currently distributed to high schools by the U.S. Department of Education. In contrast to PROFILE, the federal form only gathers income information one year previous to the year the student is expected to enter college. Also, the form does not request home equity information, a significant family asset in many cases; the PROFILE does collect this information. The FAFSA does not ask about the student's expected summer or school-year income.

Once the free application is submitted, a federal processor calculates the Expected Family Contribution (EFC) and then sends a Student Aid Report (SAR) to the family. The EFC and other FAFSA data is simultaneously sent to all listed colleges and state aid agencies. The SAR can be used by the family to confirm/correct FAFSA data. State agencies use EFC and other FAFSA information to determine potential student eligibility for need-based state aid. The various states report any awards to colleges; colleges make the final decision.

# UNUSUAL FAMILY CIRCUMSTANCES

There is room for unusual circumstances. In other words, there is room for a family to appeal the size of an award or even the denial of such, because the financial and family circumstances of some students cannot be appropriately addressed by the standard FAFSA questions; circumstances can change after filing. Federal aid regulations allow financial aid officers to make adjustments for unusual situations through an appeal process.

## *Special Circumstances Defined*

A special circumstance is one which materially affects a family's income or assets, e.g., unusual medical or dental expenses, school tuition expenses, lost wages caused by illness or unemployment, or loss of parental financial support and/or cooperation in meeting college costs.

Consider the following in working with your families:

- Aid applicants can apply for consideration of unusual financial circumstances, but the appeal can *only* be made through the financial aid office of the college in which he or she is interested.

- The earliest time an appeal may be submitted is *after* the FAFSA has been filed and the EFC (Expected Family Contribution) has been calculated.

- An early step in the appeal process should be the gathering of documentation. Such documentation could include paid tuition bills or unreimbursed medical expenses for the treatment of major or chronic illness or disability.

- There is no standard form for the appeal process. Each college or university has its own procedures, and the family should follow instructions from the financial aid office. Any appeal should be addressed to the director of financial aid at the given institution.

- The initial appeal letter should contain, among other things, the student's full name and social security number, a brief statement of the reason(s) for the appeal, and a summary of the supporting documentation to be offered.

# EIGHT BIG FINANCIAL AID MISTAKES MADE BY FAMILIES

1. *Rushing through the application process:* It is *not* first come, first served—or, for that matter, the early bird gets the worm. Such maxims may at times hold true for the college application process, but what's important in the financial aid process is an errorless application. Errorless applications result from careful and thorough preparation. The reason some students are denied aid is not because mom and dad make too much money. It's because the preparer rushed through the aid-application process and committed too many errors. Remember, it was the tortoise that won the race.

2. *Underestimating one's financial aid eligibility:* It's unfortunate that many people believe they make too much money and therefore don't qualify for assistance. An accompanying danger is the tendency for the family to limit the college search, e.g., exploring only those colleges and universities they think they can afford. Families forget that there is a wide range of costs. They might not qualify for aid with a school of $14,000, but are very much in the picture with a school that costs twice that amount.

3. *Overestimating one's financial eligibility:* Some families assume the boat will be coming in loaded with money. Such irrational thinking can lead to the even more dangerous situation of applying to only the most expensive schools. A family has to apply to one or two "financial safety" schools—schools where the applicant has a good chance of admittance *and* where the family can afford the price if little or no aid is offered.

4. *Thinking that all public colleges and universities are inexpensive—even the out-of-state:* Two of the most expensive public universities in America for out-of-state students are the University of Vermont and the University of Michigan. The gap between tuition at out-of-state public schools and that of private schools has narrowed greatly in the past decade. Out-of-state public schools are no longer the bargains they once were. A family that has high need might want to proceed carefully with out-of-state institutions, since most of these schools give first priority to the needs of their in-state students. What *is* interesting and often overlooked is the fact that if you can demonstrate need, you'll usually do better at the more expensive private schools than at the less expensive out-of-state public schools.

5. *Floating a personal bank loan for that needed extra money:* Before a family goes running to their bank for personal loan funds, they should check with the financial aid office of the college the student will be attending. State, federal, and private commercial vendors can usually offer more attractive arrangements.

6. *Turning down student loan money because parents don't want to see a debt hanging over their youngster's head:* Aside from the fact that education is probably the best investment one will ever make, Perkins and Stafford loan programs are very attractive, in that there is no interest charged and no repayment of principal until several months after the student graduates.

7. *Prematurely responding to an offer of aid:* The applicant usually has until May 1 to respond to both the offer of admission and to the financial aid package. Responding to a package of financial aid too early can be troublesome, in that a better offer might come along. For better or worse, for richer or poorer, today's families can be seen using the attractive offer of one school to bargain for a better deal with another that the student prefers to attend. The name of the game is keeping options open and under wraps for as long as possible. There is no advantage to responding (other than the pressured but modest dormitory space deposit) to a school before the deadline.

8. *Waiting until the senior year to get moving on financial aid:* Here is where the word "early" takes on new meaning. Early planning is where it's at, folks! A family needs to think about financial aid considerations when their offspring is in ninth grade—even earlier, if warranted. Decisions can then be rendered intelligently with the absence of

haste and emotion. A family can hire an *independent* financial planner, and/or use a money guidebook that contains worksheets and formulas for determining eligibility. Corporations such as Peterson's Guides and the College Board have user-friendly computerized programs for early analysis and planning.

# SCHOLARSHIP SEARCH COMPANIES: CAVEAT EMPTOR!

Since we wrote *Making a Difference in College Admission* in 1989, there has been a significant increase in the number of scholarship search companies offering their services to students and their families. Many of these companies have been targeting low-income families who cannot afford the requisite fees; so there is reason to suspect that not all of these search groups are above-board. You can help your families make a more informed decision using the handout given in Figure 29-1.

# SUPPORT FOR THE LOW-INCOME OR "AT-RISK" STUDENT

There were originally three aspects to the federal TRIO program, hence its name: Talent Search, Upward Bound, and Student Support Services. Two more have been added: the Robert E. McNair Post-Baccalaureate Achievement program and the Educational Opportunity Center program. All TRIO programs have historically targeted low-income or first-generation college-bound students who are "at risk" for dropping out of school.

TRIO programs have proven to be effective and are usually spared the ax when Congress is looking to cut federal expenditures. Currently the five programs are receiving some 450 million dollars in federal funds.

- More than 300,000 students, grades six through twelve, participate in **Talent Search** which provides counseling services and information on college admissions and financial aid.

- **Upward Bound** helps 50,000 high schoolers prepare for the rigors of college. Enrollees attend classes in mathematics, science, and literature on selected college campuses after school, on weekends, and during the summer months.

- **Educational Opportunity Centers** around the nation help some 150,000 people who are either unemployed or underemployed obtain a college education.

- Once students are in attendance at a college or university, they can take advantage of TRIO's **Student Support Services**, which offers counseling, tutoring, and remediation to over 170,000 "at risk" collegians yearly. A chief thrust of the services is to improve retention rates.

- Finally, the **Ronald E. McNair Post-Baccalaureate Achievement** program provides faculty mentors and research opportunities to 2,000 undergraduate students who are encouraged to seek advanced degrees and ultimately pursue careers in college teaching.

FIGURE 29-1

## FINANCIAL AID MATCHING SERVICES: QUESTIONS FOR FAMILIES TO RAISE

As funds for higher education have become harder to get, many families are turning to financial aid "matchmakers." The number of these computerized matching service firms has significantly increased, as well. Since the first of these companies opened its door some 25 years ago, the advertising message has remained much the same: "Big dollars are going begging. There are literally millions of unclaimed dollars just waiting for you and others like you."

But buyer beware! Researchers say it is an unproved claim that significant amounts of educational monies are going untapped. So, before plunging into any such plan, you might want to procure answers to the following questions:

1. What is the size of the data bank for financial aid sources? Does the company maintain its own file of sources, or does it use the file of another service?

2. How many leads will the company supply for the fee? What percentage of these leads are in the form of scholarships, loans, work study programs, or contests? More important, do they include federal and state programs for which students are considered through normal financial-aid channels?

3. How often does the company update its list of aid sources? Is the company willing to confirm that these sources exist and that deadline dates and eligibility criteria are current?

4. What characteristics are used to match students with aid sources?

5. What has been the track record of the company? In other words, how successful have former participants been in securing financial aid from company-recommended sources?

6. What is the company's refund policy? Will it return all or a portion of the fee if (1) aid sources are incorrectly matched with student's qualifications, (2) aid sources no longer exist or fail to respond to the student, (3) an application deadline has passed when the information is received?

Answers to these six questions should help you establish the credibility of a particular search company. But remember: There is no guarantee that your son or daughter will actually receive any funds should you decide to use this type of service.

# FINANCING WITHOUT MOM/DAD OR SCHOLARSHIPS

Every once in a while you'll come across a counselee who is interested in a cooperative education program, such as those offered at Drexel University in Philadelphia, or Northeastern University in Boston. Cooperative education combines coursework with off-campus employment related to the student-employee's major area of study; in most cases, money earned on the job covers college costs. History is replete with the many thousands of satisfied undergrads who have worked their way through college, thanks to a cooperative education program. It's not for everyone, but it certainly is for some.

Depending on institutional policy, students can rotate between work and school each semester, or divide their days between the two. Some programs are with private employers, others with federal departments or agencies. Cooperative education can open doors for eventual full-time employment. (More than a few coop students have been offered a permanent position upon graduation.)

Then there is the federal Student Educational Employment Program that offers students at all levels (high school through graduate school) work opportunities to help pay their college bills. The program has two components: (1) The Student Temporary Employment Program which offers students the flexibility of earning a salary while working on their studies. The employment may be during the summer or school year and need not be related to the student's major field of study. (2) The Student Career Experience Program provides students with work experience directly related to their academic field of study. Students alternate formal periods of work and study and may be eligible for permanent employment with the federal government upon graduation from college or graduate school.

Much of the aforementioned information is detailed in *Earn & Learn*, a forty-page pamphlet by Joseph M. Re, and obtainable through Octameron Associates, P.O. Box 2748, Alexandria, Virginia 22301.

The military also offers an assortment of programs that can help students fund all or part of their college education. Military Academies are free, albeit intensely competitive for admission. They also require a certain amount of military service after graduation. ROTC programs are operated through individual colleges and universities and in conjunction with the various branches of service. Such programs provide cadets with small monthly stipends that can help defray some of the cost of undergraduate education.

For those willing to serve the nation prior to attending college, there is the Montgomery GI Bill. Under the bill, military personnel on active duty who can stash away $100 a month into an education fund are rewarded at the end of a two-year enlistment with an additional $10,500 by the Veteran's Administration; if they do a four-year enlistment program, they would receive $13,200.

# SUGGESTED READING

Cassidy, Daniel J. (1996), *The Scholarship Book*, 4th ed. Englewood Cliffs: Prentice-Hall, Inc. (A complete guide to 50,000 private-sector funding sources for undergraduates.)

# CHAPTER 30

# SENIORS, GRADS, AND PARENTS IN THE ADMISSION PROCESS

## HOMEWORK FOR PARENTS

In doing college planning, it is important that communication with parents be open and honest, with special attention paid to their expectations. Most parents don't have the background experience, the time to discover current trends, or the objectivity to have a *realistic* assessment of their youngster's chances in the competitive world of college admissions. Parents often see their offspring through colored glasses—sometimes rosy, sometimes shadowed gray. Your conferring with students *and* parents should help bring things more into focus.

An effective means of dealing with parental expectations is to ask them to share with you in writing *their* perceptions as to their youngster's personal strengths, concerns, attitudes, and accomplishments. (See Figure 30-1 on page 241.) This activity can broaden lines of communication between home and school, and enable you to receive early warnings of unrealistic expectations and/or special problems. Such written input can also expand your knowledge of a particular counselee, providing you with insight into the family situation, including the individual youngster's position within the family structure.

While parent "brag sheets" are now quite common, in many schools they are not as strong a "must do" as they could be. In one school system, the letter and form are sent to the parents the August before the senior year; if there is no response, they are sent home with the student in the fall, with the admonition that completing the "brag sheet" will be most helpful in counselor recommendations.

The quality of the invitational letter is of prime importance. Note the personal nature of the letter, and the fact that it is sent from the counselor, not the department. The number of questions posed should be kept to a minimum. Hopefully, all of this will ensure a response—and a quality piece, at that.

# ENLISTING HELP FROM FORMER STUDENTS

## *The Lawrenceville Project*

Students at the Lawrenceville School in New Jersey get to browse through a looseleaf binder of comments from former schoolmates about the colleges and universities they now attend. "Page two" of a biannual follow-up survey of graduates, supervised by Arthur Thomas, director of counseling, provides for direct feedback from previous Lawrenceville students on their collegiate experiences. Surveys are mailed to students at their respective colleges. The response sheets, placed in a binder and organized by name of institution, become available to juniors and seniors in a kind of coffee-table arrangement in the counseling department's outer office. It is a great early planning activity, as well as a way for seniors to see what grads have to say about the schools they are attending. It's yet another method by which professional staff can update themselves on particular institutions. Thomas and colleagues naturally encourage students to use the material, but to read it judiciously. (It might be said, though, that the personal biases of former Lawrenceville students probably don't differ appreciably from the views expressed in such "tell it like it is" publications as the *Insider's Guide to the Colleges* by the Yale University Press.)

## *Alumni/Senior Exchange*

It is not at all uncommon for secondary schools to support some sort of program whereby graduates return to the building or campus to speak with students about college life. A popular time is when the collegians are on winter break—early December to late January. There's nothing like hearing it from those who are presently going through the process. Youth counseling youth doesn't hurt, either.

One high school aptly calls its program an alumni/senior exchange. With this special affair, participating graduates are encouraged to wear their college sweatshirts, are provided with tall neatly-lettered signs that announce their respective colleges, and are invited to eat lunch in the faculty dining room when not manning tables in the main cafeteria. The letter of invitation shown in Figure 30-2 on page 243 to senior students describes the activity well.

CHEROKEE MISSION HIGH SCHOOL
CHEROKEE MISSION
OKLAHOMA 55555

Dear Parent:

Whether it be the tragic loss of a loved one, or something wonderful, like a community award, there can be aspects of a youngster's growth and development that may not be apparent to the school counselor. These same experiences could play an important role in the youngster's pursuit of an appropriate college or university at which to matriculate.

In order to provide me with pertinent information, I am asking my students' parents to complete a "brag sheet" on their sons and daughters. Your personal responses can go a long way toward helping me write a more informed and substantive evaluation.

Your comments on the enclosed form can either be placed in a sealed envelope and marked to my attention, or delivered to me in person.

Your remarks will remain confidential. If you would rather discuss a particular situation than write about it, please feel free to make an appointment to see me or telephone me.

Thank you for your cooperation!

Sincerely,

Ralph Diorio
Counselor

FIGURE 30-1 *CONTINUED*

PARENT "BRAG SHEET" FOR
COLLEGE RECOMMENDATION

Name of Student: _____

1. What do you believe to be your child's outstanding accomplishments during the past several years? *Why* did you select these particular accomplishments?

2. In what developmental areas has your child shown the most growth during the past several years?

3. What do you consider to be your child's outstanding personality traits?

4. Are there any unusual and/or personal circumstances (negative or positive) that have affected your child's academic performance or growth process?

Additional comments, if any. Please feel free to use the back or enclose a second sheet.

_____          _____
Name of Counselor                                    Parent Signature

**FIGURE 30-2**

---

December 12, 199X

Dear Senior:

The Counseling Department and Administration invite you to attend our fifth annual Alumni/Senior Exchange to be held Friday, January 4, 199X in the cafeteria.

The purpose of the program is to afford you the opportunity of speaking with last year's graduates who are currently enrolled in college. We hope you will use this time to alleviate any concerns you might have regarding adjustment to college living.

The affair will run during the three lunch periods. Last year's graduates will represent nearly 45 different colleges and universities.

Enclosed please find some sample questions you might like to pose to the student representatives.

---

Graduates of the preceding year are invited by postcard, and this particular counseling department wisely builds a sufficient amount of planning time (about ten weeks) into the program. As with most other events, there is always the concluding evaluation form (see page 244). This one is as simple and straightforward as you can get.

### *"What I Would Have Done Differently"*

An excellent exercise conducted in late spring by senior English teachers—if you can get their cooperation, that is, which you most probably can do—is to have the seniors write 150-word graded essays on the topic, "What I Would Have Done Differently in the College Admission Process." The contents of the completed essays are summarized by the Counseling Department, bound in booklet form, and then shared with junior students. It's yet another example of students helping students.

### *It Can Take More Than You*

It certainly can. Effective precollege planning is a team effort—parents, teachers, alumni, current seniors—and *you* should be the captain. You do have a special role in tying together the education of your counselees, and post-secondary planning is a critical aspect of a youngster's total educational experience. So when it comes to college selection, it can indeed take more than you—as each *unique* applicant moves closer and closer to his or her most *appropriate* choice.

FIGURE 30-3

**Evaluation of Alumni/Senior Exchange**

Please rate the following items:

|  | Excellent | Good | Fair | Poor |
|---|---|---|---|---|
| Library Orientation of Participants | | | | |
| Classroom Visitations | | | | |
| Cafeteria Mini-Fair | | | | |
| Lunch w/ Faculty | | | | |

What one or two aspects of the exchange did you find most enjoyable?

Would you change or eliminate any aspect of the program?

Would you add anything to the program?

General Comments:

# CHAPTER 31

# THE MEDIA AND TECHNOLOGY IN COLLEGE PLANNING

The use of the Common Application has been making students nervous for decades, as they've fretted about the impression the generic application would make once submitted. With the advent of computer technology and the handy diskette application, or on-line application processing, nervousness has turned to panic for more than a few students. As one youngster remarked, "It's taken me years to grow into the realization that I am one very important person in the world, only to find myself reduced to a mere blip on a computer screen."

But it's here—and it's gaining a full head of steam. "Applying to college is moving from the paper chase to the electronic chase," says William Conley, Dean of Undergraduate Admissions at Case Western Reserve University. But a good number of students and counselors don't like the chase. They'd rather do a slow walk through a process that is already too impersonalized. Applying by computer, they argue, will reduce students to a number, making it impossible for them to stand "far from the maddening crowd."

School counselors worry that increased computerization, especially the variety that directly link applicant and college, will remove them, the counselors, from the picture. But the picture has many pieces. "My fears were not justified," said Vincent Poisella, guidance coordinator at Hopatcong (New Jersey) High School, in the July 22, 1994 issue of the *Chronicle of Higher Education*. Poisella had been concerned that bringing computers into the guidance office would reduce personal interaction with students. He now uses interactive programs to help students narrow their choices, which leaves him more time to help other students deal with serious personal issues. And so goes the argument: Computer technology can free counselors to spend more advisement time with their clients on the all-important selection and refining process, as well as gather sufficient information from families and elsewhere to compose a more informed counselor recommendation. In short, a growing number of colleges are permitting students to forgo the frustrations of paperwork and apply to college electronically.

The State University of New York with its 34 campuses is but one of the many institutions that have joined the trend. Two other leaders have been Massachusetts Institute of Technology and Georgia Institute of Technology. Much of the movement to electronic admissions has been spearheaded by students and high school counselors. For computer-literate youngsters, disks can be easier than paper. SUNY applicants need only to obtain a copy of the university's admissions software. After the disk arrives by mail, the applicant simply fills in the blanks, then mails the disk back to the university. Once the disk is returned to the university, the entered information is loaded into the university's computer system. Higher education officials argue that electronic admissions is less time consuming and less expensive than paper application processing.

Another leader in the method is the University of Southern California, where in 1995, nearly 40 percent of the 15,000 applications were filed on disk. Georgia Tech has taken the process a step further: instead of mailing a disk, applicants can file directly on-line from their home computers with a modem—over the telephone lines and directly into the university computer database. This is known as Electronic Data Interchange (EDI).

Not every student has a sophisticated home computer, however. Yet some of these same students are not missing out. Using advanced technology in more than 500 high schools nationwide, these students can apply to several hundred colleges by using the College Board's new *ExPan* program.

Aside from all this, paper applications are not going to go the way of the 78 rpm record any time soon. Higher education isn't about to leave large numbers of youngsters stranded if they do not have access to a computer.

## A REVIEW OF WHAT'S AVAILABLE

Just how long private electronic application services will remain in demand is anybody's guess, as more and more colleges and universities bring electronic applications in-house with disks of their own or on-line application processing. The following is a review of some of the programs available from both profit and not-for-profit organizations.

### Common Application on Disk

The paper version of the common application is a program that was developed a quarter of a century ago by certain very selective colleges and universities. The intent of the founders was to simplify the college application process for American families. It has been a highly successful endeavor as indicated by the increasing number of collegiate institutions that have climbed on board this express vehicle.

Now we have the common application on diskette. Families can write directly to the National Association of Secondary School Principals in Reston, Virginia for a disk; or high schools can make copies for their students from a master disk. In the latter case, the high school usually requests that the student bring in a blank disk. Whatever the case, computerization of the common application was an inevitable happening, and to date, things appear to be going well.

If your student is planning to use disk, he or she should check each member college for its policy on accepting disk or printout. Some schools do not accept disk. Each college's requirements are noted in italics at the end of its admission information. Software versions available include Macintosh (MAC), and Windows and DOS for IBM-compatibles. (IBM).

For further information on this program you can telephone NASSP at (703) 860-0200, ext. 289.

### College Board's ExPan

This Windows-based software program centers on a student portfolio in which the user can enter, store, and revise information related to personal data, academic matters, co-curricular participation, and general correspondence throughout his or her high school career. The Board maintains an annually updated library of vital statistics on some 3,000 undergraduate colleges and universities, as well as hundreds of graduate and professional schools. *ExPan* (Explorer Plus Guidance and Application Network) helps students select and apply to various colleges and universities, enables school counselors to monitor their students in the application process, and offers colleges the opportunity to reduce application processing costs.

*ExPan* was first piloted in Washington State in 1993. Washington State counselors found *ExPan* to be a great way for students to organize a personal portfolio beginning as early as the ninth grade. Each year students can update their information as to activities, grades, and personal accomplishments. At a later point in time, some of the data can be transferred into a college admission application piece.

Since the Washington State pilot, the College Board has added new features, such as counselor reports and user electronic mail capability. (Users can send e-mail to other participants on the network.) About 500 secondary schools and 800 colleges and universities are currently using the program. *ExPan* provides a secondary school and its students the option of sending common applications *and* individual institutional applications electronically through the *ExPan* Network or by way of print format. Of course, the program is free to students provided that the secondary school opts to participate and purchase the package.

Information on *ExPan* can be obtained by writing the College Board at 45 Columbus Avenue, New York, NY 10023-6992, or telephoning (212) 713-8000.

### College Connector by ACT

American College Testing (ACT) has a long tradition of making it easier for the secondary school student to move from high school to college. ACT's *Discover* program has been a one-of-a-kind phenomenon. In keeping with that tradition, ACT has now developed *College Connector*, a computer-based college planning and application service.

*College Connector* provides college-bound students with a comprehensive set of electronic tools to assist students in selecting and applying to colleges and universities. The software includes the following on-line modules:

- A **College Search** whereby students can become better informed about particular schools and readily identify those that meet their individual needs.

- A two-way **Inquiry Service** that permits students to request information from participating colleges and universities, as well as allows the same participating colleges and universities to learn about prospective applicants.

- An **Application Service** that students can utilize to complete their applications and apply electronically to the participating colleges and universities.

- A **Financial Aid Need Estimator** that allows families to receive college-cost data and early estimates of their eligibility for federal financial aid programs.

*College Connector* is available to high schools that wish to license the service for student use. Families can also purchase a modified package for use on their home computers. To learn about *College Connector*, telephone ACT at (319) 337-1215; FAX: (319) 339-3020.

## Peterson's Career & College Quest

*Career & College Quest* is a three-part integrated program using intuitive, easy-to-use, pulldown menus to take career- or college-bound students on a search that will help them orient themselves. Users can determine what kinds of careers best match their particular skills, interests, and motivations. They can then select a college, university, or vocational school that will deliver the best educational experience based on their career goals; and they can build a financial package that addresses their specific financial profile and ability to pay. The "College Center" profiles nearly 3,000 collegiate institutions, allowing users to conduct searches combining multiple criteria, produce inquiry letters, complete electronic applications, request materials, and more. The financial aid component estimates financial need and provides access to over 800 million dollars in private funds. Peterson also has some 400 career fields, 900 specific job descriptions, and 6,000 vocational schools in its computer base. Career & College Quest is available in MAC or Windows software.

## CollegeLink™

One of the most successful private ventures in the college admission scene, *CollegeLink*™, based in Concord, Massachusetts, offers subscribing students the opportunity of completing *one* application on a personal computer that the company then formats to each collegiate institution's liking. Students can then send their applications to as many as a dozen schools that they select from the more than 800 colleges and universities that participate in the service. The personal software kit *and* preparation of the student's first application are free—the applicant pays only shipping fees. Additional applications are five dollars each. Link does not charge applicants who qualify for fee waivers. If essays are required, there's more good news: Link's agreement with participating colleges and universities means a single essay will fulfill the requirements for *most* of the participating institutions.

If it wishes to do so, a secondary school can send transcripts and other related materials to *CollegeLink*™, which in turn scans and merges the documents with each student's application. Colleges and universities receive the completed application packet on *both* paper and diskette. Copies of all documents are returned to the high school for record-keeping and to the students for their verification. The software is available in both Macintosh and IBM (or compatible) versions. *CollegeLink*™ offers free subscriptions to secondary schools. Some secondary schools maintain a supply of Link brochures and application materials, or the student can request the materials directly from the company.

### CollegeView

*CollegeView* is an interactive CD-ROM program that helps high school students search, discover, and connect with colleges. By combining a database of 3,000 two- and four-year colleges with engaging multimedia "tours," *CollegeView* provides students with a picture of what college life is all about.

Students begin their search by focusing on information *they* feel is important. They usually start with the KeyFact database: a comprehensive data source of critical information that includes cost, majors offered, athletics, student services, religious affiliations, and more. Students can print the acquired material for future reference.

Then there are the QuickView presentations, kind of a "slide show" glimpse of what a college has to offer. Even more impressive is the FullView program which is the next best thing to being there. Students can see college-designed presentations on more than 200 schools that offer engaging interactive information including the benefits of a degree from the particular institution. FullView incorporates audio clips, full-motion video, and eye-catching graphics.

The program also has AppZap and InfoZap. With AppZap the student can easily complete a custom application form and send it electronically. InfoZap connects the secondary school electronically with QuickView and FullView schools. The system creates immediate personal contact between student and admission office.

# SMOKE AND MIRRORS WITH GUIDEBOOKS AND MAGAZINES

The eyes of parents of budding college students can glaze over as they watch tuition costs escalate each year, knowing that they will soon be facing big tuition bills. These same parents are turning for counsel in alarming numbers to college rankings as published in popular magazines and specialty guides. What's even more alarming is that they're taking the rankings as gospel. All the while, the preachers, in the guise of college deans and directors of admission, are now so obsessed with moving up or down a notch in the rankings that they freely admit to padding the numbers.

Case in point: In *The New York Times* "Education Life Supplement" of January 8, 1995, Richard Fuller, Dean of Admission at Hamilton College in New York, states that he simply started doing what many other prestigious colleges and universities do, and that is fudge the statistics. To revive his sagging image with *U.S. News & World Report*, Fuller instituted a two-part application process at Hamilton to make his figures look better. Students were asked to make an initial commitment to Hamilton by sending in Part I of the application. School counselors are aware that some students never complete the second step of the process. But that doesn't seem to matter to certain admission officials. When deans are asked by ranking guides and magazines how many students apply, they have a larger number to report—and thus a smaller percentage of acceptances—because that's the name of the game: giving the impression that you're very selective.

Thomas Anthony would agree. The former dean of admission at Colgate University is quoted in the April 5, 1995 issue of *The Wall Street Journal* as saying, "This is awful stuff. But when the American public comes to you and says you're not in the top 20 and they're going to make their decision based on that, it puts incredible pressure on you to have the right-looking numbers."

Guidebooks and magazines primarily measure a school's quality by determining how many students apply, how many are accepted, and how many actually matriculate. Harvard is the uncontested leader—it get tons of applications, but only accepts 17 percent of its applicant pool!

Dean Fuller goes on to say in the *Times* article, "You have to remember that we work for the colleges, not for the students." That's quite a statement. You can't get more frank than that. Thank heavens, school counselors work for the students!

Most colleges and universities have been playing it straight. In all fairness, in the past decade much of higher education has been trying—albeit not very successfully—to live with the rating of their institutions by outsiders. Issues of public relations and marketing now play a major role on campuses due to the significance assigned by the general public to rankings and statistical comparisons. As do school counselors, most college administrators have serious doubts about the value of rankings.

Are students getting hurt by these shenanigans? Yes. If the published numbers are not reliable, thousands of students are making important decisions based on false data.

To gauge the accuracy of reported numbers, *The Wall Street Journal* compared data colleges provide to various guides and magazines with similar statistics they provide to debt-rating agencies and investors, such as Moody's Investors Services and Standard & Poor's. More than two dozen discrepancies surfaced in SAT scores, acceptance rates and other enrollment data. In nearly every case, the Moody's and S&P numbers were less favorable to the colleges than the guidebook and magazine figures.

Does anyone really care whether Williams is ranked slightly higher than Haverford in the East, or that Oberlin has edged out Carleton in the Midwest? Maybe the college presidents. But as a school counselor, you can work with your families to set the record straight.

## *Tips on Handling the Situation*

- Work toward convincing parents and students that college rankings such as those found in *Money Magazine* and *U.S. News & World Report* are suspect at best, completely without merit at worst. Some people believe these annual rankings are nothing more than the commercial equivalent of magazine swimsuit editions. Maybe we should rank colleges on a weekly basis like Division I football teams.

- Be open with your families as to how higher education manipulates the numbers.

- Be careful not to overrate certain colleges and universities as you and your counselee work to construct a selectivity ladder of reaches, targets, and safeties.

- There is a proliferation of guides (300) on the market today, ranging from the mediocre to the excellent. Lobby your department to develop a recommended list of specialty and comprehensive guides on which families can rely.

- Take two aspirins. On a more serious note, these superficial rankings can adversely affect the development of student decision-making skills. The frivolous endeavor detracts from the serious examination of the college admission picture by students as they try to select the most "appropriate" schools to which to apply. Through the years, more than a few students have made their final decision for all the wrong reasons.

- Examine the selectivity indexes of such guidebooks as *Barron's* with a jaundiced eye. You might want to develop (as some high schools have done) your own list of the 150-some colleges and universities that are "hung up" on SAT/ACT scores. Divide the list into three basic selectivity categories: "most," "highly," and "very." Utilizing reputable guidebooks as a resource, place about 50 schools in each category. Never mind that the engineering department of a particular university is under "highly" and that arts and sciences is under "very." Lump them together under one heading. As you and your department create a list with which you can live, keep reminding yourself that the remaining 2,850 schools in the nation are more interested in quality of coursework and grade point average, and that most of the hoopla is over only 150-some institutions.

# SUGGESTED READING/CONTACTS

Hunter, Bruce (1995), *Hunter's Guide to the College Guides*, P.O. Box 9647, Naples, Florida 33941. (Reviews 140 college reference books and guidebooks grouped by category.)

*CollegeLink*™. 200 Baker Avenue, Concord, Massachusetts 01742. 800-394-0404.

*CollegeView*, 10200 Alliance Road, Cincinnati, Ohio 45242. 800-927-VIEW.

# CHAPTER 32

# THE COUNSELOR AND THE WRITTEN WORD

Communication is the exchange of information, thought, or messages by signals, speech, or writing. Communication, especially of the oral variety, is the heart and soul of school counseling; in fact, it is the reason for our existence. It seems obvious, then, that we should hone our communication skills to the highest possible degree.

If good listening is the first component of good communication, as many believe it to be, then *respect* has got to be up there as well. Some of us have left the classroom, believing that we have "stepped up" to a counseling position. We don't intend to be pretentious, but sometimes our speech and writing betray us. Humility is truth. Each of us knows things *differently*; we don't necessarily know them better. It is important to remember that each person you deal with has his or her expertise. If you really *believe* that you are having an *exchange* of information or insight, your speech and writing will project that good counselor image. It's not only what you say, but how you say it—and this is precisely where the counselor's personality comes through.

## A NOTE ABOUT YOUR SECOND MOST IMPORTANT PUBLIC

After your students, the most important people you work with are those most directly involved with the welfare of your counselees: the teachers. Human relations and communications skills must be the sharpest when dealing with the teaching faculty; you and they work very hard for the students, and you and they are human beings. Teachers need to hear a kind word now and then. And counselors who get along well with teachers are usually those who in some way convey a strong message: "I respect you and I admire the quality of your teaching." Some of that conveying can be done in writing. For example, you might occasionally pass along positive comments from students, mentioning to Mr. J. that Mary had commented on the great job he had done with Calculus I in preparing her for her first college math course; or sending a note to Mrs. C., telling her that one of your junior counselees thought she was of great help in improving the student's writing skills.

Incidentally, once a teacher has approached you with a student problem and you've told her that you will take some specific action, be sure to do it promptly. Then pen a brief note to the teacher, thanking her for her interest, and informing her that you did indeed take the action.

## TOWARD BETTER TEACHER RECOMMENDATIONS

When you take the time and make the effort to assist teachers involved in the college admission process to do a better job of writing personal recommendations, you are making a difference in a student's chances of acceptance. Teacher recommendations, for those colleges that require them, become an integral part of an applicant's folder. Colleges that use such information are seeking additional objective assessment data in order to view the candidate from yet another perspective.

Such writing can have its abuses, such as: devoting an inordinate amount of space to discussing a student's co-curricular program; or writing identical recommendations for two different students to the same college; or pirating student/parent "brag" sheets specifically designed for the counselor's personal use, and thereby running the danger of two people quoting the same words.

When it comes to recommendation writing, the same teachers get "hit hard" each year with requests. (A good English or social studies teacher gets no rest.) Since the 1980s much material has been published in pamphlets and paperback books on more effective teacher recommendation writing, so we're not going to spend much time on the topic. However, since classroom teachers can find themselves pressed for time, Figure 32-1 is a handy handout that reflects what we believe to be the six key points of teacher recommendation writing.

You can do more than just consulting with teachers on how to write effective recommendations. Just as you "gain a few points" by sending along comments of former students, you can also compliment the teachers by letting them know in writing what the faculty has accomplished within the admission process. For, after all, excellence of teaching has had something to do with some of those acceptances. A few colleges take the time to send thank-you notes to involved teachers. So should you.

Note the judicious timing of the memorandum in Figure 32-2 which is sent to faculty members as they are about to face an onslaught of new requests.

FIGURE 32-1

---

**Teacher Recommendation Writing:
Six Key Points**

1. Introduce yourself and briefly explain your relationship to the applicant. If you are familiar with the applicant in more than one setting, mention it.

2. Focus on the student's accomplishments in your classroom, and the skills he/she has developed. Do not mention the importance of the course.

3. Negative comments can become positive, e.g., "Although she makes careless errors, Mary develops formulas with considerable logical reasoning."

4. Never litanize co-curricular activities. Stick to the classroom! You don't even need to peruse a transcript.

5. Ask the student to give you written input where necessary. You might want to know, for example, which part of the course the student found most meaningful, and where he/she found the most success.

6. Be as specific as possible. Admission folk love anecdotal information, but they want it short: keep your recommendation to one page.

---

FIGURE 32-2

---

September 13, 199X

TO:      Faculty & Staff

FROM:  Marjorie Whitherspoon, Counseling Chair

RE:      Heartfelt Thanks.

Since last year's seniors clutched their diplomas and left us for parts *known*, we thought you'd enjoy knowing about some of those parts, too. Enclosed please find a list of colleges and universities at which our most recent graduates are matriculated.

The counseling department is grateful for your past writing efforts! So are the kids!

# COUNSELOR RECOMMENDATIONS: MOSTLY A WASTE OF TIME

"This is mostly a waste of time!" Scott sighed, as he flopped down at the keyboard to compose yet another counselor evaluation. At least he said "mostly." The word denotes "extensively"; it doesn't mean completely, utterly, or absolutely. Thank heavens, Scott saw some wiggle room—because the counselor evaluation *can* play a significant role in determining the acceptance of applicants to at least *some* of the colleges and universities in the nation.

It is true there are colleges and universities that pay little or no attention to teacher and counselor comments. Hearing and/or reading of such disinterest can be a discouraging factor for some counselors, resulting in their taking their writing responsibilities less seriously. They feel no one out there is listening. Of course, nothing could be further from the truth, because we *can* make a difference in the lives of our counselees, if nowhere else than at those one hundred "highly" selective schools, where the quality and perception of counselor comments are critical.

We encourage our students to spread their final choices up and down a selectivity ladder, from "reaches" at the top to "safeties" at the bottom. Since many harried public school counselors write generic evaluations—one size must fit all—that *same* evaluation will go out to "reach" schools as well as to "safety" schools. It's vital to remember that what might not be an important piece for Penn State might be a consequential "hook" at Washington University in St. Louis. The evaluation should be written, then, as if it were aimed at admission to a really tough "reach."

Note the use of the term "evaluation" instead of "recommendation." That's more than semantics. College admission folk would like you to describe and evaluate rather than recommend.

When we first began writing on this topic, we believed it necessary that counselor evaluations be complete—that is, that they encompass five *categories*: academic program, academic achievement, academic capability, personal qualities, and extracurricular participation. We've largely given up on that idea for varying reasons, including the reality of counselor caseloads. We now urge our busy colleagues to focus instead on five powerful *characteristics* of their evaluation: it should be supportive, evaluative, substantive, specific, and honest. Let's define these adjectives.

*Supportive:* promoting the interest or cause of; advocating for

*Evaluative:* carefully appraising, in part by way of description

*Substantive:* having meaning; solid

*Specific:* including detail; free from ambiguity

*Honest:* free from deception; genuine

Now we take our finished piece in hand to see if it meets the test. To what extent am I *supporting* this candidate? Have I carefully *evaluated* and described his or her personality and actions? Is there real *substance* to this piece of writing? Have I been *specific* and used anecdotal material where appropriate? Have I been *honest* in my writing?

### Creating a Generic Evaluation

A counseling department would do well to sit down and discuss the entire evaluation process, reviewing departmental policy and procedures. It might also be helpful for the group to share each other's evaluations—or peruse samples—and critique these writings for the five characteristics. Another method of improving skills is to create a hypothetical case, such as the one displayed in Figure 32-3. An evaluation can then be composed by the group or through individual effort. The final copy should be critiqued by all concerned.

FIGURE 32-3

---

#### Writing a Counselor Evaluation

**Instructions:**

1. Write a lean generic evaluation of some 125 words (three short paragraphs).
2. In doing so, make a group decision as to what material below is suitable for use.
3. Pay special attention to opening and closing comments.
4. Does the final evaluation meet the five-adjective test: supportive, evaluative, substantive, specific, and honest?

SHANNON BURKE

SAT/GPA Profile: 625 Verbal, 570 Math (recentered) 3.40 on a 4.0 Scale

Senior Courses: World Literature (H), Precalculus, Humanities, AP French, Anatomy & Physiology (H), Intro to Psychology, Health & PE 4

—one of the *nicest* students of my 25-year career

—has developed into a mature, caring, and creative individual

—has become an excellent communicator, with some of this excellence being achieved *via* her drama and chorus activities

—a most talented actress and singer

—once was in three plays at the same time, and still managed to keep up with her *school work*

—father passed away suddenly in the *freshman* year

—has a myriad of friends

—I saw her in *Pajama Game*, and she lit up the stage in the role of Mabel

—a *tall, comely* young woman

—willingly shares her joy, love, and life with others, and genuinely cares about people

—chosen by the Guidance Department, along with eleven others, to work with counselors in presenting an orientation program to rising ninth graders

—enjoys the biological sciences

---

In composing any evaluation, it is most important to use words that convey the most accurate picture of the counselee. Some suggestions are given in Figure 32-4.

FIGURE 32-4

---

### The Power Of Word Choice

1. **In your writing, try to avoid the following personal judgment words:**

| | | | | |
|---|---|---|---|---|
| cute | strapping | womanly | manly | nervous |
| buxom | virile | unwomanly | unmanly | anxious |
| pretty | obsessive | good-looking | handsome | tense |

2. **Avoid words that suggest any reference to race, sex, religion, appearance, or politics.**

3. **Nondescript words can weaken the effectiveness of an evaluation:**

| | | | | |
|---|---|---|---|---|
| solid | likable | pleasant | somewhat | apt |
| good | nice | reasonable | very | civil |
| decent | ordinary | meaningful | fairly | warm |

4. **Use words that are powerful to increase the effectiveness of an evaluation:**

| | | | | |
|---|---|---|---|---|
| edge | expressive | reputation | witty | significant |
| focus | persevering | survival | mature | purposeful |
| impact | brilliant | acclaim | assertive | charismatic |
| force | imaginative | prestige | driven | sophisticated |
| capacity | innovative | poise | intelligent | urbane |

5. **Use words that add specifics:**
   a. *Mental qualities:*

| | | | | |
|---|---|---|---|---|
| educated | erudite | scholarly | learned | wise |
| astute | talented | intellectual | precocious | capable |
| gifted | reasonable | rational | sensible | shrewd |
| prudent | observant | clever | ingenious | inventive |
| subtle | witty | | | |

   b. *Moral qualities:*

| | | | | |
|---|---|---|---|---|
| idealistic | exemplary | temperate | truthful | honorable |
| trustworthy | respectable | altruistic | giving | straightforward |
| open | | | | |

FIGURE 32-4 CONTINUED

c. *Social qualities:*

| | | | | |
|---|---|---|---|---|
| tactful | courteous | polite | cooperative | genial |
| affable | gracious | amiable | cordial | amicable |
| sociable | cheerful | sensitive | convivial | ebullient |

d. *General personal qualities:*

| | | | | |
|---|---|---|---|---|
| distinguished | eminent | admirable | influential | impressive |
| imposing | generous | benevolent | charitable | magnanimous |
| humane | gentle | patient | considerate | compassionate |
| sympathetic | tolerant | ambitious | conscientious | persevering |
| industrious | persistent | efficient | assiduous | diligent |
| resourceful | scrupulous | punctual | earnest | uncompromising |
| zealous | enthusiastic | strong-willed | determined | resolute |
| confident | self-reliant | self-starter | intrepid | courageous |
| indomitable | solemn | serious | sedate | discreet |
| garrulous | wary | eloquent | persuasive | reserved |
| taciturn | laconic | droll | cautious | imperturbable |
| responsive | natural | candid | unaffected | ingenuous |
| reticent | humble | self-effacing | modest | unassuming |
| amenable | serene | nonchalant | indifferent | philosophical |
| pensive | sober | valorous | munificent | witty |

## More Tips on Writing the Evaluation

1. Brevity *is* the soul of wit. It is much better to have 200 well-written words than 400 that are general, flowery, and clichéd. "Enlightening" does not have to mean "lengthy!" Don't be afraid to write a single-page piece, or even a half-page piece. You *can* meet all of the adjectival requirements in a short presentation.

2. Write lean! Use no unnecessary adverbs and adjectives. (Writing lean is one of the most difficult tasks for the writer to master.) Choose your adverbs and adjectives carefully; vary them as you keep a synonym finder nearby. Use the *present* voice, remembering that your students are *still involved*; they are still in school. You'd be surprised at the number of counselors who write in the past tense.

3. Speaking of involvement: don't sacrifice your evaluation by "laundry listing" your counselee's extracurricular activities. There is nothing wrong with *expanding* on a particular involvement, however, especially if it can underscore commitment or certain personality traits.

4. A few universities—Rutgers, for instance—handle their applicant folders in batches from the same secondary school. They don't like to see counselors using the same phraseology in describing each of their counselees.

5. Some counselors write a personal note at the bottom of their generic piece, or they'll write a few words on the Secondary School Report form in an attempt to "tie" their counselee to a particular school. Good idea! Always mention the school by name, and use blue ink, not black.

6. A good evaluation simply *presents*. Beware of becoming too subjective.

7. Look for discrepancies in the record. Do a three-minute study of the transcript and ask yourself if there is anything that is likely to raise questions. Why did my counselee *start* a second language in her senior year? Are there any glaring inconsistencies between what I've written and what the record reflects? Do the check marks on the Secondary School Report reasonably match my open comments?

8. Save the word "recommend" for the end—if you use it at all. "Highly" is different from "enthusiastically." And "mostly" *is* different from "completely."

### *When in Doubt, Go Composite*

Counselors can sometimes be found playing "catch up" in writing their evaluations of certain counselees. That is, they'll be scurrying to gather assorted information from various sources to construct evaluations because they don't know particular students very well. Get a few words from a parent here, from a teacher there, a few from the student him- or herself, and the counselor has what is known as a composite evaluation. There is absolutely nothing wrong with a composite evaluation when you do not know your counselee. As a matter of fact, give yourself a pat on the back for having the concern and ambition for wanting to put something together of value.

Even in schools where there are reasonable caseloads (200 to 1), the composite approach can be a most appropriate choice. A composite can provide a more interesting and complete treatment, so when in doubt, go composite. A vehicle should be in place in every counseling department whereby external input can be procured. (See Figure 32-5.) Many high schools have sophisticated mechanisms for gathering such data that include the use of printed forms.

One method of enlisting the assistance of your counselees in the writing of the evaluation is to encourage or even require them to complete and submit a brief questionnaire. You'll want to shoot for *revealing* questions—questions that will elicit responses that could be purposeful in building a solid evaluation. Figure 32-6 is a sample questionnaire of eleven telling questions.

FIGURE 32-5

Council Rock High School
Council Rock
South Dakota

TO: _____
           (teacher name)

FROM: Rick Bryant

RE: Counselor Evaluation

  Shannon Cassaday   is working on her applications for college and mentioned your
(student name)

name as a potential resource person for my evaluation. Any appropriate comments

you care to make about this student would be most helpful to me in my completion

of the counselor evaluation.

                               Thank you!

## COUNSELING ON THE PERSONAL ESSAY

You are no doubt aware that many public colleges and universities pay scant attention to an applicant's personal characteristics in their selection process. You also know that almost all of the "most" and "highly" selective private schools zero in on such qualities. In fact, one might say that the more selective the school, the more emphasis is placed on personal characteristics. Most admission officers agree that the application document where these qualities can best be discovered is the personal essay.

In his pamphlet, *How to Prepare a Great College Application*, G. Gary Ripple, Dean of Admissions at Lafayette College in Pennsylvania, writes, "In selective college admissions, applicants who fail to understand the importance of the essay and don't put forth the necessary effort, seriously jeopardize their chance to position themselves, and lose the opportunity to enhance their academic credentials in the competition for a limited number of great opportunities."

School counselors often have considerable control over the final application packet submitted by the student. But to what extent should the counselor become involved in the writing of the personal essay? The counselor can certainly *advise*, and he or she is in an excellent position to do so. A skilled counselor should: (1) know the young writer well, having worked with him or her over the years in developing greater self-awareness; (2) be

FIGURE 32-6

## ABOUT MYSELF

_____
(Student Name)

Dear Student:

My responsibility in preparing the Secondary School Report for colleges and universities is to provide a summary of your academic and extracurricular achievement. The counselor also presents some sense of the student's promise for further personal and intellectual growth. Conveying your _unique_ qualities is not an easy task. Therefore, I would appreciate your giving me an honest estimation of yourself, what you have done, and what you have left to do.

Don't limit your discussion to what has happened to you in school. Rather, include experiences drawn from any part of your life.

Sincerely,

_____
Counselor

1. Which course(s) have you enjoyed most? Why?

2. Which course(s) have given you the most difficulty? Why?

3. What do you choose to learn, when you can learn on your own?

4. What books have you read _on your own_ in the past year?

5. What has been your most stimulating intellectual experience in recent years?

6. Is your high school academic record an accurate measure of your ability and potential? If not, what do you consider the best measure of your potential for success in college?

7. What circumstances, if any, have interfered with your academic performance?

8. Has any summer experience, job, or study been of significant importance to you? Please explain.

9. Describe yourself in five adjectives.

10. What are your proudest _personal_ accomplishments?

11. Is there any other information you would like to share with me so that I can make an accurate appraisal of you to colleges and universities?

familiar with important approaches to and techniques of expository writing, particularly as they apply to the special demands of writing an essay for college admission; (3) be knowledgeable about, and have a real feel and understanding for, what these institutions are seeking in terms of the personal essay.

This doesn't mean that you're expected to advise on sentence structure and points of grammar, although if you majored in English you probably possess the requisite expertise. It also doesn't imply that you should review a series of rough drafts and peruse the final copy, although you might choose to do so. But you *can*:

1. promote the feeling that a personal statement can and should breathe some life into the application,
2. counsel on such fundamentals as: essay topics, including selection and focus; attitude; approach; and content organization; and
3. understand the different ways essays are handled by colleges and universities:

   to screen out less able applicants;

   as a marketing tool ( to attract specific constituencies to the applicant pool);

   or conversely, to widen the net;

   to acquire autobiographical data on the applicants;

   to measure the writing skills and level of thinking of each applicant.

What is *not* needed is "after-the-fact" involvement, whereby counselors, teachers, and parents give essays cursory readings, along with the "It sounds good to me" comments. A developmental approach *is* needed, whereby counselors can get to know their students well, and can help them to examine their own values, interests, aspirations—and help these same students with self-assessment. This places school counselors in a favorable position to help students determine what they will write about. It's a natural. After working with your counselees on developing their self-perception so they can be true to themselves on the printed page, all you have to do is sit back and pull it out of them. Then you will have helped your counselees *write* a good essay because you will have helped them *create* a good essay.

## DESIGNING YOUR OWN SECONDARY SCHOOL REPORT FORM

They can come in salmon, aqua, chartreuse, or coffee. No, not spring sweaters—Secondary School Report forms, in single sheets, four-page openers, or fancy six-page fold-outs. And it doesn't matter whether they're titled "High School Reports," "Secondary School Reports," or "School Profile Questionnaires," they are virtually the same: paper on which you must blip, check, "x," or circle.

So there you are on Monday A.M., picking up where you had left off on Friday P.M., maneuvering through a formidable stack—trying to figure out whether Tufts' "exceptional" is the same as Washington University's "enthusiastically," or Cornell's "poor" is as bad as Johns Hopkins' "below average."

But the real test of your mettle, memory—and, alas, maturity—is in the general rating section, where you are asked whether or not the applicant is "one of the few I have ever encountered in my career." What a challenge! No real problem for the practitioner who has only been in the business a couple of years, but a real memory test for the 30-year veteran. Of course, this is one of the most abused items in the general ratings section. Some counselors nominate a half dozen or so students each year; other counselors nominate a half dozen or so each decade. What *are* the guidelines for properly responding to this question? Perhaps the key word is "few." Everything aside, counselors need to understand that the overrating of students can damage the applicant, the counselor, and the sending high school. Credibility can be on the line! Or that other term: integrity.

Tired of wrestling with a myriad of forms, as well as with the pushing of an unending amount of paper, more and more secondary schools are asserting themselves and developing their own time-saving reporting forms.

Would you like to construct your own form? Figure 32-7 is well focused and purposeful, devoid of such inane questions as, "What are the first words that come to mind?" and "Has the applicant ever been suspended or expelled?" (If the student had been expelled, would he be around to apply to college?)

## WRITING FOR PUBLICATION

Where are the counselor-writers? Seldom found in the quarterly journals or the newsletters of the profession, we're afraid. The editors of these publications continue to report a lack of submissions from school counselors, especially from those in the public sector. A large number of today's journal and newsletter pieces are written by counselor educators, sometimes in collaboration with their interns or research assistants, so it seems that a real contribution would be material from school counselors who are out in the trenches. You know, less theoretical and more practical stuff; issues, including the controversial, that can stimulate the emotions and thought processes, and at the same time spawn an increased number of letters to the editor.

Why *aren't* more school counselors writing for publication? Some would argue that they are interested but are (1) experiencing difficulty getting started; (2) unfamiliar with the publishing process, confused as to what to do; (3) fearful of rejection; (4) lacking confidence in their writing capability. For most counselors, it's probably a little bit of each of these factors.

Incidentally, this is not a topic that receives much attention in graduate school. Then again, would you expect otherwise? Since graduate programs often give short shrift to the more substantive issue of counseling for college, would you expect them to devote instructional time to the less significant topic of writing for publication?

Beginning writers tend to fret over a suitable topic; that is, they believe they must soar above and beyond into order to break into print. This attitude manifests itself in what might be termed the "new idea syndrome," the need to discover something totally different from what's been published. It can be a self-defeating attitude, because the majority of issues in school counseling have already been addressed in one form or another by someone in the profession. "New" is what's needed, of course, but not necessarily a new *topic*. It could be a new method of handling a well-worn procedure; a new revision of an aged policy; a new look at an old problem; a new perspective on a thorny issue. So you're not going to reinvent the wheel; you're simply going to rebuild it.

FIGURE 32-7

SCOTT MORROW HIGH SCHOOL
Delray, California 05555
(415) 623-7777

**Secondary School Report Counselor Evaluation**

*Please type or print in black ink.*

**Student Section:**
*After completing the information below, give this form to your counselor.*

Student name: _____
                         *Last*           *First*        *Middle*       *Jr., etc.*

Address: _____
                      *Street*

_____
               *City*             *State*       *Zip*

Social Security number: _____

Signature: _____    Date: _____

**Counselor Section:**

This candidate ranks in the _____ percentile from the top in a class of _____ students, and has a cumulative grade point average of _____ on a 4.0 + scale. The rank covers a period from _____ to _____ . The rank is weighted for honors and advanced placement courses only.

Of last year's graduating class _____% attended a four-year college, and _____% attended a two-year college.

In comparison to other college preparatory students *at our school*, the applicant's course selection is:

    __ most rigorous    __ very rigorous    __ rigorous    __ average

Note: Current year courses appear on the transcript.

Counselor's name: _____  _____
                            *Print*                      *Signature*

School: ___Scott Morrow High School_____

School Address: ___Point View Road, Delray, CA 05555_____

Office telephone: __415/ 623-0800___    Date: _____

School CEEB/ACT Code: 516478

FIGURE 32-7 CONTINUED

Comparison of this applicant to the entire class:

| | No basis for judgment | Average | Good | Excellent | One of the top few I have encountered in my career of _____ years |
|---|---|---|---|---|---|
| Academic Achievement | _____ | _____ | _____ | _____ | _____ |
| Academic Potential | _____ | _____ | _____ | _____ | _____ |
| Co-curricular/ Community Contributions | _____ | _____ | _____ | _____ | _____ |
| Character/ Personal Qualities | _____ | _____ | _____ | _____ | _____ |
| Creativity | _____ | _____ | _____ | _____ | _____ |
| Overall Rating | _____ | _____ | _____ | _____ | _____ |

This report is based upon personal contact with the applicant, school records, and teachers' comments.

Please refer to the enclosed counselor comments and school profile for additional information. We will notify the admission office of any significant academic changes subsequent to the submission of this report.

Scott Morrow High School welcomes dialogue between college admission counselors and secondary school counselors. If you require further information or if you would like to discuss a student's circumstances, please telephone us at (415) 623-0800, or fax us at (415) 623-1743.

Thank you for your consideration.

SCOTT MORROW HIGH SCHOOL
Delray, California 05555

© 1996 by John Wiley & Sons, Inc.

266

Three national organizations that would like to examine some of your rebuilding materials are: the American School Counselor Association (ASCA), the National Association for College Admission Counseling (NACAC), and the College Board. These organizations provide the writer with the opportunity of communicating with their colleagues through book reviews, practitioner articles, and issue-oriented/opinion pieces. ASCA's *School Counselor* has a "Things That Work" section; NACAC's *Journal of College Admission* has an "Open Forum" section, as well as an "On the Lighter Side" section where the writer can judiciously employ humor to jolt the reader's senses on pertinent and substantive issues.

Book reviews are a necessity in the profession; they keep us up to date on the latest publications in the field. Few counselors have the time or energy to read the myriad of material that is published; consequently, we depend on reviews to separate the wheat from the chaff.

### You're the Expert

As a counseling practitioner, you are very much involved in delivering counseling services. Who better than you, then, to write about the process, to share what you do in practice and why? Of course, it will be up to you to determine how innovative your procedure is. But you could bounce your ideas off a colleague or two, because you *can* get hung up with underestimation: you hesitate because you believe that what you or your department is doing is not all that different. When in doubt, *let the journal editor make that judgment.* A quick and painless way to test the waters is by way of a query letter—a cover letter and a one-page description of your program. Some people believe query letters are a waste of time, in that most editors will encourage submission if the manuscript is even remotely a possible fit. The extent of the fit can often be discovered by simply reading a journal section entitled "author guidelines." Also, editors don't want to miss a really good piece. At the same time, no editor is going to endorse an unseen product.

As you write, bear in mind that occasionally what might be of interest to counselors at the state or local level might have little or no relevance to counselors on the national scene. More than half of the states in the nation publish school counseling journals and newsletters that can be a great forum in which the beginning writer can test a new concept or program.

### Determination and Discipline

Writing calls for both determination and discipline. Determination has much to do with commitment—making a firm decision to begin, and then committing yourself to seeing the project through to completion. Discipline works within determination; it means finding the time in your life to write and includes the establishment of some sort of schedule. (Serious fiction and nonfiction authors discipline themselves to write *every* day, even for as little as one hour.) Most of these same individuals hold other full-time jobs.

"Success breeds success." Once you see yourself in print, it can serve as an impetus to keep writing. You might want to consider penning another piece (determination and discipline) as you wait for the acceptance or rejection of your original work.

After you have submitted your work, don't be shocked to receive a request for revision. Few authors ever receive a blanket letter of acceptance. Indeed, a request that an article be revised and then resubmitted can be a positive sign. Editors usually spell out their required changes. Believe it or not, some authors get their backs up and refuse to comply with an editor's request for changes. This is a regrettable move for the nonestablished writer. In our judgment, if revision suggestions don't compromise a work or the writer's integrity, then it makes no sense to lose a chance for publication over a few words or even a few sentences. Writers do have the opportunity to rebut suggested revisions. Make sure, however, that your rebuttal comments are presented in a professional and tactful manner.

So go to it! Take pen to paper or start pounding on a keyboard. Just *completing* and then *submitting* a piece of writing can be a rewarding experience, though at times a humbling one. Remember that even the most respected authors occasionally have some of their works rejected. Also remember that most people become increasingly successful as they acquire more experience.

## WHERE TO SEND YOUR MATERIAL

Editor, *College Prep*, The College Board, 45 Columbus Avenue, New York, NY 10023-6992. (The College Board pays a small honorarium.)

Editor, *Journal of College Admission*, National Association for College Admission Counseling (NACAC), 1631 Prince Street, Alexandria, VA 22314-2818.

Editor, *School Counselor*, American School Counselor Association (ASCA), 5999 Stevenson Avenue, Alexandria, VA 22304-3300.

## SUGGESTED READINGS

Ripple, G. Gary (1993), *How to Prepare a Great College Application, Fifth Edition*. Alexandria: Octameron Associates.

Safire, William (1992), *Good Advice on Writing Well*. New York: Simon & Schuster, (Great quotations from writers past and present on how to write well.)

Zinsser, William (1990), *On Writing Well*. New York: HarperCollins. (A classic informal guide to writing nonfiction.)

# CHAPTER 33

# ETHICAL CONSIDERATIONS IN THE COLLEGE-ADMISSION PROCESS

Ethics in recruiting students for college admission, as well as for awarding grant monies to the same students, provided the impetus in 1937 for creating the National Association of College Admission Counselors, now renamed the National Association for College Admission Counseling (NACAC). The founders developed a code of ethics which, after many years of redesigning and updating, has become today's *Statement of Principles of Good Practice*.

While the code originally was formulated and then applied only to NACAC members, the importance of ethical practices in the college-admission process for all secondary schools and colleges and universities has since been recognized by most people in the profession. The four-page statement is reviewed annually and revised to reflect new concerns regarding ethical admission policies and practices.

All of this emanates from a national organization that now boasts a membership of some 6,000 individuals and institutions. Approximately half of the colleges and universities in the nation are members of NACAC. Private and parochial schools dominate the secondary school scene, but the list of member public schools is growing steadily. Indeed, NACAC membership has been on the upswing since the mid-1980s. At the national conference in Boston in 1995, more than half of the organization's members were in attendance—a phenomenal showing for a national affair.

# NEED-BLIND ADMISSIONS

It was at that same Boston conference that the issue of need-blind admissions took a battering. Some of the leaders of NACAC had previously spent two years arguing to preserve a concept that for many families is gospel: the idea that while colleges reject students because of low grades, questionable test scores, or mediocre recommendations, they won't reject students because they're poor. Now they will. In fact, what happened in Boston was that some colleges and universities are now more likely than ever to examine income as closely as they examine SAT I results. The flip side of all of this, of course, is that if a family is solvent enough to pay the nearly $30,000 it costs to attend a private college or university, the applicant might have a better shot at getting into his or her "reach" school.

So the line in NACAC's *Statement of Principles of Good Practice* that stated, "No college may use income as an admission standard," was rewritten, and the entire issue of need-blind admissions went down hard one late September day.

The membership voted to compromise. They voted to modify the code so that basing college admission on a candidate's wealth was no longer a clear violation of ethical standards. Call it affirmative action for the rich, if you will; that has a nicer ring to it than discrimination against the poor. It might be said that school counselors and college admission officials, who for decades contended that it was unethical to discriminate against the poor or middle class, have now acquiesced to the demands of collegiate business offices. As we said in this book's introduction: "The times they are a-changin'."

### *Other Position Statements from NACAC Available to You*

- Statement on Pre-College Guidance and Counseling/ Role of the School Counselor
- Statement on Recruitment and Admission of Student Athletes
- Guidelines for the Traditionally Underrepresented in Higher Education
- Guidelines for Admission Decision Options in Higher Education

## UNDERMINING THE DEVELOPMENT OF STUDENT DECISION-MAKING SKILLS WITH EARLY DECISION/EARLY ACTION

One of the best pieces of writing to appear in the National Association for College Admission Counseling's *Journal of College Admission* is an article by Jean Ballard Terepka entitled, "Pangloss' Wisdom: College Counseling as an Ethical Activity" (*Journal*, Winter 1988). "College counselors are links between secondary school and college, between the location of childhood and the larger more risky terrain of first adulthood. . . . Every aspect of what college counselors do raises explicitly the moral issues that classroom teachers address usually only implicitly: self-knowledge and its consequences, critical judgment of the world around one, and discovery of one's own values within the ethical confusions that characterize our culture. These are all included in the work of the college counselor."

Regrettably, however, in more than a few high schools, the implementation of a sound college-planning process has given way to offensive consumerism that includes the violation of early-decision agreements, double depositing, and the placement of oneself on more than one waiting list. All are unethical tactics. Even more regrettably, some colleges are condoning—if not encouraging—such tactics. College selection should be a refining process that includes a prioritizing of interests, aspirations, and *values* so as to arrive at the "most appropriate" institution or the "best possible fit." Applying to two early-decision institutions concurrently is an example of what some counselors believe undermines the development of student decision-making skills, including the adoption of a more thoughtful approach to the college-planning process.

This past quarter-century has witnessed public, independent, and parochial elementary and secondary schools making a greater effort to work with students on building decision-making skills. In this fast-paced society of ours, one must start making choices and decisions at an ever earlier point in the passage to adult responsibility. One of the best times to hone adolescent decision-making skills is during the preparation for transition to higher education.

At the Texas ACAC Leadership Conference at Southern Methodist University in the summer of 1994, a spirited debate ensued concerning the issue of early decision. The discussion centered on whether or not students should be allowed to apply to more than one Early Decision program. NACAC guidelines stipulate that Early Decision programs are a *recognized exception* to general admission policies and practices, and that a student "may have only one early decision application pending at one time." Of course, it is possible for a student to apply to two different early decision programs, but only in succession, *not* concurrently.

Now the original intent of the colleges that created the Early Decision program was to develop a "first choice" plan. That does seem to make sense. Yet there are counselors today who endorse the idea of submitting more than one early decision application, arguing that if you ask students to withdraw other applications once accepted, that implies that students are free to apply to other programs, including early decisions. I'd say that's quite a stretch: How can you say that each of two different schools is your first choice?

Early decision has been around for some thirty years, but because of an abuse of the system perceived by both colleges and secondary schools, school counselors have become major cooperating players by providing endorsement signatures. This is as it should be. In fact, counselors should be playing an even greater role in that the program continues to be administered unevenly, e.g., some colleges require counselors to sign off and some do not. A serious consequence of this unevenness and partial accountability is that students are simultaneously applying to more than one early-decision school, *and* on occasion even with counselor approval. In these secondary schools, students who have applied to a college or university under an Early Decision program are requesting transcripts and letters of recommendation for yet another such program. Some counselors see themselves as legally bound to process the requested transcripts, but are holding the line on including letters of recommendation on ethical grounds. Others are acquiescing to the submission of both documents. With early-decision candidates, most counselors attempt to personalize their recommendations to the particular institution. It must be interesting to read such recommendations where the candidate is applying to more than one early-decision school.

To address the Early Decision/Early Action issue, we suggest the following reforms:

1.  *All* colleges and universities that support Early Decision programs should require *both* applicant and counselor to sign-off.
2.  The statement of conditions, including the two signature positions, should be on the student application, *not* on the Secondary School Report form.
3.  For early-decision candidates, colleges and universities should mandate that *all* pertinent materials be submitted and then mailed together in one package by the guidance department, *even* where the Secondary School Report form is part of the packet. Such a pulling together of documents would bring a heightened sense of importance to this special program for everyone involved.

Terepka rightly argues that counselors must teach ethical behavior by acting accordingly: "Students need to know that their college counselor's advocacy is placed within a caring context of explicitly discussed standards and values which secondary school counselors and college admission officers share. We do not merely explain the [admission] process to our students; we also actually participate in it, and we must be able to justify our actions. The ethical task of the college counselor, therefore, is to help students understand that the application and admission process constitutes a balance between caring and toughness."

Some of that toughness can be witnessed in school counselors' attempts to work against the pervasiveness of unethical behavior in today's society. There are those who would suggest that this pervasiveness implies that school counselors are losing ground, no longer able to accomplish their mission. If any or all of that is true, then what is needed is a recapturing of lost territory to help our students better clarify their goals, aspirations, and thought processes. For, after all, has not this been our historical mission? But to take and hold the high ground we need energetic and courageous counselors with reasonable caseloads. We know the reasons for "energetic" and "reasonable caseloads." But we must say "courageous" because it's easier to acquiesce to low standards than to stand for what we believe to be the better course. We must repeatedly publicize the drawbacks of trying to "beat the system," and that message must reach our most influential and concerned public: the parents.

As Terepka says, "We must teach and support our students by our example and our results. We must convey a sense that the humanistic values we hope they will cherish are in fact applicable in the competitive, sometimes vicious world to which they are making eager application. By means of our work both with our students and on their behalf, we must strive to create within them a conviction that a morally coherent world view is in fact possible."

The issue of student and family manipulation of the "early" programs brings to mind the school superintendent who once remarked that it's not the school's role to teach responsibility. Not only is it in the school's purview to teach responsibility, there is now a recognized need for schools to teach basic values—honesty being one of them.

## EARLY DECISION AS A MARKETING TOOL

You need to be aware that, to some extent, early decision has become a marketing ploy as colleges vie for an ever-shrinking pool of high-achieving applicants.

As a "come on," schools such as Franklin & Marshall College in Pennsylvania are now offering to accepted early-decision candidates tuition at last year's rate; class registration preference; temporary ID cards to high school seniors so that they can use the college library, as well as attend plays, concerts, and athletic events; and assurance that financial need will be met in full. It's quite an enticing package, and something you wouldn't have seen a decade ago.

Most school counselors regard the Early Decision program, with all of its nuances, very seriously. Our advice to you and your students, for now and in the future, is to proceed with great caution as higher educational institutions more and more test the waters of ethical conduct.

## SENIOR-YEAR COURSE CHANGES

On occasion, your senior counselee might opt to drop a course or simply change levels, all within the school's established time frame. Or, perhaps, the drop or level change might be *beyond* deadlines, but the reason for the alteration in the student's schedule is so pressing as to warrant the move. Question: Should you notify a college or university of any schedule modifications *once the transcript has been submitted?* The University of Michigan asks you to do so.

Again, should a college be made aware of major changes in an applicant's program of studies while it is in the process of evaluating his or her application? For example, is it important for a college or university to know that the student has dropped Advanced Placement Calculus and is now enrolled in Academic Calculus? Or how about a complete drop of Academic Physics for semester courses in Sociology and Psychology? If your school is a member of the National Association for College Admission Counseling, you know it's important to do so. If you're not a member, you are nonetheless faced with an ethical dilemma.

Figure 33-1 shows how one high school deals with the problem, including notification. The key word is "significant"; another descriptor might be "major."

**FIGURE 33-1**

To Whom It May Concern:

In accordance with the *Statement of Principles of Good Practice* of the National Association for College Admission Counseling, we are informing you of (a) significant change(s) in the program of study of _____, an applicant to your school.

The following change(s) has been enacted:

Dropped Course:                     Added Course:

_____              _____

_____              _____

Sincerely,
Mark Haverstadt
Counselor

Having a notification policy in place can eventually cause rising seniors to pay more attention to the course-selection process. It's very much the commitment issue that was addressed in Chapter 13. You and the transcript secretary will have to monitor all significant changes. Still, major senior-year schedule modifications tend to be few and far between once school has started.

# WAIVING THE TIME LIMIT

Are school counselors increasingly being asked to be party to a sham—in this case, an untimed testing sham? According to a *Boston Globe* article of January 16, 1996, a "growing number of high school students are willing to be labeled 'learning disabled' so that they can take the Scholastic Assessment [Aptitude] Test without time limits." Evidently more than a few counselors—including some in the Boston area—are being pressed to join with parents who believe that their child will get higher SAT/ACT scores without time limits, and that a Learning Disabled label will make that same child's course grades look better; the parents then search for psychologists and learning disability specialists willing to state that the child has a learning disability.

The recent doubling of exceptions to the three-hour time limit might have less to do with savvy parents, and more to do with society's increased knowledge of learning disabilities. At least the College Board thinks so. Maureen Welsh, director of school services for the College Board points out that 16,000 members of the 1995 graduating class, or 1.5 percent of the nation's test-takers, were granted extra time for the taking of one or more admission tests. The Board believes that abuse of the program is neither widespread nor common.

The number of requests vary with geographic region; maybe there's something in the air or water in certain sections of the country. Demand for extra time services is especially heavy in the states of New York and New Jersey, some of this undoubtedly due to the extraordinary amount of state funds allocated to local school districts for special education programs.

Educational Testing Service has been leaning on school counselors to "do the right thing" professionally, although counselors' shoulders seem to be sagging more lately. There continues to be unresolved questions of accountability. For example, is it wise to place the responsibility for authenticity and quality of out-of-school documentation with the school system itself?

Figure 33-2 shows an "anything goes" letter from an out-of-school East coast clinical psychologist that should *not* have been accepted by the school and placed in the student's file—but it was.

Note that the disabling condition isn't even mentioned, nor is there a request for extra time—two requirements of Educational Testing Service. If the school's responsibility in this matter is going to continue, should not ETS develop more sophisticated guidelines as to the content and substance of these documents? Maybe ETS should screen all extra-time documents for those students not covered by in-school IEPs. Currently, school counselors simply "X" a box stating that the required document is in the affected student's file.

FIGURE 33-2

To Whom It May Concern:

On July 3, 1993 I administered a WISC to _____. He achieved a verbal IQ of 118, a performance IQ of 85, and a Full Scale IQ of 103.

It is my impression both from the test and from what I know about _____, that he will do best in situations that are well structured. He may need some help in breaking down tasks into parts he can handle. He also may need help in developing a "plan of attack" for his work.

Sincerely,

If you find yourself being sucked into the maelstrom, here are some key points to keep in mind as you work with your parents:

- *One* (it used to be two) document from an outside professional is required for a student not covered by a Child Study Team Individual Educational Plan (IEP).

- Waiving any time limits causes test results to carry a note of "Nonstandard Administration."

- Considering that most Learning Disabled students don't significantly improve their scores through the absolute waiving of time limits, an extra 90 minutes (called "extended time") usually suffices and can be more convenient for both student and proctor. The problem here is that you and your counselee will need to stay on top of things. The extended time option is offered only twice yearly—November and May. Also, Learning Disabled students are not eligible to use the penalty date window.

- College admission officials look askance at nonstandard test scores where disability recognition comes late, e.g., junior or senior year. Such late recognition can send up a warning flag to admission folk.

- Counsel your families as to the positives and negatives of the extended and untimed programs. The problem appears not to be so much with legitimately classified youngsters, as it is with those who seek outside documentation of a particular disability. Some believe that the increased attention paid to Attention Deficit Disorder (ADD) is a contributing factor in the increased demand for extra time.

Working together, the College Board and secondary schools must apply greater pressure on those outside professionals who are willing to "write anything." Parents are even using general practice physicians to diagnose learning disabilities. This is akin to the unethical behavior of physicians who will put anything down to get a student excused from physical education—even where a school system supports an adaptive program.

Some school counselors believe that "none of this stuff is my job." But it is! It's a case of not shying away from the obvious, and not compromising one's ethics. It is also the school counselor's chance to exert leadership regarding the issue both within the school setting *and* in the community-at-large.

# SUGGESTED READINGS

Huey, Wayne, and Remley, Theodore, Jr. (1992), *Ethical & Legal Issues in School Counseling.* American School Counselor Association, 801 North Fairfax Street, Suite 310, Alexandria, VA 22314.

*Statement of Principles of Good Practice*, National Association for College Admission Counseling, 1631 Prince Street, Alexandria, VA 22314-2818.

# SECTION IV

# CAREER DEVELOPMENT FOR THE SECONDARY STUDENT

◆ ◆ ◆ ◆ ◆

Career education is big stuff today. A number of states mandate that the subject be infused into a school's regular curriculum or offered as a specific course at some point between grades 9 and 12. Some of the mandating has been an effort to temper student comments such as, "What does this have to do with what I'm gonna need in the real world?" On a more substantive and practical note, the increased emphasis is because, like diamonds, career development is forever. Projections indicate that workers of the 21st century will alter their career paths several times over their work lives and will change jobs six times—sometimes by choice, sometimes by employer request, sometimes because their jobs have been restructured or obsolete due to changed technology.

The first article in *Education Week's* "Learning to Earn" series entitled "Bridging the Gap," January 26, 1994, addresses the "relevancy" issue and highlights various approaches that educators and employers are now utilizing to assist students to make a successful transition from school to workplace: apprenticeships, tech-prep programs, career academies, cooperative education, etc.

In this age of instant communication, accurate and comprehensive knowledge of the job market can be a powerful tool, especially since the economy is shifting from the production of goods to the production of services. Chapter 35, which reflects employment trends and new demographics, along with Chapters 38 and 39, which contain specific information related to on-the-job expectations and advice on interviewing, should help you work with your students more effectively.

Through one-on-one or group career counseling, you *can* make a definite impact on your students' lifelong development. As you assist them in this regard, it's important to realize that in today's world everybody needs to be in on the action: the conceptualization base should be broadened to include support from faculty, parents, and various segments of the community, including people from the professions, labor, and industry. As English departments press for an emphasis on writing across the curriculum, so, too, should you press for an across-the-board emphasis on career education. Most importantly: Career counseling is needed by *all* students!

# CHAPTER 34

# LIFE-SPAN CAREER DEVELOPMENT

In the past twenty years or so, career education has certainly come into its own in American schools. "Career" is the totality of work one does in his or her lifetime. The term should *not* be used interchangeably with two other terms that *are* synonymous: job and occupation. Career education, then, is the totality of experiences through which one becomes knowledgeable about, and makes preparation for work as part of his or her way of living. A "career" is developmental, beginning early in one's life and continuing well into retirement. The term "education" is most appropriate in that it extends through the same time span, and encompasses far more than an individual's program of formal education.

The cornerstone to all of this is *career development*—a process, hopefully sequential, by which elementary and secondary students learn the relationship of schooling to work. It includes not only specific and well-structured programs, like Tech-Prep, but also *comprehensive* career development programs.

And so, career development *links* education and the world of work! It enables students to acquire skills, or enhance already existing ones; and it assists these same students to make decisions about their work life. It's a process that should be present in every public and private school in the nation. Incidentally, if a particular career education activity is worthwhile, then it should be available to *all* students in a given school system. This can be problematic at the elementary level where teachers are more free to "do their thing," and are more constrained by the limited work experiences available to them and their students. In contrast, secondary level teachers have access to more resources and experience greater standardization, which is as it should be.

In a 1992 American Counseling Association (ACA) position paper, *The School Counselor and Comprehensive Programs for Work-Bound Youth*, Edwin Herr asserted that schooling, human growth and development, and economic development are now linked in this nation in a virtual synergistic fashion. Connecting students' learning in school with the world of work is more critical than ever. Today's students must not only demonstrate the basic skills of reading, writing, arithmetic, and mathematical operations, but also higher-order thinking skills in making decisions and solving problems. The effective development and consequent application of personal qualities in self-management is high on the list, as well. (*SCANS Report*, U.S. Department of Labor, 1991.) If our schools fail to produce a sufficient number of students with *all* of the aforementioned skills, graduates will not be able to successfully compete in the global marketplace.

ACA and Edwin Herr have taken the position that it is the *quality* of human resources, not so much the raw material or equipment, that must be developed and refined. As cited in the ACA position paper, "The key factor in this or any other nation's ability to compete in the emerging international economic environment is the quality of the nation's work force as defined by its literacy, numeracy, flexibility, and teachability."

# SCHOOL-TO-WORK OPPORTUNITIES

To help ensure that America remains globally competitive, the *School to Work Opportunities Act* was signed into law by President Clinton on May 4, 1994. The law is an innovative approach to education that seeks to better prepare high school students for college and careers by linking what is learned in school with work. Jointly administered by the U.S. Departments of Education and Labor, *School to Work* establishes a national framework that enables partnerships between educators and employers, parents, labor, and community-based organizations to develop these new learning opportunities.

The United States is one of the few industrialized nations that does not have an organized, comprehensive system to assist young people to prepare for and then enter the workforce. Because of the increasing demands of a competitive global economy, American employers have been experiencing difficulty locating workers with the needed academic, analytical, and technical skills.

The Act expands traditional vocational training programs by offering a wider variety of occupational and professional instruction and it brings industry more into the picture as training partners. Workplaces will now become learning environments: Employers will become joint partners with educators to train students through paid work experiences for jobs that exist in the local economy, for *School to Work* is not intended to be a top-down mandate—it is a movement that must spring from strong partnerships at the state and local levels.

Federal monies fund the establishment of *School to Work* systems at the state level, which in turn support transition programs such as tech-prep, cooperative education, and youth apprenticeships. School-to-work transitioning will mean changes in the way some teachers teach, as well as in the manner by which students learn within the school setting.

It demands a considerable amount of educational restructuring as set forth in *GOALS 2000*, the keystone of the federal government's initiative to identify and classify those skills workers need to perform successfully in the workplace and for the nation to do well in the global marketplace. Educational criteria for obtaining grant money must include curricula that is dedicated to high standards; has delivery of instruction that integrates work and school; effectively links secondary school and junior colleges; and provides for the use of workplace monitoring and instruction.

Industry supports *School to Work* because it represents the solid investment in "human resources" about which Edwin Herr speaks. Only time will tell how successful this national thrust will be. If the endeavor is successful, the country should have a more competent and highly educated workforce capable of performing at top levels, and prospering in a global economy.

Improving guidance and counseling initiatives can go a long way toward enhancing the quality of the nation and its workforce. We serve as professional consultants in developing our human resources that includes helping young people link their education to the world of work.

## SUGGESTED READINGS/CONTACTS

Herr, Edwin L. (1992) *The School Counselor and Comprehensive Programs for Work-Bound Youth*. American Counseling Association/National Occupational Information Coordinating Committee, Alexandria, VA.

National School-to-Work Opportunities Information Center, 400 Virginia Avenue, Washington, DC 20202 Tel: (202) 401-6222.

U.S. Department of Labor (1991) *What Work Requires of Schools: A SCANS Report for America 2000*. U.S. Government Printing Office, Washington, DC

# CHAPTER 35

# THE WORLD OF WORK

Today's adolescents will be part of a workforce with new demographics. Some 75% of the *entering* labor force in the United States is currently composed of minorities, women, and immigrants. By the year 2000, minorities and women are expected to account for more than 90% of said entering force. In addition to changing demographics, higher levels of skill and educational training will be required. Three out of four workers currently employed will need retraining for the new jobs of the next century. Anyone with less than a high school education will encounter a troublesome job search.

Census figures indicate that the majority of public school students after the year 2000 will have racially and culturally diverse backgrounds (U.S. Bureau of the Census, 1990); such diversification will have major implications for school counselors and administrators. Counseling programs will have to be developed to meet the needs of the various minority populations who heretofore have been underserved by the schools (Commission on Precollege Guidance and Counseling, 1986). Studies continue to uncover the fact that minority students are less likely to utilize guidance and counseling services for making important educational and career decisions than their white counterparts. All of this must change, including counselors being more sensitive to the educational and career needs of different ethnic minority students.

Technology is creating a demand for highly skilled workers, and most employers are presently hiring people with specific job skills. A certain number of industries are doing their own retraining in order to fill job openings—teaching everything from reading and writing to highly sophisticated computer skills—such training taking place in the workplace *and* on company time. The U.S. Department of Labor estimates the majority of jobs through the year 2000 will require a trade or technical education.

## FACTORY JOBS OF THE 1990s

There will continue to be jobs that will require only a high school diploma, however. What industry do you think is creating the best substitute for the "factory jobs" (positions open to high school graduates with little or no work experience) of the old days? Answer? Retail discount stores. Of the nearly 2 million jobs born since the end of the recession in 1991, 340,000 have been in retail discount stores. Wal-Mart alone has added some 150,000 more workers since 1991, employing people with virtually no work experience or people who had been laid off from other jobs. Service jobs will not pay as well as the blue-collar jobs they are replacing.

## IS A COLLEGE EDUCATION WORTH IT?

Nationally, some 55 percent of secondary school students move on to higher education; but, regrettably, society continues to be too focused on getting into the "right" college or university as opposed to getting into the "most appropriate" one—the one that will best serve the youngster's needs once graduated. "But why worry about the future?" parents argue. "Just go to college and things will take care of themselves." The colleges themselves fuel the fire with their continual reminders of how studies indicate that a growing number of jobs in the future will require a college degree. What's glossed over, however, is the fact that these same studies assume degree completion *and* the acquisition of meaningful skills—"meaningful," as in a marketable degree.

Is it in the best interest of the country to pack our youth into colleges from which they will ultimately drop out? At the root of the problem is the press for everyone, the disinterested and the poorly educated alike, to attend college. In essence, we thumb our noses at society's economic need for a highly skilled workforce, as we encourage thousands of disaffected youth to head off to colleges where they will ultimately experience further failure. Some of the fallout can be seen in the vast amount of retraining that's necessary for the college graduates of today.

Then we have the other problem: that of individuals who do go on to graduate but find themselves sitting home with no jobs to go to—they're either over- or under-qualified for a particular occupation. The fact that a good number of that figure are jobless is stupefying, but the fact that only 60% of young people complete college in five years is a rather jarring statistic in itself. States love to flaunt statistics that reflect record-breaking college enrollments as a sign of the strength of their higher education systems. Colleges and universities long ago made it clear they know how to admit students—the problem is that they don't know how to graduate them four or five years later.

The Ivy League schools with their separate personalities and varying strengths and weaknesses in major subject areas are not exempt from this problem, either. Not only does a college degree *not* guarantee a job at the end of the line, but neither does attending an Ivy League institution. The economy of the 21st century will be driven by automation and high-tech inventions. Engineers, scientists, and mathematicians will be the professionals most in demand. Manufacturing, business, government, and academia will be looking hard for them.

# PSYCHOLOGY AND LAW

It seems everyone wants to be a psychology or a pre-law major these days. Students must remember that certain entry-level positions will require some graduate study, and so should be prepared to attend graduate school. Psychology and law are but two occupations that require such advanced study.

There are some 800,000 lawyers in America, and the number is expected to reach one million by the year 2000. Two-thirds of the attorneys surveyed by *California Lawyer* said they'd change jobs if they could do so. Twenty-five percent of the 1993 law school graduates did not find jobs in the field, and the salary average has dropped from $40,000 to $36,000.

But they keep coming. Despite well-publicized negatives, thousands of our brightest and most ambitious men and women vie each year for law school admissions, to spend the next three years in the most intensive study of their lives. (Then again, conditions in other fields, e.g., business and medicine, aren't much rosier.)

The employment picture *has* tightened, but each year there are still thousands of good jobs awaiting new law graduates. There are 42,000 law firms with more than one lawyer; the 67 largest firms, with more than 300 lawyers each, employ 31,000 individuals. Competition among law firms is intense and each works hard to enhance its reputation.

The emergence of women in the field has been most impressive. In the early 1970s, only 4 percent of law school graduates were women. That figure is 45 percent today. And women currently fill nine of the top thirteen positions at the U.S. Department of Justice, beginning with Attorney General Janet Reno. Marcia Clark hasn't hurt matters either; if nothing else, the O.J. Simpson trial has increased interest in the legal profession.

# ON THE OTHER SIDE OF THE IVY WALL

What *is* out there as we move within striking distance of a new century? And with all of the discussion about job placement once graduated, what becomes your role in the advisement of your students? Certainly you shouldn't be dissuading a student from majoring in a particular field of interest just because few job openings exist, for you can run the risk of "turning off" the next Leonardo DaVinci or Isaac Newton. On the other hand, it's important to share with families specific information as to the potential employability of a given major, and then help them decide whether or not to pursue that option. Factual and specific information of both a negative and positive nature needs to include the intrinsic social, personal, and professional advantages of earning a college degree.

So what's waiting on the other side of that ivy-covered wall? Not open arms waiting to embrace even more young people into the legal profession, for example. Figure 35-1 is a table of just a few promising job possibilities culled from data obtained from the United States Office of Education. Note that not all occupations require a college degree.

A wonderful sourcebook for researching specific jobs is the *Occupational Outlook Handbook* published by the United States Department of Labor, Washington, D.C.

# WOMEN IN THE WORKPLACE

The number of employed women will soar from 55 million in 1988 to some 65 million by the year 2000—a phenomenon that will continue to have a far-reaching impact on home *and* workplace. All of the issues that relate to women will be exacerbated in the next decade: child care, elder care, home-office employment, paid maternity and parental leave, sexual harassment, nontraditional occupations, flexible hours, and opportunities for advancement. Accommodating the needs of female employees will be quite a challenge for those businesses and industries that seek success. The reality of more professionally trained women in the workplace will be an impetus for *management* to include additional women in their ranks. Even now, school counselors hear the concern voiced by fathers who want their young daughters to have every opportunity.

### America's Impending Labor Shortage

Because of impending labor shortages in the United States, the country will become a land of opportunity for *skilled* workers, regardless of age, sex, or ethnicity. Some industries are so desperate that they're hiring headhunters to locate the talent. The Chrysler Corporation needs 200,000 additional skilled workers by the year 2003 just to replace some 150,000 retirees.

Despite the continuing debate over affirmative action, employers in coming years will support equal employment using it as a recruitment tool rather than as a concept to be fought. It will become a case of economic necessity: Everyone will be swept up by employers, provided the prospective employee has the requisite education and skills for the workplace. By the end of the 20th century, the United States will finally be able to deliver on its promise: a job for everyone who wants one.

There seems to be a difference of opinion about the areas of female employment and the quality of such employment. Some see women in every kind of job across the board; others believe that, although women will account for the majority of the workforce growth, they will still have a disproportionate share of the lower-paying jobs. The key that should unlock the "door of equality" will be appropriate training. For example, women will need to learn the skills of the fast-growing service sector of our economy: communications, mathematics, information processing, and computer literacy. If any or all of these skills are not mastered, an underclass will emerge. Women will be that underclass.

FIGURE 35-1

## Hot Professions for the Twenty-first Century

| Occupation | Commentary | Entry-Level Salaries | Training Required | Best Possibilities |
|---|---|---|---|---|
| Bilingual Education Teacher | Growing numbers of school children have limited English proficiency. Big need exists for teachers to teach the basics utilizing two languages. | $25,000 | | Southwest, Florida, California, New York, New Jersey |
| Geriatrics | One fifth of the nation will soon be 65 or older. Needed: more specialists skilled in working with the aging. | | | |
| Claims Adjuster | Multiple factors including increased natural disasters and more complex liability laws create demand. | $17,000 | 2- or 4-year degree plus on-the-job training | Insurance company headquarters in major cities; nationwide |
| Clinical Laboratory Technician | Expanded health coverage will call for more medical testing. Discoveries/equipment will create demand. | $18,000 | 2- or 4-year degree | Any medical center |
| Computer Engineer | Expanded use of computers will bring a need for software and hardware engineers. | $35,000 | B.S. and/or M.S. | Near large cities where software corporations are located |
| Home-Care Aide | To cut hospital costs, more health services will be in the home. | $11,000 | No formal training but Medicare aides need 75 hours special training | Across nation, especially where there are pockets of elderly |

FIGURE 35-1 CONTINUED

| Protein Chemist | Specially trained chemists needed to research and develop products. | $48,000 | Ph.D. in bio-chemistry | Seattle; Boston; California |
|---|---|---|---|---|
| Sales and Marketing Specialist | Banks and investment houses need to sell their services. | $29,000 | B.S. or B.A. plus mar-keting skills; MBA helps | New York; Boston; San Francisco; Charlotte, NC |
| Travel Agent | Travel-related demands will increase. | $14,000 | 2-year college or vocational training | Suburbs/ city, esp.in AZ, NY, CA, FL |
| Tax Accountant | Fewer accounting grads plus growing complexity of laws. | $29,000 | B.S. in accounting, CPA certi-fication; MA taxation helps | New York, D.C., Los Angeles, Philadelphia |
| Systems Analyst | Experts needed to link computer hardware and software to meet organizational needs. | $32,000 | B.S. or M.S. in science, computer sci-ence, business management | Anywhere |
| Information Broker | Increased data bases and other sources of info cause demand for persons to identify useful resources. | $22,000 | B.S. in library science or specialized field plus research experience | Major cities |

# THE GRAYING OF AMERICA

One-third of the population will be 50 years of age or older by the turn of the century. At that time, the average age of the American worker will be 40, compared to 35 in 1990. The largest age-group of workers will be those who are 35 to 55 years old, and many of the country's 75 million baby boomers will be in that number.

Whether the hair is gray, white, or red, or the skin color is black, purple, or pink, there will be a "new diversity": the employment door will open to *anyone* who is qualified. As one personnel manager put it: "When you are growing at 300 percent a year, you grab whoever walks in who can get the job done."

The graying of America signifies more jobs for the 50-and-older folk who qualify. Barriers are slowly falling for older, qualified workers, in spite of continuing reports of age discrimination. Increasing numbers of the mature are being considered because of their strong work ethic, experience, and special skills. The federal government reports that half of the Americans 65 and over work part-time. AARP reports that of their 30 million members, 10 million are working and another 10 million wish they were.

# THE ILLITERATE AT RISK

Educators will have their work cut out for them in the 21st century. According to the U.S. Bureau of Labor Statistics, some 30 percent of the current workforce is illiterate, that is, workers who cannot read or write on an eighth grade level or higher. The very fact that so many of these same individuals have skills that don't correspond to the needs of the coming century spells double trouble, considering the jobs with the highest growth rate in the 1990s and beyond will be those requiring the *most* education and training. Nearly half of all new jobs will be in the three highest-skill categories: technicians, managers, and professionals. More specifically, the demand will be great for engineers, health care specialists, educators, computer programmers and analysts, correction officials, social workers, environmentalists, lawyers, and maintenance and repair technicians—all occupations that stand in need of postsecondary education.

An increasing number of companies reports having real difficulty in finding qualified workers to fill professional and technical positions. These same companies are bemoaning the fact that new entry-level applicants lack such basic skills as reading, communications, writing, mathematics, and problem solving.

Teachers and counselors will face a two-fold challenge: to rectify the vast illiteracy problem, and to do a more effective job in advising students toward postsecondary education and training opportunities.

# SUGGESTED READINGS

Commission on Precollege Guidance and Counseling (1986) *Keeping the Options Open.* New York: The College Board.

Kleiman, Carol (1992) *The 100 Best Jobs for the 1990s & Beyond*, Dearborn Financial Publishing, Inc., Chicago, IL 60610.

# CHAPTER 36

# THE STUDENT'S INTERESTS, ABILITIES, AND EXPERIENCES

As we stated in Chapter 34, dedicated educators and employers have been working on diverse approaches to help students make a successful transition from school to workplace: apprenticeships, tech-prep programs, career academies, and cooperative education, just to name a few.

The best school-to-work transition programs in the world are ineffective at best, useless at worst, unless students have some idea prior to entering them what they'd like to do, what career path they'd like to follow. The School-to-Work Opportunities Act passed by Congress in May of 1994 recognizes this vital component. Again, the Act highlights the importance of career awareness and career exploration at an *early* stage in a student's growth and development, as well as an *initial* selection of a career major by at least the first semester of the eleventh grade.

Of course, this means that we must teach our counselees to explore their own interests, abilities, and experiences, and then link them to the unlimited possibilities in the workplace. We have to counsel them so they can utilize acquired information to *discover* which career paths might be appropriate for their needs. But we can't wait until our counselees enter high school. If we do, then they will not be prepared to select the appropriate courses of study or make even rudimentary career-planning decisions.

The career-development decision-making process is not ancillary to successful school-to-work programs: It is an integral part of such programs. Comprehensive career development links education and work. It enables students to acquire skills that will assist them in making *meaningful* decisions regarding their work life.

One program that does a beautiful job of tying one's interests, abilities, and experiences together, is American College Testing's DISCOVER system.

## ACT'S COMMITMENT TO THE PLANNING PROCESS

The American College Testing Program (ACT) has a long-standing commitment to excellence in a variety of programs that support effective career and educational planning for secondary school students. DISCOVER, now some fifteen years of age, is but one of many programs produced by ACT personnel. DISCOVER provides all of the important elements of a complete career and educational planning program, while offering the widest variety of self-awareness activities of any system of its type. The content of the program is closely tied to the theories of leading career-development authorities. Additionally, research and development staff responsible for DISCOVER content have established credibility in the field and continually update the system to provide users with the most current and comprehensive career-planning information possible.

The system has always contained on-line assessments and ratings of interests, abilities, and experiences. But now it has become more economical for a department to offer these important self-awareness experiences to students. To save time on the computer, the exercises can be accomplished in paper-and-pencil format with the results scanned or key-entered as a batch into the DISCOVER computer. This method is ideal for group counseling activities.

Your counselees can receive current data on almost every post-secondary educational option in the country, along with the jobs of 95 percent of the workforce. The system also offers information concerning financial aid procedures and suggestions for improving one's job-seeking skills.

Results from other ACT programs, such as ACT Assessment, PLAN, CPP, and VIESA, can be easily integrated with DISCOVER, thereby enhancing the effectiveness of both DISCOVER and the other programs.

When a counseling department licenses DISCOVER, it probably gives its students one of the most well-organized and extensive approaches to career planning available today.

## SUGGESTED CONTACTS

American College Testing Program, Iowa City, Iowa

# CHAPTER 37

# COUNSELING A STUDENT WITH AN INTEREST IN . . .

Pamela, discussing her plans to attend a four-year college, explains to you how much she enjoys helping people and how she is taken with scientific things. You ask her for her favorite science to date; she responds that she found chemistry and biology to be equally interesting, but adds that she's not having a very good experience with physics.

Less-responsive and less-decisive Matthew, also bound for a senior college, slouches in his chair. Matt has given little or no thought to the future. But that's Matt—very much a live-for-today type.

Computers with their search capability are good, and career development programs that begin at the elementary level are great; but it appears that large numbers of young people remain "at sea" as to what they want to do with their lives.

Does your counselee enjoy helping people, working with his or her hands, working with information and numbers, creating, designing, being outdoors? Identification of one's interests can translate into career possibilities. One of the most important factors in career satisfaction is liking what you do.

Work will occupy a significant portion of a person's life. Most men and women work an average of forty years and change jobs as many as five or six times. To help ensure job satisfaction, young people should take the time to explore a career tailored to their interests.

# A WORKSHEET TO USE WITH STUDENTS

Figure 37-1 is a hands-on, in-your-office resource that you can employ as a post-secondary educational-planning device to use with all your students. The Pamelas of the world, responsive and self-directed as they may be, can often benefit from exposure to additional alternatives. The exercise is even more appropriate for students like Matt, who can be totally unsure about their future.

You know better than most that students tend to dismiss certain of their interests and hobbies as irrelevant, and similarly view their participation in certain activities as trivial. How unfortunate! Such involvement can be the key to unlocking eventual college majors and/or occupations.

What we've attempted to do is pull together 23 general interest areas, 134 college majors, thousands of colleges and universities, and more than 200 occupations. The exercise can move the student from general interest areas to possible college majors, to the collegiate institutions he or she might attend, to a final, "What job can I get with this major?"

The first step would be for your counselee to familiarize him or herself with each general interest area and then complete a worksheet.

FIGURE 37-1

## WORKSHEET

Dear Student:

Many high school students are uncertain as to what major to pursue once in college. They can be equally unsure about occupational choice. You need to understand that such indecision is perfectly normal and quite common among young people.

The world of work is filled with people stuck in jobs selected for reasons *other than* consideration of their personal interests. The result is often called "job dissatisfaction."

To avoid that situation, you and your counselor will be closely examining your own personal interests to help make the eventual selection of a college major and consequent occupation as appropriate an experience as possible. The completion of this worksheet is an important step in that process.

First, carefully read the descriptions of *all* 23 general interest areas. Then, *as best you can*, rate your interest on each item: heavy, moderate, light, or none. Finally, *as best you can*, select six areas in which you have the greatest interest (those with the highest scores), then list them in *descending order* of importance to you.

### 23 GENERAL INTEREST AREAS

*Animals:* You love animals. Perhaps you've had experience raising pets. Observing the behavior of animals and caring for them could be of genuine interest to you.

*Athletics:* You don't have to be an athlete or even be athletically inclined, but it helps. If you are a player of one or more sports and/or a fan of several, athletics could be an important part of your life.

*Children:* You thoroughly enjoy working with children of varying ages. Perhaps you've worked as a baby-sitter or day-camp instructor, and know the pleasures that only children can bring. You might delight in personal contact with them.

*Computers:* Whether you are learning the theoretical constructs of computer language or doing more practical tasks, the computer fascinates you with its speed and capabilities. You see it in the future and want to be a part of it.

FIGURE 37-1 CONTINUED

*Fashion:*     You are "taken" with fashion. Perhaps you have a flair for design, or enjoy shopping and are confident in your taste in selection of garments.

*Government/ Politics:*     You might have an interest in the structure of various levels of government and how they conduct their business. Perhaps you've gained practical experience by working on a political campaign or by interning with a government agency.

*Helping Others:*     Whether you're helping an elderly woman cross a street, reaching out as a member of your rescue squad, or periodically volunteering for local causes, you find happiness in helping other people.

*History/Social Studies:*     For the longest time you've been interested in history; past happenings with their tie to present and future intrigue you. Or maybe you have a concern for other cultures and locations.

*Languages:*     You appreciate languages other than your native tongue. Indeed, you may have studied more than one language, and not only enjoy learning the new one but find it relatively easy to do.

*Law Enforcement:*     Someone has to enforce the law, and you have an appreciation for the men and women who wear the badge. Whether it be the FBI, CIA, state or local authorities, police activities hold a special appeal to you.

*Life Sciences:*     You are fascinated by life and living things. Perhaps a field like biology, agriculture, forestry, and the like could hold a special interest for you.

*Management Activities:*     It's not that you like running the show, but you do find yourself good at managing people and things. You have your share of good ideas, have a sense of organization, enjoy working with people, and can often persuade them to your point of view.

*Mathematics:*     Numbers "turn you on." Some people call it a head for math. You enjoy the challenge of solving complex mathematical problems and/or working with straight numbers in a practical sense.

*Music:*     It could either be performance (vocal or instrumental) or history/ appreciation, but the world of music is a world of enjoyment for you. Maybe you see yourself as performer or composer; anything musical is for you.

FIGURE 37-1 *CONTINUED*

*Outdoor Activities:* You love to be outdoors; a good deal of your life has been spent in the open air. A job that would take you outdoors much of the time might be good.

*Performing Arts:* You love to perform, whether it be on a stage, in front of a camera, or facing a microphone. You enjoy entertaining others and might see yourself as being rather talented.

*Physical Sciences:* You are a good conceptual thinker. You want to know why things work and have enjoyed such sciences as chemistry and/or physics. You want to be a part of the contribution the physical sciences are making toward the betterment of society.

*Religious Activities:* There is a "something beyond" that fascinates you. You might see religion as fulfillment for yourself and others, and want to take part in that process.

*Sales Activities:* You've enjoyed the world of selling and trading since your lemonade stand or baseball card exchange. You might not want to sell the Brooklyn Bridge, but you find "wheeling and dealing" to be pleasurable and productive.

*Social Consciousness:* You are aware that you are more fortunate than others and want to offer them your help. Or you see the interdependence of all of us and want to contribute to the good of the whole. You see beyond your corner of the world and want to take part in it.

*Visual Arts:* Whether you are talking about fine arts, commercial design, or three-dimensional art such as crafts and sculpture, you have a penchant for and talent in this medium. "Art" has many specializations and you delight in working in it.

*Working with Hands:* It's called manual dexterity. Both gross and fine motor skills will play a major role in the ability to work with your hands. You may not only like a "hands on" experience, but discover that you're quite good at it.

*Writing:* You love to write—it's as simple as that. It's also becoming apparent to you that you have a certain facility for expressing your thoughts on paper. Perhaps you've won a writing contest or contribute articles to the school or local paper. In any case, you want to improve your craft.

FIGURE 37-1 CONTINUED

Student Name: _____     Date: _____

Rate your interest level on each of the 23 interest areas by circling the  appropriate number. Review your ratings, then select your 6 favorite areas and place them in *descending* order of importance to you.

| Intensity Rating Scale | Heavy | Moderate | Slight | None |
|---|---|---|---|---|
| Animals | 3 | 2 | 1 | 0 |
| Athletics | 3 | 2 | 1 | 0 |
| Children | 3 | 2 | 1 | 0 |
| Computers | 3 | 2 | 1 | 0 |
| Fashion | 3 | 2 | 1 | 0 |
| Government/Politics | 3 | 2 | 1 | 0 |
| Helping Others | 3 | 2 | 1 | 0 |
| History/Social Studies | 3 | 2 | 1 | 0 |
| Languages | 3 | 2 | 1 | 0 |
| Law Enforcement | 3 | 2 | 1 | 0 |
| Life Sciences | 3 | 2 | 1 | 0 |
| Management Activities | 3 | 2 | 1 | 0 |
| Mathematics | 3 | 2 | 1 | 0 |
| Music | 3 | 2 | 1 | 0 |
| Outdoor Activities | 3 | 2 | 1 | 0 |
| Performing Arts | 3 | 2 | 1 | 0 |
| Physical Sciences | 3 | 2 | 1 | 0 |
| Religious Activities | 3 | 2 | 1 | 0 |
| Sales Activities | 3 | 2 | 1 | 0 |
| Social Consciousness | 3 | 2 | 1 | 0 |
| Visual Arts | 3 | 2 | 1 | 0 |
| Working with Hands | 3 | 2 | 1 | 0 |
| Writing | 3 | 2 | 1 | 0 |

## MY TOP SIX

1. _____

2. _____

3. _____

4. _____

5. _____

6. _____

Once a student has identified and analyzed his or her interests, an Interest-Major Match sheet can be utilized to acquaint him or her with major fields of study that relate to the personal interests. A college major is first listed *under* the general interest area that seems in our judgment to be the strongest in its pursuit. You can make your own additions and/or modifications in the listings. For example, oceanography is listed under "Life Sciences," even though an interest in animals and physical sciences is also implied. Scanning related interest areas will provide you with more possibilities to suggest. The symbol (G) indicates the requirement for graduate study.

## *Interest Areas and College Majors*

ANIMALS
    Animal Science
    Veterinarian

ATHLETICS
    Athletic Trainer/Sports Medicine
    Physical Education
    Professional Athlete
    Sports Management

CHILDREN
    School Psychology (G)
    Teaching
        Early Childhood
        Elementary
        Hearing Impaired
        Preschool
        Secondary
        Special Education
        Speech Impaired
        Visually Impaired

COMPUTERS
    Computer Engineering
    Computer Information Sciences
    Computer Mathematics

FASHION
    Fashion Design
    Fashion Merchandising

GOVERNMENT/POLITICS
    International Relations
    Law (G)
    Political Science
    Public Administration

HELPING OTHERS
    Gerontology/Geriatrics
    Nursing
    Occupational Therapy
    Physical Therapy
    Physician (G)
    Psychology
    Recreation/Leisure Studies
    Respiratory Therapy
    School Counseling

HISTORY/SOCIAL STUDIES
    Archaeology
    Anthropology
    Economics
    Geography
    History
    Museum Studies
    Sociology

LANGUAGES
    Comparative Literature
    Linguistics
    Chinese
    English
    French
    German
    Greek
    Hebrew
    Italian
    Japanese
    Latin
    Russian
    Spanish

LAW ENFORCEMENT
 Criminology
 Police Science

LIFE SCIENCES
 Agriculture/Horticulture
 Agronomy
 Biochemistry
 Biology
 Biophysics
 Cytology
 Dental Hygiene
 Dietetics/Nutrition
 Ecology/Environmental Science
 Forestry
 Genetics
 Geology
 Microbiology
 Oceanography/Marine Biology
 Physiology
 Zoology

MANAGEMENT ACTIVITIES
 Business Management
 Hotel & Restaurant Management
 Hospital Administration
 Industrial Management
 Industrial Relations & Labor
 Insurance Management
 Library Science
 Medical Record Administration
 Real Estate
 Textile Management

MATHEMATICS
 Accounting
 Actuarial Science
 Engineering
 Finance
 Robotics

MUSIC
 Instrumental Music
 Music Composition
 Music Management
 Music Merchandising

Musical Theater
Music Therapy
Vocal Music

OUTDOOR ACTIVITIES
 Commercial Fishing
 Conservation/Wildlife Management
 Parks and Recreation Management

PERFORMING ARTS
 Acting
 Dance
 Dance Management
 Dance Therapy
 Radio & Television Announcing

PHYSICAL SCIENCES
 Astronomy
 Astrophysics
 Chemistry
 Earth Science
 Geology
 Pharmacy
 Physics

RELIGION/PHILOSOPHY
 Ministerial Studies
 Philosophy

SALES ACTIVITIES
 Advertising
 Insurance
 Marketing
 Merchandising
 Real Estate

SOCIAL CONSCIOUSNESS
 Black Studies
 Health Education
 Social Work
 Women's Studies

VISUAL ARTS
 Architecture
 Art Therapy
 Cinematography/Film
 Fine Arts

Graphic Design
Illustration
Illustration, Medical
Industrial Design
Interior Design
Landscape Architecture
Ornamental Horticulture
Photography
Photojournalism

Technical Theater
Textile Design

WORKING WITH HANDS
Ceramic Engineering

WRITING
Creative Writing
Journalism
Scientific Writing

### Interest—Major Match

Here are just five samples that depict how interest areas and college major can be tied together. You can create additional matches with your students in either an individual or group guidance session.

ATHLETICS . . . . . . . . . . . . . . . . . . . . . . . . . . . . . . . . . . . . . professional athlete
   & HELPING OTHERS . . . . . . . . . . . . . . . . . . . . . . . . . . teacher, physical ed.
   & HELPING OTHERS & LIFE SCIENCES . . . . . . . . . . . . . . sports medicine,
   . . . . . . . . . . . . . . . . . . . . . . . . . . . . . . . . . . . . . . . . athletic trainer
   & MANAGEMENT . . . . . . . . . . . . . . . . . . . . . . . . . . . . sports management

COMPUTERS . . . . . . . . . . . . . . . . . . . . . . . . . . . . . . . . . . . . computer info. science
   & MATHEMATICS . . . . . . . . . . . . . . . . . . . . . . . . . . . . . computer math
   & MATHEMATICS & PHYSICAL SCIENCE . . . . . . . . . . . computer engineering

HELPING OTHERS . . . . . . . . . . . . . . . . . . . . . . . . . . . . . . . recreation/leisure study
   & CHILDREN . . . . . . . . . . . . . . . . . . . . . . . . . . . . . . . . school counselor
   & LIFE SCIENCES . . . . . . . . . . . . . . . . . . . . . . . . . . . . nursing
   . . . . . . . . . . . . . . . . . . . . . . . . . . . . . . . . . . . . . . . . psychology
   . . . . . . . . . . . . . . . . . . . . . . . . . . . . . . . . . . . . . . . . occupational therapy
   . . . . . . . . . . . . . . . . . . . . . . . . . . . . . . . . . . . . . . . . gerontology/geriatrics
   & LIFE SCIENCES & PHYSICAL SCIENCES . . . . . . . . . . . physician
   . . . . . . . . . . . . . . . . . . . . . . . . . . . . . . . . . . . . . . . . physical therapy
   . . . . . . . . . . . . . . . . . . . . . . . . . . . . . . . . . . . . . . . . respiratory therapy

LIFE SCIENCES . . . . . . . . . . . . . . . . . . . . . . . . . . . . . . . . . biology, etc.
   & ANIMALS . . . . . . . . . . . . . . . . . . . . . . . . . . . . . . . . zoology
   & HELPING OTHERS . . . . . . . . . . . . . . . . . . . . . . . . . . dental hygiene
   . . . . . . . . . . . . . . . . . . . . . . . . . . . . . . . . . . . . . . . . dietetics/nutrition
   . . . . . . . . . . . . . . . . . . . . . . . . . . . . . . . . . . . . . . . . psychobiology
   & MANAGEMENT & HISTORY/SOC. STUDY . . . . . . . . . . agricultural economics
   & OUTDOORS . . . . . . . . . . . . . . . . . . . . . . . . . . . . . . ecology/environment
   . . . . . . . . . . . . . . . . . . . . . . . . . . . . . . . . . . . . . . . . forestry

```
& OUTDOORS & MANAGEMENT . . . . . . . . . . . . . . . . agriculture
. . . . . . . . . . . . . . . . . . . . . . . . . . . . . . . . . . . . agronomy
. . . . . . . . . . . . . . . . . . . . . . . . . . . . . . . . . . . . turf management
& OUTDOORS & PHYSICAL SCIENCES . . . . . . . . . . . . oceanography
& PHYSICAL SCIENCES . . . . . . . . . . . . . . . . . . . . . . biochemistry
. . . . . . . . . . . . . . . . . . . . . . . . . . . . . . . . . . . . biophysics

VISUAL ARTS . . . . . . . . . . . . . . . . . . . . . . . . . . . . fine arts, illustration
& HELPING OTHERS . . . . . . . . . . . . . . . . . . . . . . art therapy
& HISTORY/SOCIAL STUDIES . . . . . . . . . . . . . . . . cinematography/film
& LIFE SCIENCES . . . . . . . . . . . . . . . . . . . . . . . . . medical illustration
& LIFE SCIENCES & WORKING WITH HANDS . . . . . . . . landscape architecture
. . . . . . . . . . . . . . . . . . . . . . . . . . . . . . . . . . . . ornamental horticulture
& MATHEMATICS . . . . . . . . . . . . . . . . . . . . . . . . graphic design
. . . . . . . . . . . . . . . . . . . . . . . . . . . . . . . . . . . . industrial design
. . . . . . . . . . . . . . . . . . . . . . . . . . . . . . . . . . . . architecture
& PHYSICAL SCIENCES . . . . . . . . . . . . . . . . . . . . . textile design
& WRITING & HISTORY/SOCIAL STUDIES . . . . . . . . . . photojournalism
```

# COLLEGE AND CAREER PLANNING

College planning and career planning: if you think about it, there's a synergism between the two. Such a relationship is especially apparent at the high school level as students search, not only for the best-choice collegiate institutions, but also for the best-choice majors and consequent careers.

*Lovejoy's College Guide* is a most worthwhile publication you can use in the next step of the process, a resource guide that enables you to engage in both college and career planning simultaneously. In the *Guide's* Career Curricula section, you can find all kinds of college majors—everything from accounting to zoology. Note, however, that in presenting their material the Lovejoy people exercise a certain amount of control over the inclusion of collegiate institutions. It's a departure from the "anything and everything" approach of other publications, and therefore can be of special benefit to the reader searching for a relatively strong major program.

Once you've developed a tentative list of colleges and universities, your final step is to crack open a copy of the *Occupational Outlook Handbook*, the pace-setting guide published every other year by the U.S. Department of Labor. You and your counselee can examine well-written descriptions of various occupations that highlight: the nature of the work; training and advancement possibilities; job outlook until the year 2005; related jobs; and the most important section of all: where one can find additional job information. The handbook is a highly respected publication—the bible of the industry since World War II.

# PERMISSION TO EXPLORE

It's vital for young people to give themselves permission to explore—to try out different things. But these same youngsters must be *encouraged* to move out and do just that. That's the key! Your students may not readily see how all the pieces fit together, but they'll develop skills, curiosity, and leadership capability in the pursuit. Most important, pursuing one's interests makes for a wiser and more complete person. All the pieces will one day come together and be an asset to the career the person ultimately selects.

So youngsters should permit themselves to change and not feel guilty about it. But they first need to explore and see what interests them. They should bring imagination to bear, and not hesitate to dream and visualize what they see as their ideal work environment. They can create a vivid picture of where they would like to be and what they would like to do. Then, and only then, can they begin their journey.

# CHAPTER 38

# ON-THE-JOB REQUIREMENTS AND EXPECTATIONS

By the year 2005, fully one quarter of today's workplace knowledge and practices will be history, according to an analysis of the *broad* skills needed to ensure future job success.

### Top Ten Skills Needed

1. Self-analysis: Being able to objectively analyze personal strengths and weaknesses and make the necessary effort to enhance both areas.
2. Cooperative learning: This promises to be more than a passing fancy at elementary and secondary educational levels.
3. Global thought capability.
4. Conflict resolution.
5. Passion for performing well.
6. Willingness to change and to accept change.
7. Networking acumen.
8. Optimism in the face of uncertainty.
9. Facility with oral and written communication.
10. Openness to criticism.

Now let's move from the broad to the more specific. As mentioned in this book's introduction, industry and business are not nearly so concerned about grade point average as they are about whether students can express themselves well both orally and in written form. It's also important that students be able to relate well to peers *and* adults. Management has become increasingly concerned with the social—or, unfortunately, anti-social—aspect of their employees' behavior. They look to hire young people who have the capabilities and the *responsibility* to be effective members of the company. (See Figure 38-1.)

FIGURE 38-1

### Qualities That Count with Employers

Figures from a Census Bureau survey of 3,000 employers nationwide, conducted in August and September of 1994. The survey was developed by the National Center on the Educational Quality of the Work Force at the University of Pennsylvania.

When you consider hiring a new non-supervisory or production worker, how important are the following in your decision to hire?

(Ranked on a scale of 1 through 5, with 1 being not important or not considered, and 5 being very important.)

| Factor | Rank |
|---|---|
| Attitude | 4.6 |
| Communication Skills | 4.2 |
| Previous work experience | 4.0 |
| Recommendations from current employees | 3.4 |
| Recommendations from previous employer | 3.4 |
| Industry-based credentials certifying skills | 3.2 |
| Years of schooling completed | 2.9 |
| Score on tests administered as part of interview | 2.5 |
| Academic performance (grades) | 2.5 |
| Experience or reputation of applicant's school | 2.4 |
| Teacher recommendations | 2.1 |

Figure 38-2 further substantiates the Census Bureau findings and reflects advice given to school counselors by the Siemens Corporation of Edison, New Jersey at an employment seminar.

FIGURE 38-2

## WHAT EMPLOYERS ARE LOOKING FOR

FROM *PROSPECTIVE* EMPLOYEES:

1.  *A positive attitude:*
    a. about oneself
    b. about work in general
    c. about the company
    d. about the particular job

2.  *Enthusiasm* that begins with a positive attitude and includes:
    a. a cheerful demeanor
    b. expressed interest in the company, based on some knowledge of its products or services
    c. eagerness to learn more about the company and the job

3.  *Ability to communicate* that includes:
    a. listening ability
    b. good oral and written English
    c. an organized thought process

4.  *Integrity:* honesty with employer and self.

5.  *Computer literacy* (the number of jobs requiring this skill will continue to increase to where it will be almost as basic as reading and writing) that includes:
    a. keyboard skills
    b. knowledge of basic terminology and the principal ways in which computers are used

FIGURE 38-2 CONTINUED

## TO *ADVANCE* IN YOUR JOB:

In addition to the five qualities listed above, to maintain your position, or for that matter, to advance in it, the employee needs:

1. *Interpersonal skills* including:

   a. willingness to listen

   b. consideration of others' feelings and differing points of view

   c. establishment of mutual respect

2. *A sense of responsibility:*

   a. for one's own actions

   b. for self-improvement

   c. for others such as colleagues or members of the same team

   d. for keeping commitments (follow-through)

3. *Dedication to quality* as a way of life, which means:

   a. doing our best, whatever we do

   b. encouraging quality consciousness in others

   c. always looking for the better way

## THE *COLLEGE DEGREE* AS A FACTOR

Does the college degree guarantee the acquisition of these eight qualities? No, but it certainly can be a contributing factor. Similarly, a college education is necessary and/or appropriate for:

1. Entering a profession such as accounting, law, engineering, or education.

2. Entry to or advancement within a field of interest where employers generally require a degree.

3. Satisfying a thirst for knowledge and academic accomplishment.

# CHAPTER 39

# JOB-INTERVIEWING TECHNIQUES

It is a rare phenomenon for a person to land a job without having had to interview for the position; the interview is usually the final hurdle in securing a position. Without a doubt, the key to a successful interview is *preparation*. Here are a few words of advice you can impart to your counselees.

## BEFORE THE INTERVIEW

1. Know the type of questions the interviewer might pose and be ready to respond appropriately.
2. Do some homework on the company. Become knowledgeable about it.
3. Think of questions you'd like to ask that are related to the job you are seeking.
4. Practice your responses with an adult or friend. Have that person play the interviewer.
5. First impressions can be lasting ones. Make a good personal appearance.

# DURING THE INTERVIEW

1.  Try to relax as much as possible. It's normal to be somewhat nervous.
2.  Be on time. Actually, be a bit early. If possible, locate the office a day or two prior to the interview.
3.  Do not bring anyone with you.
4.  Bring a pen and be prepared to take notes and/or sign documents.
5.  Do not chew gum!
6.  Sit erect and look the interviewer in the eye.
7.  Your responses to questions should rarely be one-word answers. Your responses should be complete. For example, if you are asked, "Do you enjoy working with people?" Instead of answering with a simple, "Yes," you might respond: "Yes, that's the reason I did volunteer work at Monmouth Medical Center."

# AFTER THE INTERVIEW

1.  Take some notes on what was asked in the interview.
2.  Write the interviewer a letter thanking him or her for the time and consideration. There's nothing wrong with mentioning your continued interest in the job. Keep the letter brief.
3.  Don't give up! Very few people get a job on their first or even second interview. Besides, the more interviewing a person does, the more relaxed he or she will become with the process.

# BEHAVIOR-BASED INTERVIEWING

These days, high school and college graduates will do well to reflect carefully on their school and/or part-time work experiences prior to going to job interviews. Many companies are now employing behavior-based interviewing techniques rather than theoretical questioning.

Instead of asking, "What do you see yourself doing in five years?" employers are now inquiring about the applicant's last held job and what were his or her responsibilities. Instead of a theoretical situation, a candidate can describe the actual situation and how it was handled. Behavior-based interviewing can be a plus for young new applicants who have to compete with more experienced persons; school counselors can help students review and analyze their past accomplishments, and how they might relate to a forthcoming interview and the position a company is looking to fill.

# WHY CANDIDATES ARE REJECTED

It is critical that young people learn how to interview well for a particular job. Many people, adults included, have little or no idea what is expected of them in the interview process, and they more often than not receive no feedback on their performance. Employers report that the most common reasons why job applicants "blow" the interview are:

1. Poor personal appearance
2. Lack of interest and enthusiasm during the actual interview
3. Poor eye contact with the interviewer
4. Showing up late to the interview
5. Failure to raise questions about the potential position
6. Overbearing "know it all" attitude
7. Inability to express oneself clearly
8. Voice quality, diction, grammar
9. Exhibiting little, if any, goal setting and/or career planning

# EPILOGUE

What makes school counseling such an invigorating challenge is that the professional counselor has the potential to make a decisive and positive impact on the growth and development of *each* student, of each unique individual.

Society seems to be more cognizant of the "other" aspects of a young person's education: character and personality traits such as diligence, commitment, and respect are now more revered; community service has taken on new importance. All educators have the opportunity *and* the responsibility to mirror the values that will bring out global community to a more peaceful and productive level; but it is the counselor's job to *directly* influence the young person's ability to choose.

Parenting seems more difficult now than it used to be; it's probably due to the amount of communication—and, therefore, the pressure—that affects children: television, movies, ease of transportation, use of the computer internet, absence of one parent, lack of time for both parents. *Because* parenting skills are so seldom taught, and *because* the school setting is the youngster's first and greatest opportunity to deal with societal values and responsibilities, someone in that school must help the parents guide that child.

Even if large numbers of parents continue to be, for all the reasons we have discussed, on the outside looking in, that stance can be changed. We can help break the cycle of parental passivity—in some cases, outright neglect—by helping our own counselees mature into caring, altruistic, participating adults. We can even lay the groundwork so that they will be involved in *their* youngsters' education. That is part of the challenge.

Counseling is a noble profession; the educative process is a determinate of the future. We'd like to quote the late Ernest L. Boyer, from a 1995 speech upon the release of his report *The Basic School: A Community of Learning*:

> *"I believe that America is losing sight of its children. In decisions made every day, we are putting them at the very bottom of the agenda. And while people endlessly criticize the schools, I've concluded that the school is probably the least imperiled institution in our culture."*

# INDEX